Arduino®
Projects
FOR

DUMMIES®
A Wiley Brand

Arduino® Projects

FOR

DUMMIES®

A Wiley Brand

by Brock Craft

FOR

DUMMIES®

A Wiley Brand

Arduino® Projects For Dummies®

Published by
John Wiley & Sons, Ltd.
The Atrium
Southern Gate
Chichester
West Sussex
PO19 8SQ
England

Email (for orders and customer service enquires): cs-books@wiley.co.uk

Visit our home page on www.wiley.com

For general information on our other products and services, please contact our Customer Care Department within the U.S. at 877-762-2974, outside the U.S. at 317-572-3993, or fax 317-572-4002.

For technical support, please visit www.wiley.com/techsupport.

Wiley also publishes its books in a variety of electronic formats and by print-on-demand. Some content that appears in standard print versions of this book may not be available in other formats. For more information about Wiley products, visit us at www.wiley.com.

British Library Cataloguing in Publication Data: A catalogue record for this book is available from the British Library.

ISBN 978-1-118-55147-9 (paperback); ISBN 978-1-118-55150-9 (ebook); 978-1-118-55151-6 (ebook)

Printed and bound in the United States at Bind-Rite

10 9 8 7 6 5 4 3 2 1

About the Author

Brock Craft is a Lecturer in the Department of Computing at Goldsmiths, University of London. He is also a Senior Tutor at the Royal College of Art. He is a specialist in physical computing, data visualization, and the Internet of Things. Brock's background is in the field of human-computer interaction, and he has over a decade of experience making interactive things that people can use, explore, and play with. He was a co-director of the design consultancy Tinker London, along with Alexandra Deschamps-Sonsino and Massimo Banzi, one of the founders of the Arduino Project. He has taught hundreds of people to create things with Arduinos.

When he is not teaching and learning, Brock likes to make interactive stuff and digital art.

Dedication

For Barbara, who has supported me steadfastly on this most incredible journey, and without whom this book would not have been possible. She has put at least as much work into this effort as I have. I also dedicate this book to my mother, Lea Gaydos, who taught me that I can do anything I put my mind to. I would like to acknowledge and dedicate this book to the memory of Craig Veal, the best teacher I ever had.

And most especially, this book is for Eleanor, who I hope will grow up to make everything in her world come alive with creativity.

Author's Acknowledgments

First and foremost, I'd like to thank Massimo Banzi and the entire Arduino crew. Their foresight has opened up the joy of programming and electronics to millions of people and revitalized my own teaching and learning.

Writing this book has been a rewarding and challenging process, which would not have been possible without the support of my many colleagues and friends. I'd like to extend special thanks to Alexandra Deschamps-Sonsino, without whose insight this book wouldn't have been undertaken. I'd also like to extend my gratitude to all the members of the TinkerLondon crew, the extraordinary Nick Weldin, and also to Peter Knight, from whom I learned so much during our extraordinary work together.

My father's mechanical acumen is, no doubt, where I got my own, and I thank him for many rewarding hours of thinking and tinkering together. I also appreciate the contributions and support of my friends Jason Geistweidt, James Larsson, Patrick Burkart, and Carl Wiedemann, whose probing questions inspired me to think a bit harder about my readers. Many of my students have made useful suggestions too, which were very helpful in deciding what should go into these pages.

Particular thanks go to my technical editor and TinkerLondon compatriot, Daniel Soltis, who spent many hours building the projects from scratch and finding errata. He has made many useful suggestions for improving both the projects and the code. Daniel's excellent insights into how people build projects, along with his edits and tweaks, have been a hugely positive contribution.

I also extend my gratitude to the team at Wiley, including the patient and supportive Craig Smith, and to Beth Taylor for her excellent editorial recommendations.

Publisher's Acknowledgments

We're proud of this book; please send us your comments at http://dummies.custhelp.com. For other comments, please contact our Customer Care Department within the U.S. at 877-762-2974, outside the U.S. at 317-572-3993, or fax 317-572-4002.

Some of the people who helped bring this book to market include the following:

Acquisitions, Editorial

Project Editor: Beth Taylor

Executive Commissioning Editor: Craig Smith

Associate Commissioning Editor: Ellie Scott

Copy Editor: Beth Taylor

Technical Editor: Daniel Soltis

Editorial Manager: Jodi Jensen

Senior Project Editor: Sara Shlaer

Editorial Assistant: Annie Sullivan

Cover Photo: Brock Craft

Marketing

Associate Marketing Director: Louise Breinholt

Marketing Manager: Lorna Mein

Composition Services

Senior Project Coordinator: Kristie Rees

Layout and Graphics: Jennifer Creasey, Joyce Haughey

Proofreaders: Debbye Butler, Jessica Kramer, Linda Seifert

Indexer: BIM Indexing and Proofreading Services

UK Tech Publishing

    Michelle Leete, VP Consumer and Technology Publishing Director

    Martin Tribe, Associate Director–Book Content Management

    Chris Webb, Associate Publisher

Publishing and Editorial for Technology Dummies

    Richard Swadley, Vice President and Executive Group Publisher

    Andy Cummings, Vice President and Publisher

    Mary Bednarek, Executive Acquisitions Director

    Mary C. Corder, Editorial Director

Publishing for Consumer Dummies

    Kathleen Nebenhaus, Vice President and Executive Publisher

Composition Services

    Debbie Stailey, Director of Composition Services

Contents at a Glance

Table of Contents

Introduction

*H*ave you heard a lot about Arduinos and wanted to get to know how they work a little bit better? Maybe you have a friend who's used an Arduino to build some crazy project or interactive gizmo. Perhaps you have an Arduino lying around that you always thought you'd get working but never had the time to do it. It's time to blow the dust off!

Maybe you just want some inspiration and fun projects to do in your spare time or on the weekends. If so, this is exactly the book for you. The projects here show off some of the amazing capabilities of an Arduino, and they can all be completed without any prior expertise or experience. It's also a great companion to other Arduino books that you may have bought or skimmed through.

Arduino Projects For Dummies is an inspiring collection of fun and interesting things you can do with an Arduino. I've packed in a wide range of cool ideas for things you can do. Best of all, I selected them so that after you've done a few of them, you'll have most of the technical knowledge you'll need to come up with your own amazing gadgets, widgets, and interactive stuff. Whether you are an Arduino newbie or a seasoned pro, these projects are super fun to build and help you to really get your creative ideas flowing.

Why Arduino?

It's no secret that Arduino has been making a lot of news lately, especially among makers, tinkerers, and hobbyists. All kinds of people are getting into the powerful and interactive things you can do with an Arduino — from school kids to university researchers, to artists and designers. One thing that sets apart Arduino from a lot of other platforms is that anyone can write new programs to use with it and share them online. Even more powerfully, special code collections called libraries extend the things Arduino can do by allowing you to connect cameras, motors, printers, scanners, remote controls — you name it. Because anyone can create code for Arduino and share it online, the community is really growing fast. It's been instrumental in renewing interest in electronics and new hacker spaces all over the country where people build cool things, such as autonomous robots, 3D printers, and interactive artwork.

Foolish Assumptions

I'm assuming in this book that you have an idea of what an Arduino is and maybe have played around with one a bit. You also may have done some basic electronics, either in a school physics class or on your own, but you may not be aware of or remember much about the basic principles of electronics. That's no problem, because I'll go over what you need to know and explain a bit about how the electronic circuits in this book work, mainly what you need to know to get the projects going.

I also figure you've tried your hand at writing a little code before. But whether you have written any code at all, I explain how all of the programs in this book work in fine detail. That way you can learn how to program your Arduino to do not just the things in this book but the things you want to do.

I'm also assuming you want to get your Arduino to do its thing on its own and without having to rely on a computer for power or a data connection. So all of the projects in this book can operate just fine without the need for keeping your Arduino connected to your desktop or laptop.

Which brings me to another assumption — that you have a computer you can work on consistently and that you're pretty familiar with how to operate it, move and save files, and generally keep your system organized. I'm also assuming you are familiar with downloading zipped files from the Internet and extracting them.

Safety and Arduino Projects

When working with electricity, safety is paramount. If you connect something incorrectly, you can easily fry your hardware or yourself, especially if you do anything with household power. That's why none of the projects in this book are connected directly to the main power. All of the projects use low voltage, direct current components. It's simply a safer way to operate.

However, it is still possible to fry something if you aren't careful. So you should pay particular attention that you are wiring things up according to the diagrams provided. There are warning icons in the margins for steps that are particularly hairy, so keep an eye out for them. And speaking of your eyes, some of the projects require a little light fabrication, so you should use those safety goggles. Also, if you do any soldering, you have to be careful about the hot soldering iron. Make sure you set up your workbench to be a safe and productive environment.

How This Book Is Organized

In general, I've organized the book with the easier projects toward the beginning and the harder ones toward the end. But if you see a project you really want to get going on, dive right in.

Check out the table of contents to see what you might want to tackle first, and if you need to look something up, the index is a handy reference.

The parts in this book are divided into chapters, so you can find what you need quickly and easily.

Part 1: Getting Started with Arduino Projects

You should check out Part I before you get started, to make sure you are ready to go and your project building workspace has everything you'll need to get your work done. I discuss the basics of setting up your workbench and getting the right project building supplies and tools in Chapter 2, and I cover setting up your Arduino on your computer.

I also describe the most popular kinds of Arduino boards and suggest which ones are good for different applications, although all of the projects in the book can be built with the basic Arduino Uno.

I also cover setting up your Arduino and provide some tips on "packaging up" your project. A lot of Arduino project guides online neglect the part about building a good enclosure, so there are some creative tips in this section.

Chapter 3 describes the basics of writing Arduino code and the basics of physically building your projects. If you know nothing about writing code for Arduino, you should definitely read this chapter. Pretty much everyone who has used an Arduino has made an LED blink, and that's what you do in Chapter 3, when you set up your Arduino. I also describe the kinds of things you can do with your Arduino — sensing things in the environment and actuating things. I give an overview of the kinds of electronic components you will find out there on the market and provide some tips on soldering and building your projects.

Part II: Basic Arduino Projects

Part II is all about lights and timing. Chapter 4 takes LEDs bit further, describing how to make lots of LEDs blink in what I call an All-Seeing Eye — think *Battlestar Galactica*. Chapter 5 describes how to make LEDs pulsate so you can create a light pet with a personality. Chapter 6 takes LEDs to a more functional application – writing with light, in which timing is a key factor. Chapter 7 rounds things off with another timing application — building an alarm clock. This is the most advanced project in Part II, so if you are just getting your feet wet, save it for last.

Part III: The Interactive Home and Garden

Turn to Part III if you are fascinated by sensors and home automation. People have been automating their homes and apartments since the 1980s, at least — but with Arduino, you can take things to a whole new level! Chapter 8 shows you how to build a keypad entry system for your door — very James Bond. When you've completed it, you can extend its capabilities with the keycard reader in Chapter 9. Only someone with a properly registered keycard will be able to gain access.

Once you've made it easier to come and go, you can build the plant irrigation system in Chapter 10. That way, when you've gone out for a long trip, you can make sure your houseplant or even a whole indoor garden stays healthy and happy.

While you are smartening up your home, you can give your pets a new voice as well. The tweeting pet door in Chapter 11 helps give your dog or cat a voice online. You'll be able to tell whenever they are coming and going by wiring up your pet door to the Internet — with no computer required, once it's set up!

The last project in Part III takes this one step further and shows you how to connect live data feeds from your house to a data tracking system online. In Chapter 12, you build your own home sensing station that posts regular information about temperature and light levels around your house — accessible from anywhere you can get an Internet connection. You can even embed data charts into your own website. Once you've got a handle on how the code works, you can hook up just about any sensor to the Internet — whether in your home, garden, or treehouse.

Part IV: Advanced Arduino Projects

I've saved some of my favorite and trickiest projects for last, in Part IV. Chapter 13 shows you how to build a GPS data logger. You don't have to settle for the GPS in your car or on your phone. You can use it just about anywhere and log the data to a standard SD data card. There are all kinds of clever uses for this, including tracking vehicles, packages, pets, and logging your own explorations in the city or country.

No electronics-related project book would be complete without a remote-controlled device of some kind. Chapter 14 shows you how to build your own remote-controlled car out of a few easily found supplies and some potato chip cans. The clever part is that you use any old remote control around your house to control the car. By the time you finish this project, you'll not only have a pretty cool vehicle, but you'll also understand the basics of using servo motors and how to use an Arduino to make just about anything remote controllable.

Chapter 15 gets back to playing around with light. LED cubes are getting really popular and if you haven't seen them already, you will. This chapter shows you how to make and program your own. There's also an online tool for building your own animated lighting patterns. Both the code and the physical construction are pretty challenging, but the results are really cool. If, like me, you are mesmerized by blinking lights, you're gonna love this one.

Part V: The Part of Tens

Every book in the *For Dummies* series has a "top ten" style list where you can find further information quickly. This part is where I get to share some of my favorite Arduino resources and some handy tips and tricks with you.

Chapter 16 describes the best suppliers and Arduino resources for the stuff you'll need to build the projects and take things even further. I also get to brag about my favorite suppliers — and friends — in the Arduino world. Every projects book should help you out with troubleshooting as much as possible. Chapter 17 provides tips for solving problems. This can be tricky, since the problems could arise from your software or your hardware — *or both!* I hope that the tips in this chapter will help you figure out why your project might not be working.

The Companion Website

This book has a companion website that offers some additional projects and a tool for creating patterns for the LED cube you build in Chapter 15. Go to www.dummies.com/go/arduinoprojectsfordummies and look on the Downloads tab. You can also find schematics and full-color parts placement diagrams here to help you build the projects in this book.

Several of the projects require additional code libraries to make them work. You can find these libraries in a .zip file on the Downloads tab of the companion website. Later, if updates become available for this book, you can also find them on the Downloads tab.

Besides this book's companion website on dummies.com, you can also go to my personal website at www.brockcraft.com. Everyone I've ever met who tinkers with Arduino is happy to help out other folks in improving their code and their projects. So, if you have any suggestions for enhancing or improving these projects, please let me know!

Icons Used in This Book

I can't highlight the most important passages in this book with my trusty Sharpie or yellow highlighter, so I've used icons to draw your attention to the important parts.

Tips highlight information that can save you time or money or just make things easier to do. You'll have a lot more fun if you keep the tips in mind as you go along, and they can help you with your own projects, too.

Building projects can be tricky or hazardous or both. I've placed warnings to highlight areas where it's easy to make a mistake or fry something or generally get something messed up. The warnings are there so that you don't have to learn the hard way — because I probably already did that for you!

Sometimes there are important points that you really need to keep in mind when you are working on a project or writing code. I've use this icon to highlight these important points. That way, you can easily find them when you are reviewing a project or building a new one of your own.

This is a pretty technical book, but sometimes there are extremely geeky topics that are either interesting or useful to know. I've identified these with this icon. You can skip this stuff because it's not essential to know in order to build the projects, but I've included it here in case you want to understand a little better how things work.

Part I
Getting Started with Arduino Projects

In this part . . .

✔ Learn how to set up your Arduino workspace

✔ Find out about the many different kinds of Arduino boards

✔ Get to know the basics of Arduino code

✔ Learn about electronics components and soldering techniques

Chapter 1

Exploring the World of Arduino

In This Chapter

▶ Discovering Arduino

▶ Understanding who uses Arduino

▶ Understanding microcontrollers

▶ Understanding Arduino capabilities

You probably wouldn't have picked up this book if you hadn't already heard about the "World of Arduino." You're probably already a part of it. I think of it as being made up of a community of creative people who are interested in making inanimate stuff do interesting and clever things with computers, programming, and *computational thinking* — which is just a fancy way of saying "writing recipes."

Computational thinking means considering problems and their potential solutions and trying to determine the best way to get to those solutions. Usually, it means deciding the best steps to take — and in what order — as well as keeping track of important decisions along the way, or getting the right information you need to make a decision. This could be doing something simple like baking cookies, in which case you probably don't need a computer. But you can use a little bit of computing power to carry out a simple sequence of steps and decisions to come up with something really creative.

Maybe you want to know when your cat is coming and going from your house. Perhaps you want to know when your houseplants need a little more water and then give it to them automatically. Or suppose that you want to be able to open your front door with a code or card, instead of a physical key. Each of these involves just a little bit of sensing what's going on in the real world, combined with decision making, and then performing some kind of action.

In the case of watering your plants, it's something a human might be prone to forgetting or something you just don't want to pay attention to all the time. Sounds like the perfect job for a computer. That's where Arduino comes to the rescue.

About Arduino

The Arduino Uno (see Figure 1-1) is a general purpose microcontroller programming and prototyping platform that you can easily program to react to things going on in the real world. You can also link between the real world and the virtual world by connecting up your Arduino to the Internet, either sending data to the Internet or responding to data on the Internet, or both.

You can use it to sense almost anything you can find an electronic sensor for, including light, temperature, pressure, sound, even smell — if you consider environmental pollution to be a smell. You can even build your own sensors. How your Arduino reacts depends on how you program it. You can use its output capabilities to sound alarms, open doors and windows, activate lights or motors — the possibilities are almost endless.

Arduino is used for *prototyping* ideas — getting them half built and then trying out what works. Prototyping means testing alternatives to come up with creative solutions to problems (see Figure 1-1). You try out part of a project to see how your sensors respond and then change how your Arduino program functions, depending on what works best for you. Although the projects in this book are like little recipes, they are just a starting point. You could — and should — use any of them to build much more elaborate ideas and projects.

Figure 1-1:
The general purpose Arduino Uno prototyping board.

Discovering Who Uses Arduino

The Arduino family is used by makers, hackers, designers, artists, architects, and even professional engineers to quickly and easily try out interactive design ideas. The Arduino Uno is inexpensive and easy to use, with a big community of supporters, tinkerers, and developers who are constantly coming up with new ways to use it and improve it. In the next sections, I go over a few of the kinds of people and communities that are using Arduinos every day.

Arduino in education

Arduino provides a really simple way to learn how to program microcontrollers to sense and react to events in the real world and even online. Because it was conceived as a way to support designers and artists — people who are not typically computer programmers — it is very easy to get started and easy to use. I have taught hundreds of people — from little kids to retirees — to get started programming with Arduino. They have gotten simple programs up and running in as little as a half-hour and built their skills to develop their own sophisticated projects in a weekend. As you see from the projects in this book, it doesn't take long to get your Arduino doing some pretty interesting stuff. And the more time you put into using it, the more you can get out of it.

Art and design schools use Arduino to design new interactive product prototypes, interactive artwork, performances, and even clothing. High schools and secondary schools teach core concepts in computer programming. University students in engineering and computer science departments use Arduino to create interactive models and prototypes as well as learn sophisticated computer-controlled engineering techniques.

Arduino in the corporate world

A growing community of industry professionals in the corporate world use Arduinos to make interactive stuff in their work. Design firms use them to develop interactive product prototypes. Software engineering companies use them to test software systems that interact with the physical world. Ad agencies use them to come up with new and creative interactive campaigns. Arduinos are used to control interactive exhibits and conferences and trade shows in both the industry and in digital media sectors. They are used as management-consulting tools to help teams coordinate problem solving and improve collaboration.

Making and hacking communities

In little pockets all over the world, a new community of tinkerers, makers, and hackers has emerged. Arduino has been a fuel for this creative fire and continues to be one of the key hardware prototyping platforms that people create projects with, talk about, and share with one another.

What are they about?

There have been small electronics and hardware clubs since the early days of the twentieth century, when teenage boys were encouraged to build their own "cat's whisker" radios to listen to the new local radio stations that were popping up all across the United States. Over the decades, a large community of radio buffs grew, especially among fans of the shortwave radio frequencies. These "ham" radio aficionados set up their own transmitters and spent long hours listening to the radio waves for new and far-flung transmissions from friends and strangers. By the 1970s, the stage was set for a whole new generation of electronics fans who started clubs around not just radios but also the newly available home computers. Lots of midnight oil was burned as tinkerers and hobbyists stayed up hacking code and trading ideas on electronic bulletin board systems. This was the breeding ground for some of today's giants, including Apple. Then the Internet exploded onto the scene and changed everything.

At about the same time Arduino was created in 2005, a small subculture emerged that was sort of an extension of the computer clubs and do-it-yourself groups and clubs. Fueled by the Internet, there was sort of a renaissance of computer clubs and do-it-yourself groups, as it became easier to use computers and electronics to make interesting interactive stuff. Some people even call it a "maker movement." The Arduino fits right in with DIY groups, makers, tinkerers, and hackers. There are now hundreds of makerspaces (also called hackspaces) around the world. If you live in a big or medium-size city, there is probably one near you. *Makerspaces* are community-operated physical space where people with common interests (like Arduino!) can meet, get ideas, collaborate, and share accomplishments. Check for a makerspace in your area. These are the best places to learn how to build even more cool stuff with your Arduino.

The open source world

The term *open source* is thrown around a lot these days. If you haven't come across it, you will, because the Arduino is one aspect of the open source world. Open source refers to both a philosophy and a software development approach that advocates for complete transparency in all the points of authorship of software. That lets anyone see how a program is built and potentially contribute to its development. The open source movement is a reaction to the tight control that software companies have had over their products. Their code is intellectual property, and they want to keep control of it both to prevent others from stealing their ideas and to maintain the quality of their products. However, the downside is that consumers are disempowered from making changes and can sometimes be locked in to buying upgrades they may not want. In principle, anyone with a little know-how can pitch in and contribute to the software development of open source projects, because the code is all online and freely downloadable. The Linux operating system, Google's Android operating system for mobile phones, and Mozilla's Firefox Web Browser are popular examples of open source software.

Thinking about computer hardware as being open source is a relatively new idea, and Arduino is at the forefront. It was conceived as a tool that anyone can build and use to do his own prototyping, using the ATmega328 micro-controller. All the plans to produce your own Arduino are freely available online, and you can put one together without paying anyone else to do so. In practice, it's usually cheaper to buy one, but the principle still holds that the plans are freely available and redistributable.

Contributing to the Arduino project

In the spirit of collaborative development, people are also invited to contribute to the development of the Arduino platform and a thriving community of enthusiasts has contributed to both the hardware development and to the many software libraries that extend Arduino's capabilities. If you want to jump in on the action, all you have to do is join the conversation in the Arduino developer discussion boards and consider writing some libraries of your own. If you are really eager, you may even be able to contribute to the development of the next Arduino board.

Understanding Microcontrollers

The heart of an Arduino is a *microcontroller,* a little computer that performs menial decision-making tasks that might be tedious, too fast, too slow, or otherwise irritating for a human to do. You can make it sense events in the real world and then react to them by doing something. This little guy is perfectly happy to wait for days until the houseplant dries out and then give it a little drink. You simply need to tell him what to wait for and what actions to take. And he's really very little.

Because it's a *micro*controller, it's very small, so it doesn't need much power and can be put into tiny spaces like a project box. How small are microcontrollers? Physically, the one on the Arduino is about as large as they come, about half the size of a pack of gum, as you can see in Figure 1-2. The micro-controller is the rectangular *integrated circuit (IC)* on the blue *printed circuit board (PCB).* It's that size because it's easy to handle with your fingers, so you can replace the microcontroller on your Arduino if it croaks for some reason. But microcontrollers start about this large and go down from there, all the way to the microscopic level. The main factors that determine their size are their capabilities and cost. In fact, the actual processor *core* on your Arduino chip is much, much smaller than the exterior IC chip itself.

Figure 1-2:
The Arduino's brain, an ATmega328 microcontroller.

Along with the processor core, which processes the instructions you give it, the silicon chip has a small memory area for storing your commands, called *program memory* and *random-access memory (RAM),* which is used to keep track of things while the program is running. It also has input and output peripherals to handle sending and receiving data, either in the real world or to other computers, and with the correct code, to the Internet.

Microcontrollers were invented in the early 1970s to do all sorts of everyday automation tasks for industry. Your Arduino uses the single-chip ATmega328 microcontroller, which is part of the AVR family of products from the chipmaker Atmel and was originally developed in the mid-1990s.

The best part about micro*controllers* is that they are inexpensive, unlike their big brothers, the micro*processors* in your computer, laptop, tablet, or phone. Microcontrollers are inexpensive because they have limited capabilities (see Figure 1-2). They are mainly designed to control things or otherwise respond to sensory input, and are called *embedded systems.* Bigger computers have more general capabilities and need more power and therefore, cost more, and use *general purpose* microprocessors.

Because they are inexpensive, you can use them for all kinds of small computing tasks that don't need a full-size computer, like opening your front door with a code. The microcontroller on your Arduino costs less than a couple of bucks. The rest of the cost of an Arduino comes from all the convenient things that are onboard that help you to send programs to it and interact with the world.

Using tiny computers to do useful stuff

Microcontrollers are the unseen helping hands that are all around us, working tirelessly all the time to make modern life convenient and pleasant. They open doors for us (literally), keep us entertained, and can make a pretty decent cup of coffee. They also ensure that we get from Point A to Point B safely, being embedded in planes, trains, and yes, automobiles. Here are a few examples of what we use them for and similar projects in this book. It's not an exhaustive list, but it should give you an idea of what microcontrollers are used for and how ubiquitous they are!

Toys and games

If you walk into a toy store these days, you come across hundreds of devices that walk, talk, blink, flash, and even respond to how you position their parts or speak to them. Even very inexpensive interactive toys have embedded microcontrollers that perform the same functions as an Arduino. They are usually very tiny and specially designed for mass production and are often hidden under a dab of epoxy on the printed circuit board (PCB) inside the toy, as shown in Figure 1-3. In fact, some products may even use a microcontroller from the same Atmel family. They are programmed at the factory to respond to input and actuate lights, sounds, and movements.

Although it's not interactive, the light pet in Chapter 5 is a simple, preprogrammed toy like many you might see in a store. It's not interactive, but by the time you finish a few projects in this book, you'll be able to make it respond interactively to light, touch, temperature, or other kinds of input.

Home appliances

Your kitchen is almost literally a digital mission control center. A major proportion of the electronic appliances you use to whip up a meal have a microcontroller in them. The microwave has a timer to control power changes and timing. The oven has similar capabilities. A coffee machine also has a timing function and different programs for brewing different cups of java. Advanced food processors sense the consistency of the food mixture and have safety shutoffs. All of these capabilities are done with embedded microcontrollers that sense and respond to the world.

The Arduino Clock in Chapter 7 gives you a taste of what's possible and describes how to build a programmable alarm. With a little further research, you could even hook up its alarm to kick off your own cup of brew!

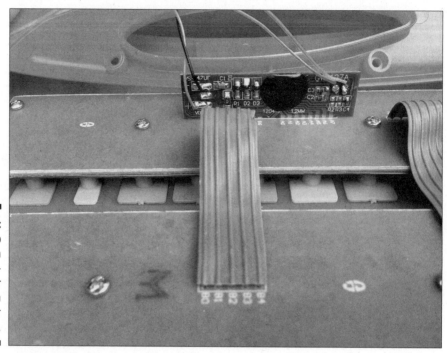

Figure 1-3:
A close-up
view of a
toy's micro-
controller
hidden
under
epoxy.

Automated manufacture

If you are building lots of components into a single product, automation is essential and microcontrollers assist with the process. Whether it's a child's toy car or a real car, microcontrollers embedded into the assembly line ensure the precise placement of parts, test for errors in manufacture, adjust the feed of subcomponents, track inventory, and perform other useful functions. Their core capability of sensing the environment and responding quickly, and according to a fixed program, ensures that manufactured products are consistently built and product inventories carefully managed.

The radio frequency ID (RFID) reader in Chapter 9 uses the same RFID technology that many inventory tracking systems use to manage raw materials, parts, and inventory warehouses.

Field sensing and response

Microcontrollers can be placed into conditions where it is simply impractical or downright dangerous to place a human. Imagine you want to ensure that a leak in a gas pipeline doesn't progress into a full-scale explosion. A microcontroller embedded in the line can ensure that the supply is switched off if a pressure leak is detected. Similarly, you wouldn't want to pay someone to monitor moisture levels in a greenhouse. A microcontroller can activate a spray of water at a fixed interval or according to measured environmental conditions.

The automated plant irrigator in Chapter 10 is a household version of this very useful capability.

Building automation

You are familiar with building security systems to keep out intruders. Along with this, many buildings are now using sensors to detect the internal climate and energy efficiency conditions. Architects now design many modern structures with a "nervous system" of embedded sensors that can adjust heating and cooling automatically, in specific zones or individual rooms, and with the use of energy-efficient heating, cooling, and air handling.

The home sensing project in Chapter 12 is a mini-sized version of a sensor network that you can build in your own home.

Process control

Microcontrollers are used in industry for things such as assembly line control and sensing. For example, microcontrollers can test to find out if all bottles in a line have been filled to the correct level. Microcontrollers attached to sensors can quickly and easily detect problems and either report the fill problem to a central computer or actuate a system to remove the bottle from the line. This can be done much faster than any human could do it. Many product manufacturing processes use microcontrollers because they are cheap and reliable. Similarly, mixing up the raw materials for batches of bread, candy, petroleum products, or concrete can be precisely monitored and controlled with microcontrollers like the one on an Arduino.

Although none of the projects in this book does quite this kind of thing, after you've built a few of them you can figure out how to modify, prototype, and pick and choose from the features you want to build into a project to control many different kinds of processes or activities.

Getting Started

If you haven't already jumped into the middle of the book to check out what you can do, stop now and take a peek. I wrote this book to get you going with some cool Arduino projects so that you can make something amazing that nobody has dreamed up yet. I hope these projects inspire you. Poking around online may provide additional fuel for your creative fire.

Before you get going, though, it's a good idea to assemble a few tools that will make your Arduino adventures a bit easier. All the projects in this book require some basic tools — and an Arduino. If you are going to dive right in, more power to you. But do take a minute to peruse Chapter 2 to get together a few of the tools you'll need. If you have never used an Arduino before, check out Chapter 3, which covers some of the basics you need to know before you dive into a project.

So what are you waiting for? Take the plunge and get going!

Chapter 2

Setting Up Your Workspace and Tools

Getting your workspace ready is the first step in building your Arduino project. You can do the first couple of projects in this book just about anywhere, but for anything a little more involved, you want to create a dedicated work area that has your necessary tools at hand.

In this chapter, I explain how to create a good workspace with the right set of tools for the projects in this book. The project chapters assume that you have the basic workspace and tools ready to go, so I only list the parts you need to build each of the projects. After you get focused on a project, interrupting your work to get some basic tool that you've overlooked is a drag. But if you have most (or all) of the basics of your workspace covered, you won't have to stop what you are doing to go get a hand tool or run to the hardware store. You also learn how to set up your Arduino software and get your Arduino connected to your computer.

Preparing to Build

You can start working on Arduino projects just about anywhere you can crack open a computer. I've worked on some basic projects at a local coffee shop — though I did get some stares! However, for the projects in this book, you want to create a better working environment. Find a good spot where you can work comfortably, see what you are doing, and fine-tune it to be the perfect laboratory for your creations.

Setting up your workspace

You need a dedicated area where you can build and test your projects — especially the bigger ones in this book, which can take a few hours. Find a spot in your house, apartment, shed, garage, studio — wherever you and your work will be undisturbed. Figure 2-1 shows my work area for building Arudino projects.

Getting the workspace right

A good Arduino project workspace has the following elements:

- ✔ A comfortable and dry environment
- ✔ A solid workbench or desk and comfortable chair
- ✔ Plenty of power outlets
- ✔ Enough room for a computer or laptop
- ✔ A nearby network connection or a place to where you can run a network cable
- ✔ Good lighting and ventilation (especially for evacuating soldering fumes)
- ✔ Shelving and storage for projects you are working on
- ✔ Small boxes and drawers for organizing parts and tools

The environment (light heat, comfort, and so on) needs to be comfortable to work in for a long stretch. If it's too cold or too hot, too noisy, or filled with distractions, completing your work may take longer. Also, if you're interrupted, you may struggle to regain your momentum.

Make yourself a sort of hideaway where you can stay focused. I like to have electronic music playing so that my little wall of sound creates a private zone where I can become engrossed in my work.

Your computer is essential to the project building process, so make sure that you have room for your desktop or laptop on the workbench. Also you will want to hunt for references online, look up datasheets, and post questions to forums, so a reliable Internet connection is vital.

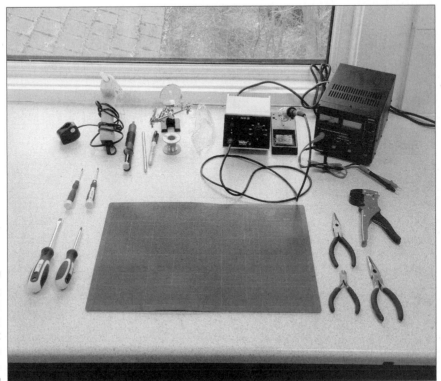

Figure 2-1:
A good
working
environment
and some
basic tools.

Fine-tuning your Arduino zone

The easier projects in this book can be completed in an hour or less. But the more complicated ones will take several hours. Inevitably, something will probably come up to interrupt you, so you need a place where you can set up incomplete projects that you can leave and come back to later.

Safety is always a factor when working with electrical circuits. Even though the projects in this book do not work with the full power available from wall sockets, you should always treat electronic projects as though they could have potentially dangerous voltages.

If you have little ones roaming around, you should take special precautions to keep them away. Curious fingers love to yank on dangling cords and wires. If a child yanks on a dangling cable, she could pull things off your workbench and onto her head! A hot soldering iron left unattended could cause severe burns. Not a nice way to introduce anyone to Arduino and electronics.

I've seen very few hacker workbenches that do not have cans of soda and snacks littered here and there. However, keeping food and drink separate from your workbench prevents costly accidents.

Empty pizza boxes can hide critical parts, and you can waste time hunting for things. Accidentally spilled drinks do not do good things to live circuits.

Now that you have the creature comforts taken care of, you need the right tools for the job.

Selecting Basic Tools

You need some basic tools for fabricating all the projects in this book. They basically fall into two categories — electronics tools and physical building and fabrication tools. You can get most or all of these components from electronics retailers, such as Radio Shack or Maplin (U.K.). Specialty electronics suppliers on the Internet also stock them and are often cheaper than retail outlets, so hunt around at DigiKey (U.S./U.K.), NKC Electronics, Rapid (U.K.), RS (U.S./U.K.), and Farnell (U.S./U.K.). Don't forget to check eBay and Amazon for deals, too.

Here's a list of the basic tools you need, which are described in more detail later in this chapter:

- **A multimeter:** A multimeter is an essential tool for most Arduino and electronic projects. You use it to perform basic tests to make sure that you have good connections in your electrical circuits. You can measure the characteristics of an electrical circuit and troubleshoot why something might not be working. A multimeter is also handy for testing and measuring individual electronic components. You should have one on hand for testing and troubleshooting your projects.

- **A breadboard and jumper wires:** All the projects in this book involve wiring up electrical components, LEDs, sensors, or actuators to your Arduino. This can be as simple as one or two wires, but some of the projects entail using dozens of connections. A breadboard is a simple tool to help you easily make all these electrical connections. You need jumper wires to make connections when you are putting a project together. Wires come in solid core and stranded versions (which contain many fine wires). Solid core jumper wires are needed for working with breadboards.

- **A soldering iron:** A breadboard is ideal for temporary connections and prototyping, but for some connections you want something more permanent. This is where a soldering iron comes in. You use it to make strong, permanent connections between components in your electrical circuit. If you want to mount buttons onto an enclosure for your project, you probably want to solder wires to the buttons and connect these to your Arduino. You can even build part of your circuit on a breadboard and use soldered connections for switches or sensors that are located some distance away. You can complete all the projects in this book without a soldering iron, but having one for your workbench is a good idea.

✔ **A power supply:** The Arduino itself can provide small amounts of power to light up a few LEDs, but for anything more, you probably need to have a power supply on hand. In this book, some projects need additional power supplies, and their exact specifications are provided in the parts list.

You also need some basic tools for light fabrication. Not all of these are essential, but you will often find that the one tool you *don't* have is the one you need, so build up a good armory of gear. These tools, shown in Figure 2-2, are listed in my own order of importance, but your needs might vary:

✔ **A selection of precision screwdrivers:** Both flathead and cross-head ("Phillips head") screwdrivers are essential. You should have several sizes of both.

✔ **"Helping hands":** A small clamp with two alligator clips to hold your work piece. They often come with an integrated magnifying glass. Essential, unless you have three arms.

✔ **Wire strippers:** Use wire strippers for cutting and stripping the insulation off of wires. These come in several different styles. Splurge a little here — a rule of thumb is to buy something costing in the midrange. Too cheap, and they will produce poor results and be frustrating to use.

✔ **Needle-nose pliers:** Pliers work well for holding fine objects. You should have both small and large ones on hand.

✔ **Angled side cutters:** Use these for clipping component leads and cutting wires.

✔ **An X-ACTO knife/craft knife:** An X-ACTO knife is a key tool for making fine cuts.

✔ **A box cutter/carpet knife with replaceable blades:** Use a box cutter to cut sturdier materials.

✔ **A cutting mat:** Protects your work surface.

✔ **A Sharpie and a pencil:** Essential tools for making cutting marks and permanent marks. I say you don't have a complete workbench without a Sharpie!

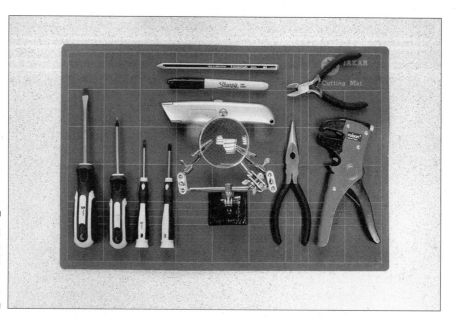

Figure 2-2:
Some
essential
light fabri-
cation tools.

Selecting and using your multimeter

A multimeter, like the one shown in Figure 2-3, is an essential tool for testing, measuring, and diagnosing problems in electronic circuits. Older multimeters used a needle and graduated scales for the display, but modern ones use a digital, numeric readout. You use a multimeter to measure several basic attributes of your circuit, including:

- **Continuity:** Determines whether you have a good connection between two points.
- **Voltage:** Measures potential electromotive force in a circuit.
- **Current:** Measures the continuous, uniform flow of electrons through an unbroken pathway in an electrical circuit.
- **Resistance:** Measures opposition to the flow of current within a circuit.

You can also measure the voltage provided by batteries and power supplies, and the characteristics of discrete electronic components, such as resistors and diodes.

As with soldering irons, different multimeters have different features, and the more expensive ones have advanced features you might not need. Higher priced ones also enable you to measure transistors and capacitors and offer features, such as auto-ranging. Inexpensive meters require you to estimate the range of measurement and set the dial accordingly. On auto-ranging multimeters, you don't have to set the dial to select the range of measurement that you are reading. Auto-ranging is particularly handy but is usually much more expensive.

Probably the most common thing you use a multimeter for is checking continuity — making sure that the things you think are connected really are connected. You don't need the Ferarri of multimeters, but you should spend a little more for one that has an audio signal for continuity. It's a pain to check continuity by holding leads on a circuit while you are also looking at the display. It's much easier to just poke around and listen for an audio signal.

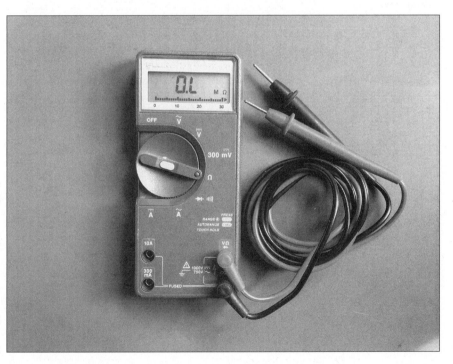

Figure 2-3:
A digital multimeter is an essential tool for your Arduino project work.

Selecting and using a power supply

Some of the projects here require you to provide additional power, separately from your Arduino, and you may want to build a project that controls a motor, solenoid, or other device that has its own power source. You can use a battery pack or a dedicated power supply — each has a different use.

A battery pack is useful for projects requiring a small amount of power for a relatively short period of time. Battery packs are also essential if you want to ditch your computer and let the Arduino roam free and untethered, such as with the robot car in Chapter 14. You can get battery holders of all kinds — from the small and convenient AAA and AA types to chunky C and D cells. And of course, you can try specialty and rechargeable batteries. In general, the larger the battery pack, the longer it lasts. Most cylindrical batteries provide 1.5 volts each, and you need a minimum of 6 volts to supply Arduino projects, so get a pack that holds at least four cells (1.5 volts each x 4 batteries = 6 volts).

If you need a longer lasting source of power for something that's permanently installed somewhere, you should use a fixed power supply that is plugged into the household power. For example, if you are using lots of motors, they need to get power from somewhere. This power can come from a wall transformer (which I call a "wall wart") with a high enough current rating to suit your needs. You can buy dedicated bench-top units that supply variable voltage and current and have digital readouts, which are useful for building and testing projects that will be installed somewhere else later. Bench-top supplies tend to cost much more, even into the triple digits! If you decide to get one, a basic power supply that offers 12 to 30 volts DC and 3 to 5 amps should be sufficient. (See Figure 2-4.) You can get by with a basic one that simply supplies 7 to 12 volts DC and 500 milliamps (mA) because that's sufficient to power an Arduino, with a little extra capacity left over.

Figure 2-4:
A bench power supply, a compact 12V transformer, and a wall transformer or "wall wart."

Regardless of the project you are working on, your power supply should be rated to provide the correct voltage and amperage for the devices you are using. You should either use the power supply that was provided with the thing you are trying to control, or you should choose a power supply that will match the voltage and exceed the current requirements of the devices you are operating.

Understanding electricity and safety

In working with electronics, safety is critical. You must take basic precautions to protect yourself. None of the projects in this book involves connecting directly to wall power, but you must use precautions anyway and develop good safety habits. Even though you may only be working with low DC voltages, if you are using components, such as motors and solenoids, which require a lot of current, you can end up working with enough current to give you a nasty bite.

Therefore, it's a good idea to follow some basic safety rules when working with all electronic projects:

Do's

✔ Always test with one hand tied behind your back. Well, at least one hand not on the work piece. If enough stray current flows between both your hands, and across you heart, it can cause arrhythmia. That's not likely at the low DC voltages you are working with here, but it's best to be safe and get into the habit.

✔ The integrated circuits on your Arduino and other components are sensitive to wayward voltages, including static electricity. Several thousand volts of static electricity can build up on you and you might not even know it, especially on carpeted floors. If it does and you touch your hardware, you can fry it in an instant. To protect against this, you can buy an inexpensive anti-static wrist strap, which will guard against unexpected sparks by connecting you at all times to ground, which diverts any electrical charge from building up on your body.

✔ Wear light, comfortable safety glasses. Clipping wires can fly around the room and hot solder can sometimes spit and splutter — you don't want any molten metal heading for your eyes.

Don'ts

✔ Don't touch metal contacts or leads in a live circuit.

✔ Don't alter a live circuit. Always disconnect power before removing or adding components to your Arduino or breadboard.

✔ Don't work barefoot. Maximize the resistance between you and the floor by wearing good, rubber soled shoes. A puddle of water is a great conductor and you don't want to be in one should something go wrong.

Working with breadboards, stripboards, and perfboards

To quickly and easily connect your project circuits, start out by using a breadboard. A *breadboard* is a small block of plastic with lots of columns and rows of holes into which you can insert jumper wires and electronic components. All the projects in this book use a breadboard for building and testing. After you've got it working properly, you can either put your Arduino and your breadboard inside an enclosure or go the more permanent route and build your circuit on a stripboard or perfboard, which requires a bit of soldering (more about these options later in the chapter).

About breadboards

Underneath the holes of a breadboard, tiny metal strips form springs that grasp wires, and the legs of components that are inserted into the holes. Because the springs are metal, if you connect wires or components to the same springs, they are electrically connected together.

Because breadboards use springs to hold the wires, you should always use solid core wire on them. Stranded wire, which is composed of multiple tiny wires, gets scrunched by the springs when you try to push them into the holes on the breadboard. It's a big pain to use stranded wire, so save yourself the trouble.

In the main work area on the board, the holes are organized into rows of five (typically) and grouped into two columns on the breadboard. There is usually a *trough* between the two columns of holes, which allows you to insert an integrated circuit (IC) into the breadboard, such that each of its legs is served by four adjacent holes.

Many breadboards have columns of holes that run the full length of either side of the board. These are not electrically connected to the main work area, and they are often labeled + (positive) and – (negative, or "ground") and may be color coded. You use these as *rails* for power and ground. When you use a breadboard with your Arduino, you always connect a wire from the Arduino pin labeled +5 to the positive rail and from the pin labeled GND ("ground") to the negative rail. You also want to connect most of your components at some point or other to power and ground, so you usually need lots of connections to them.

You should have on hand a large size breadboard with 830 contact points and a couple of half-size boards with 400 contact points. If you run out of room, you can connect together two boards by using the notches and fingers on the sides of the breadboards. But be warned, there's no standard for these, so they usually need to be from the same manufacturer to do so.

About stripboards and perfboards

Stripboards and perfboards are similar to breadboards, in that they supply lots of holes to connect things together. However, they are designed for permanent connections that are soldered together.

- ✔ **Stripboards** are coated with adhesive strips of conductive copper that run underneath the holes and components are soldered to the strips of copper, providing an electrical connection and a strong physical bond.

- ✔ **Perfboards** simply have metallic pads that surround each individual hole, into which you can solder parts, and which you can solder together to create electrical circuits.

Stripboards and perfboards come in a huge range of sizes and configurations, so if and when you are ready to go for a more permanent solution, you should shop around for the size and type you need (see Figure 2-5).

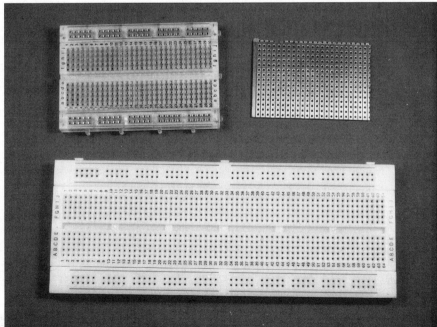

Figure 2-5:
Mini and full-size breadboards and a piece of stripboard.

Choosing Your Soldering Iron and Accessories

Soldering (pronounced "sodd"-ering in the U.S. and "sold"-ering in the U.K.) is simply melting solder, which has a relatively low meting point (about 700 °F!), and allowing it to cool, creating a strong, conductive joint. You can join wires to each other and join wires to components. You can bond wires to circuit prototyping boards, such as perfboards or stripboards, and also secure components in place, while creating a good electrical connection for a more permanent, lasting project. You can also simply solder some of the components (like switches and displays) to wires that lead to your breadboard. That way, you can mount them in a project box. On some projects in this book, you want to move buttons or switches from the breadboard to the project enclosure, which means that you need to solder extension wires on them.

Also, you will probably buy project kits to provide additional features to your Arduino projects. The Arduino clock in Chapter 7 uses a kit that requires you to solder the parts together onto a printed circuit board (PCB). Selling things as kits keeps their cost down, but it means that you have to do a little of the work to solder them together.

You use a soldering iron to heat up both the solder and the components that are being joined together. When the components are hot enough, the solder will flow onto them, at which point, you remove the tip of the soldering iron (and thus, the heat supply). The solder cools rapidly and if done correctly, forms a reliable bond.

The key soldering tools you need are:

- **Soldering iron:** Your main tool for the job. Irons can be very inexpensive, but the professional ones will set you back hundreds. If you want to save money, avoid the cheapest ones and aim for one that is at the top end of low-range options. You need one that supplies at least 30 watts. Irons come in both fixed and adjustable power output. Having adjustable power is nice, but probably not essential for most light soldering work.

- **Solder:** This is the main raw material you use to create soldered joints. There are both leaded and lead-free varieties. Some purists prefer leaded 60/40 solder (60 percent tin, 40 percent lead), but lead is toxic. So unless you have a particular need for it, go for the lead-free variety, with a rosin core. The rosin core melts and helps to clean the surfaces you are joining. Solder comes in a variety of diameters, but 0.032 diameter is ideal for most electronics soldering needs.

- **Extra tips:** Tips come in a variety of shapes and sizes. For most electronics work you need a cone-shaped tip rather than a chisel tip. Eventually through use or abuse, the soldering iron tip will wear out. Different manufacturers have different tip mounting systems, so you should buy a couple of extra tips when you buy your iron to avoid having to hunt for the right product later.

✔ **Soldering stand:** A device that holds the wand safely while it's hot, and which may have a sponge for cleaning the tip. These are often included with soldering iron kits.

✔ **Regular sponge and brass wire sponge:** These sponges are used to clean the tip of your iron. The tip is cleaned while the iron is hot. The regular sponge can be any garden variety cellulose kitchen sponge from the grocery store. The brass wire sponge costs a little more, but it has the benefit that it doesn't cool down the tip of the iron when you're cleaning it. If you clean regularly, your tip will last longer.

✔ **Desoldering tools:** You can find both soldering wick and soldering suckers (see Figure 2-6). The sucker is a spring-loaded pen that you can use to suck liquefied solder away from your work piece. A desoldering wick is simply braided flat copper ribbon, which you press against your work while heating it. Capillary action draws the liquefied solder onto the braid and away from your work. I tend to prefer wick, which is cheaper and usually more effective.

✔ **Tip cleaning paste:** This is pretty important to have on hand. Your tip may develop an oxidation coating, especially if you don't clean it regularly. Oxidation makes it very difficult to coat the tip and control the way your solder flows. Cleaning paste can help to remove oxidation and debris. It's a good idea to clean the tip with paste every now and then to ensure a good tip surface.

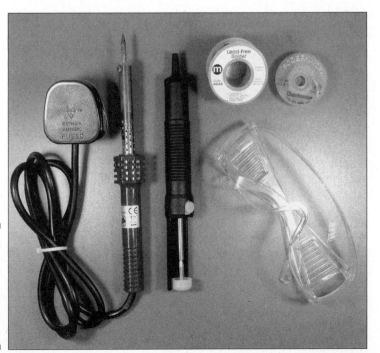

Figure 2-6:
An entry-level soldering iron and essential accessories.

Soldering basics are covered in Chapter 3 if you want to have a first try, or brush up on your skills.

Selecting Project Boxes and Housings

All the projects in this book are built on a breadboard because it's a fast and easy way to get going. If you want to protect the project, you can transfer it to a dedicated enclosure. Although I don't show this for the simpler projects in Part II, you may want to transfer them. If so, look around for a housing that will be suitable for your Arduino and electronics.

Potential project housings are everywhere, and almost anything that can be used as a small box will do. Some of the most creative and clever project enclosures were never intended to be Arduino projects. I've seen old discarded mantelpiece clocks repurposed as temperature and barometric pressure displays. There is a whole fanatical subculture of people who build Arduino projects using metals Altoids tins. Do you have Prince Albert in a can? Well, let him out, and use the can for your Arduino project!

When you go to a store, start to imagine what you could use to hold your project together. Pretty soon, you will start to see almost everything as a potential raw material for a project. It's a bit of a weird habit, but you will really start to see things in a different way. It's quirky and cool to geek out on packaging.

Department stores and "big box" stores, like Target, IKEA, and Costco, sell lots of home furnishings, knick-knacks, and housewares with an eye for decoration and design. Small boxes and inexpensive cases can be repurposed as a new home for your Arduino project and give it a little style. Figure 2-7 shows a little light from the kids' section at IKEA. Take out his guts and he makes a perfect Arduino enclosure.

Thinking outside the box, electronics suppliers usually stock a range of generic enclosures, in both metal and plastic. When selecting one of these, make sure you have the correct tools to fabricate your housing. If you are going to mount switches, buttons, or a display on the project box, you will need to be able to cut through the material cleanly. It is really difficult to drill a hole into thick materials and metals without the right saws, drills, and bits, so make sure to select a housing that you can work with.

Figure 2-7:
A quirky
housing.

A final source of project enclosures is one of the new and popular laser cutting or 3D printing services, such as thinginverse, ponoko, pololu, or shapeways. You send off your design to them, and they will ship you your finished custom laser cut or 3D-printed design. Many of these companies also have templates you can download for boxes and enclosures.

You don't have to limit yourself to things you can buy. You can make a perfectly good project enclosure out of thick cardboard, matt board, or plastic and a little bit of adhesive.

Choosing Your Arduino or Arduino Kit

The Arduino project has come a very long way in only a few years. It started out with just a single simple board that offered basic features and did not have a USB connector. You can now find over a dozen Arduino boards, each with its own unique characteristics and features. All the projects in this book were written for the current flagship product, the Arduino Uno. The current full listing of Arduino products is on the Arduino website (`http://arduino.cc`). Select the Arduino that best matches your needs and your budget.

The most important ones to be familiar with, shown in Figure 2-8, are:

- ✔ **Arduino Uno:** This is the main workhorse in the Arduino family. All the projects in this book were built and tested with it. The Uno is based on the ATmega328 microcontroller and operates at 16MHz. It has 14 digital input/output (I/O) pins and 6 analog input pins. Power can be provided over the USB connection or DC Barrel connector, or by using power input pin headers. The onboard power regulator is smart enough to know which one is being used. It has a handy onboard "utility" LED connected to digital Pin 13, and a reset button for when things get weird.

    A key difference of the Uno from all previous boards is that it has a USB controller chip integrated onboard. This feature makes it much easier to hit the ground running because you simply plug it into your computer and the device will be recognized. Previous versions required you to install software drivers for a USB interface provided by FTDI.

- ✔ **Arduino Mega:** The Mega 2560 is the Uno's big brother. It has all the basic functionality and is fully compatible, but benefits from a ton of extra connections — 54 digital IO pins and 16 analog input pins! It also has more pins that offer pulse-width modulation (PWM), which is useful for dimming LEDs and controlling motors. It costs a little more, but if you want to control an army of devices or read in a fistful of sensors, this Mega is the way to go.

- ✔ **Arduino Leonardo:** The Leonardo is similar to the Uno but has more digital I/Os (20) and analog (12) inputs. Where it really stands apart, though, is that it has a second serial port. It can also do some nifty tricks like emulating a keyboard and a mouse. It can be programmed to control these input devices using the Keyboard and Mouse classes and your computer will act as if it's receiving keyboard and mouse input. Nifty!

- ✔ **Arduino Due:** The Arduino Due boasts a much beefier processor and is really a full-fledged computer on a board, similar to a Raspberry Pi or a BeagleBoard. It has an Atmel SAM3X8E ARM Cortex-M3 CPU that runs at the brisk pace of 84MHz, and 54 digital ports. It's more robust than what you need for anything in this book and uses 3.3V DC onboard rather than 5V DC, so you should avoid it for the projects here.

- ✔ **Lilypad Arduino:** The Lilypad is an Arduino with personality! It's a favorite of people who want a little style and designed for sewing into wearables and textiles and clothing. It has almost the same number of digital input/output pins as a regular Arduino, but they are arranged in a circle and the connections can be sewn into clothing with conductive thread. Running at 8MHz, it's "fast fashion"!

- ✔ **Arduino Micro:** The Micro is super cute and perfect for tight spaces. It has only the essential requirements — a built-in micro USB connector and 20 digital input/output pins. It has no pin headers, so you solder connections directly onto the board itself. You can also solder on headers so that it can be inserted into a breadboard.

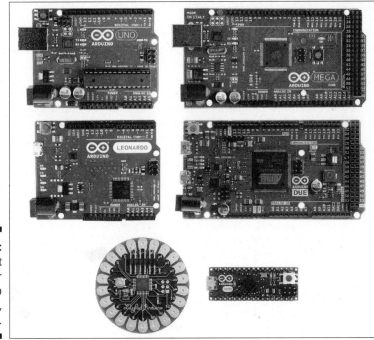

Figure 2-8:
The most popular Arduino boards, currently.

You may also come across older boards and want to use them for your project. Older Arduinos you may encounter are Diecimila, Duemilanove, NG, and Bluetooth.

Be aware that the Arduino IDE has changed a bit as the hardware has evolved and not all the older boards will work with the most current IDE. Also, some software libraries that offer extended features are not compatible with some of the older boards. If you have trouble with a project in this book using one of the older boards, you may want to try it out with an Arduino Uno instead.

Getting to know Arduino shields

A huge number of products build on the Arduino platform, providing additional capabilities for sensing and controlling things. The Arduino has *pin headers* at the top and bottom of the board that allow you to insert wires to make easy electric connections for these accessories. The "footprint" of these headers provides an easy, standardized layout to add circuit boards to provide these extra features, such as Ethernet, Wi-Fi, wireless radio, GPS, audio playback, and motor control, to name just a few. These accessory boards are known in the Arduino community as *shields*.

Arduino shields contain all the necessary electronics for the features they offer and have pins on the underside that match the input pin headers of the Arduino. The Ethernet shield in Figure 2-9 allows you connect an Arduino to your router and the Internet. Because they have the same footprint as the Arduino, you can simply insert shields on top of the Arduino (or Arduino Mega) to make a nice little sandwich of coolness.

Most shields still provide access to some or all of the Arduino's digital and analog pins. However, the additional features that a shield offers require the use of some of those pins. You have to check the shield's data sheet to make sure that the pins you want to use for a project are not also required by your shield.

In addition to shields, you'll come across other devices known as break-out boards. These are mini printed circuit boards that are built around an integrated circuit with a dedicated function, such as a real time clock (see Chapter 7), LED controller, or accelerometer. There are literally dozens of kinds of breakout boards, so named because they "break out" the tiny pins of the integrated circuit chip, making it easier to physically connect the chip to breadboards, Arduinos, or other components.

Chapters 7, 9, 11, and 13 contain projects that use shields or breakout boards.

Figure 2-9:
An Arduino
Ethernet
shield.

Setting Up Your Arduino on Your Computer

This section is written with the Uno or Mega in mind, but should also work with Micro, Lilypad, and older boards, such as Duemilanove and Diecimila. (You need to use a special connector if you are working with a Lilypad.) If you are installing a different Arduino, you should check for installation instructions on the official Arduino website (http://arduino.cc). Older Arduinos have a special chip onboard that handles the USB connection, made by a company called FTDI. Setting up older Arduinos, such as the Diecimila, Duemilanove, requires the installation of drivers for this chip.

When you've got your supplies ready and have an Arduino to play with, you need to set it up. You connect it to your computer's USB port via a USB A-to-B cable, which provides both power to run the board and a communication channel to send and receive programs and data. The communication channel is referred to as a *serial port,* and you can also use this to monitor activity while you are running a program. Some of the tiny specialty Arduino boards, such as the Mini ProMini and Lilypad, do not have an onboard USB connector. If you have one of these, you will need to use a special connector to attach the board to your computer. The suppliers of these boards usually offer suitable connectors for them, as well.

Installing the Arduino IDE

You write code for your Arduino projects with specially designed programming software called an Integrated Development Environment (IDE). The Arduino IDE (see Figure 2-10) also prepares the code for the microcontroller on your Arduino, and when you're ready to run it, handles uploading it to the board.

To install the development environment, follow these steps:

1. **Download Arduino IDE from the official Arduino website (http://arduino.cc).**

   Because the software is open-source, it's free. Make sure to choose the correct version for your computer operating system: Windows PC, Mac, or Linux.

   It's a good idea to check the Arduino website regularly because the software is updated frequently as improvements are made by the development team.

2. **Double-click on the archive to extract the compressed files.**

3. **Move the extracted files to the right location on your computer.**

   On a Mac, the extracted archive will yield an Arduino icon, which you can drag into your Applications folder and you are finished. On a

Windows computer, you will end up with a folder that contains several subfolders. You can place this into any convenient location, but most people drag it into Program Files.

On Windows machines, you need to install some drivers to connect to your board.

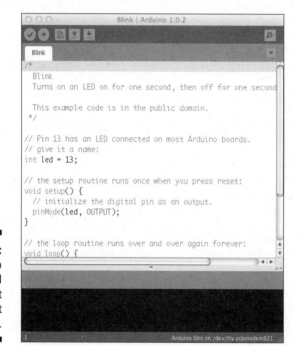

Figure 2-10:
The Arduino Integrated Development Environment (IDE).

Installing drivers on Windows computers

On Windows 7, Vista, and XP, you need to tell the operating system about your new Arduino and provide it with the correct software drivers so that it can use the board. Complete the following steps:

1. **After you plug in your board, Windows will detect the new hardware and begin the driver installation process.**

   The process will fail after a few moments, but don't worry. This just happens.

2. **Click on the Start Menu and then open the Control Panel.**

3. **In the Control Panel, click System and Security in the upper-left corner.**

   (On Windows XP, you may need to select Classic View to see the System icon.)

4. **Under the System heading (or system icon on XP), open the Device Manager.**

   Look for your newly connected Arduino under Ports (COM & LPT). You should see an open port named Arduino UNO (COMxx). If you don't, the computer has not detected that your Arduino was connected. Disconnect and reconnect it.

5. **Right-click on the Arduino UNO (COMxx) port and select Update Driver.**

   Doing this launches the Hardware Update Wizard. Do not connect to Windows Update to search for software. Click the Next button.

6. **Select the Install from a Specific Location option, and then click the Browse button to locate the folders that you just extracted from the zip archive.**

7. **Finally, navigate to and select the driver file for the Arduino Uno, which is called ArduinoUNO.inf.**

   It's located in the Drivers folder (not the FTDI USB Drivers folder).

   At this point, Windows will complete the installation for you. If everything goes smoothly, you should be ready to attach your board.

Connecting your Arduino

Now you're ready to fire up the Arduino and get going with building a project.

Make sure that your board is on a non-conductive surface. The connection points on the bottom of the board are exposed, so if your board happens to be resting on a metal laptop or other metal surface, these could be short-circuited, which at best could cause your board to function erratically and at worst, fry the microcontroller.

When you connect your board, the LED labeled ON (or PWR on earlier boards) should turn green and stay on continuously. You'll also notice that the LED labeled "L" flickers briefly, as the microcontroller starts up. Then it should flash on and off regularly at half-second intervals. It's running a demo program (the Blink program) that was loaded at the factory.

If you are building a big project, you can have multiple Arduinos on multiple USB ports; however, they *won't* be able to communicate with each other directly through their USB connections.

Installing Arduino drivers on Linux

Ubuntu, Fedora, Debian, openSUSE — Linux comes in many different flavors and distributions! Because of this, there is some variation in the installation procedure for different Linux distributions. Generally, Linux users are used to tweaking things at an advanced level, so I'm assuming that if you are running Linux already, you are comfortable with tweaking your system a bit. You should hunt around on the forums for installation instructions for your particular distribution and shell because detailed instructions for each one would take up more space than I have to write!

Now that you've hopefully got your Arduino installed and the little LED is flashing, you are ready to begin any of the projects in this book. You can skip over to what interests you and dive right in. However, if you're a complete beginner to programming, I encourage you take a peek at Chapter 3 first. That will help you become familiar with the IDE and the basics of the Arduino programming language.

Chapter 3

Understanding the Basics

. . . .

In This Chapter

▶ Understanding key Arduino concepts

▶ Reviewing basic electronics and components

▶ Understanding sensors and actuators

▶ Learning soldering basics

. . . .

*Y*ou've probably already connected your Arduino and tried out some of the example sketches that come with it, but you might not know about all the useful features in the Arduino programming environment. Also, there are a few things to keep in mind when connecting your Arduino to electronic circuits and putting everything into a protective enclosure.

This chapter covers how to get started with Arduino and the basic programming concepts you use to make your project work. Because you are working with electricity, you need to know some of the basics of how electronic circuits work. I also describe how to identify electronic components and how to read the circuit diagrams you find in each chapter.

Building your project sometimes requires a little light soldering. If you haven't done any soldering before, these projects are easy enough to give you a good start. After you hone your skills, you can tackle bigger projects or even add external components. I cover the basic technique here.

Understanding Key Concepts

You need to know a few basic concepts to get your Arduino running, write programs, and upload your programs to your Arduino. As I mention in Chapter 2, you use the Arduino integrated development environment (IDE), so that you can write code in a simplified language that is easy to read and understand.

When you send your code to your Arduino, the IDE converts it to the native machine code that your microcontroller understands, but which most humans have difficulty making sense of. This process is called *compiling* the code, and your IDE has a *compiler* built into it called "avrdude" (AVR Downloader/UploaDEr). If there are any basic problems compiling your code, like a missing letter or character, your compiler lets you know so that you don't upload code that simply won't work.

Figure 3-1 shows the Arduino IDE. You can see several controls above the programming window. Clicking the check mark makes the compiler verify that your code will run correctly. The right-pointing arrow sends your code to your board. The page icon creates a new Arduino file. The up arrow opens an existing sketch, and the down arrow saves the current sketch.

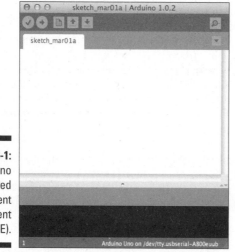

Figure 3-1:
The Arduino
integrated
development
environment
(IDE).

Below these controls is a blank, white area where you write and edit your code. Underneath the editing window is a reporting window with a black background. If your compiler wants to tell you anything, it'll be reported here. Status messages are displayed in white text. Errors are shown in orange.

The IDE also identifies the equipment and the communication port that Arduino is connected to. The IDE in Figure 3-1 is connected to an Arduino Uno (which uses an ATmega328 CPU), and it's on a communication port called tty.usbserial-A900euub on a Mac or Linux machine. On a Windows machine, this would show a COM port and its number.

Connecting your Arduino

You connect your Arduino to your computer with a USB cable, as described in Chapter 2. This provides both power from the USB port to run your Arduino and a communication channel, called a *serial port,* so that you can send and receive data from your Arduino.

Understanding your power supply

Your Arduino has a power supply on board that is smart enough to know whether it is connected to a USB port on a computer or to a battery or external power supply. It draws power from the USB port when you are connected. When you want to run it without a computer, you simply connect a 7 to 12 volt DC power supply to the barrel connector. You can use a battery or a power transformer.

You can also use the Arduino's power input pins to supply power. These are below the POWER label on your board. You insert power wires into the Vin and GND pins to supply 7 to 12 volts DC operating power to your Arduino. You can input higher voltages up to about 20 volts — though your power regulator on board might grow pretty hot, so it's not recommended. Also, you must be extremely careful not to connect things incorrectly because these pins bypass the Arduino's components that protect the Arduino from reverse voltage and short circuits.

Communicating with your Arduino

You use the serial port for programming, and you can also get your Arduino to report data to other programs on your computer or even to the Internet. The serial port is also handy for debugging when programs aren't operating correctly.

To the right of your IDE control menu is a magnifying glass icon. Clicking this icon opens a window that displays the serial communication channel that your Arduino is using. You can program your Arduino sketch to print statements to this window, which is useful for displaying data from sensors and for debugging problems with your code.

Programming your Arduino using the IDE

Arduino programs are referred to as *sketches* because you can quickly edit them and play around with how the software and the hardware work. The whole idea behind Arduino is that you can sketch out interactive project ideas, gradually arriving at a solution, as you try out ideas, keeping some, discarding others, and refining your work.

Like any design activity, working with Arduino is an iterative process. Although the projects in this book are complete and working, you should definitely take them further. Consider them as one instantiation of a final idea that you can refine and make your own. To do that, you need to know how Arduino code works.

Understanding Arduino code

All Arduino sketches have a standardized code structure. This keeps the code easy to read and modify later. The compiler doesn't care what order you put these things in, but by convention, people tend to structure their Arduino code in the following order:

1. **Comments:** You describe what the code does.

2. **Libraries:** You specify which libraries you want to use in your code. All libraries must be in your Arduino libraries folder or your compiler will complain.

3. **Variable declarations:** You specify what variables you are going to use in your code and what their initial values are. You learn more about the different kinds of variables you can use, as you build the projects in this book.

4. **Setup:** You define how your Arduino will be used and set up any pins and communications you will be using. This section is indicated by the instruction `setup(){` and it is always concluded with a closing curly bracket `:}`. Code in your setup is executed first and one time only.

5. **Loop:** You place the main instructions for your code. The loop is executed after setup and for as long as your Arduino is powered up. Any code between the curly brackets `{}` is processed sequentially and then repeated forever. The loop is processed as fast as the Arduino can go — around 16 million calculations per second.

6. **User-defined functions:** You create your own reusable functions that describe how to do something useful. If you need to repeat an operation or calculation many times as your Arduino is running, I recommend that you create a function to do this. This modular way of coding makes it easy to make a change to how your code works.

Setup and Loop are actually special functions. You can spot functions in Arduino code because they are followed by parentheses, which may contain *parameters*. `Setup()` and `Loop()` don't have any parameters, so you will see these functions preceded by the word *void*. The code that is executed by a function is always contained within curly brackets `{}`.

After you've sent code to an Arduino you can't get it back off again. You will never be able to read off the code that has already been uploaded, so make sure to keep your sketches organized. I even tape the name of the sketch to my Arduino, so I can remember what I loaded onto it last.

Each chapter in this book has code that you upload to your Arduino to make your project work. I provide a code listing and explain how it works in detail so that you understand how it works and learn how to enhance the projects and create your own new Arduino programs along the way. What follows is an example of this, using the most basic Arduino sketch, called Blink.

Understanding the Blink sketch

All programming languages have what's known as a "Hello World!" program, which demonstrates that the program code is up and running properly. The Arduino has one, and it's called "Blink" because it blinks an LED that is connected to Pin 13 on your board.

TECHNICAL STUFF

Because using an LED as an indicator is such a handy thing to do, the Arduino team put an LED right onto the board itself, labeled *L*. It's just to the right of the pin labeled AREF, and it should be blinking regularly if you have connected your Arduino for the first time and it has power. That's because it is running a LED Blink sketch that was programmed onto the CPU at the factory.

To see how it works, load the Blink sketch into the Arduino IDE. From the application menus, choose File➪Examples➪Basics➪Blink to load the demo sketch. You see the code shown in Figure 3-2. The first section contains comments that describe what the code does. Giving a summary of what your sketch does at the top of your code is a good idea.

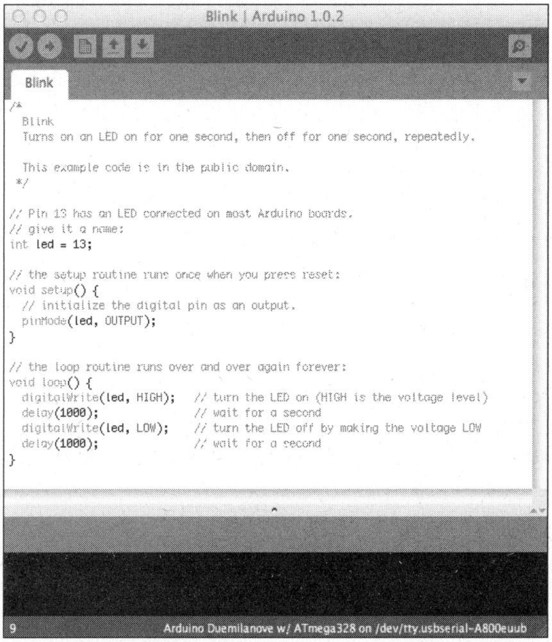
Blink | Arduino 1.0.2
Blink
/*
Blink
Turns on an LED on for one second, then off for one second, repeatedly.
This example code is in the public domain.
*/
// Pin 13 has an LED connected on most Arduino boards.
// give it a name:
int led = 13;
// the setup routine runs once when you press reset:
void setup() {
// initialize the digital pin as an output.
pinMode(led, OUTPUT);
}
// the loop routine runs over and over again forever:
void loop() {
digitalWrite(led, HIGH); // turn the LED on (HIGH is the voltage level)
delay(1000); // wait for a second
digitalWrite(led, LOW); // turn the LED off by making the voltage LOW
delay(1000); // wait for a second
}
9
Arduino Duemilanove w/ ATmega328 on /dev/tty.usbserial-A800euub

Figure 3-2: The Blink program loaded into the Arduino IDE.

You can create comments in your code by adding **/*** to a line, writing your comments on several lines, and finishing with ***/**. The compiler ignores any comments between these symbols. If you just want to add a comment on a single line, start it out with **//**:

```
/*
  Blink
  Turns on an LED for one second, then off for one second, repeatedly.

  This example code is in the public domain.
*/

// Pin 13 has an LED connected on most Arduino boards.
// give it a name:
```

The next section creates a variable. It is an *integer* variable, which is simply a whole number, and it is assigned the value 13, using the = (equal) sign.

```
int led = 13;
```

The setup() function tells your Arduino how it should be set up. This code tells it to use digital Pin 13 to output electricity, using a function called pinMode(). The flow of electricity on this pin is what turns the LED on and off because the LED on your board is connected to this pin. The parameters of pinMode() are which pin is being set (in this case, using the variable led, which was just defined as Pin 13), and whether it is used for input or output — in this case, OUTPUT. If you look at your Arduino board, you see a pin labeled "13" in the area labeled DIGITAL. The code controls the output on that pin.

```
// the setup routine runs once when you press reset:
void setup() {
  // initialize the digital pin as an output.
  pinMode(led, OUTPUT);
}
```

Note that the setup() function is terminated with a closing curly bracket. Then the loop function specifies what will happen while your Arduino is running.

Two functions are in the next section of code. The first function allows electricity to be controlled on a digital pin: digitalWrite(). You indicate which pin to write to (Pin 13 again) and whether it is high or low. If it is HIGH, 5 volts of electricity to the pin is turned on, making 5 volts available to any components connected to the pin. If it is low, the electricity to that pin is turned off.

The second function is `delay()`, which causes your Arduino to stop executing code for the duration specified in milliseconds. This code sets a delay of 1000 milliseconds, or one second:

```
// the loop routine runs over and over again forever:
void loop() {
  digitalWrite(led, HIGH);    // turn the LED on (HIGH is the voltage level)
  delay(1000);                // wait for a second
  digitalWrite(led, LOW);     // turn the LED off by making the voltage LOW
  delay(1000);                // wait for a second
}
```

When your Arduino executes this section of code, it first turns on power to an LED (the one on Pin 13). It then waits for one second before turning the power to that same pin off. Finally, it waits another second before repeating the process indefinitely.

Uploading your code

After getting to know how the code works for each project, you upload it to your board. Now, if you haven't already done so, try out this code on your Arduino. Do the following steps:

1. **Tell your IDE which Arduino board you are using. From the Ide menu, choose Tools⇨Board and then choose the board you are using.**

   The Arduino Uno used for all the projects in this book is at the top of the list.

2. **Tell the IDE to which serial port your Arduino is connected and choose Tools⇨Serial Port.**

   If you are using Windows, it will most likely be the COM port with the highest number in the list. You may need to try uploading to a couple of different COM ports before you find the correct one that your computer has assigned to your board. If you are using a Mac or Linux, the serial port will be something like this: /dev/tty.usbserial-A800euub and will likely be either the topmost or bottom entry in your list.

3. **When you have selected your board and port, click the upload button (the right arrow).**

   You should see two LEDs labeled TX and RX flashing on your Arduino for a moment.

   If all is well, your code will begin running automatically as soon as this process is finished.

You only need to do Steps 1 and 2 the first time you connect an Arduino to your computer. The IDE remembers your selections until you connect another board.

When you get an Arduino Uno from the factory, it is already preloaded with the Blink program. For this reason, you might not see any change to the LED if you upload the Blink program. Try changing the —`delay` values to see what effect this has on the behavior of the LED.

Debugging

One of the tricky parts of building Arduino projects is figuring out what's going on when something's not working correctly. That's because problems can crop up either in the hardware, in the software, or in *both!* Correcting them sometimes means you have to check both. So, when troubleshooting, always do the following:

1. **Check your connections.**

   Make sure your hardware is wired up properly. Each chapter has both an electrical schematic diagram and a parts placement diagram to help you make sure you've built your project correctly. Even one wire out of place can cause unexpected or confusing results.

2. **Check your software.**

   If there's a fundamental problem, your IDE's compiler will let you know by highlighting in orange the offending line. It also displays an orange message at the bottom of your code window. The message may at first be confusing or hard to understand. But if you read carefully and look on forums online, you can usually figure out what went wrong.

   Some other common problems are misspellings and letters of the wrong case, uploading to a board that isn't connected or is not ready, uploading to a board of the wrong type, or trying to upload to a board that is not connected to the serial port that you are using for your IDE.

Chapter 17 has ten troubleshooting tips to help you diagnose and correct the most common Arduino problems.

Extending your reach with libraries

One of the best things about Arduino is that if you want to use it to do something new or control a display or a motor or other device, someone has probably already thought about doing just that and made it easier for you. Instead of writing the code to control devices yourself, you can often find code written by others and packaged up as *code libraries.* There are many popular libraries, and you can often find reference to them in the Arduino forums.

Understanding libraries

By including code libraries in the code you write for your project, you can extend what your Arduino can do. After you install a library, you access its code from the Sketch⇨Import Library menu in the Arduino IDE to add the code library to your own code.

Some libraries are so useful that they've been included with the Arduino IDE. These include:

- **EEPROM** for writing to the onboard memory that is preserved when your Arduino is switched off
- **Ethernet** for communicating on Local Area Networks and the Internet
- **Firmata** for communicating with applications on your computer
- **LiquidCrystal** for writing to liquid crystal displays (LCDs)
- **SD** for reading from and writing to SD memory cards
- **Servo** for controlling servo motors
- **SPI** for using the Serial Peripheral Interface bus, a special communication standard
- **SoftwareSerial** for creating additional serial communications channels beyond the one that is built in to your Arduino
- **Stepper** for controlling stepper motors
- **WiFi** for communicating via Wi-Fi networks
- **Wire** for using the Two-Wire interface and I2C protocols to connect to devices or sensors

Some libraries are written by coders and shared with the community. These do an amazing variety of things and range from LED controllers to card readers to cameras and other specialty device controllers. The list is huge.

If it's a popular library, you can often download it from the Arduino website. More obscure libraries can be found on a library author's website, a code-sharing website, such as github or Google Code, or sometimes from the websites of Arduino specialty suppliers. Both Adafruit Industries and SparkFun supply code libraries for use with their specialized Arduino products.

Installing libraries

When you want to add a non-standard library to your project, you need to first download it, usually as a zipped archive. You then extract the Zip file by double-clicking on it. Doing this usually produces a folder bearing the name of the library. Inside the folder will likely be files ending in `.h` and `.cpp`, which contain the code of the library itself. You may also see an Examples folder, which contains some example sketches demonstrating how to use the library. If you do not see the `.h` and `.cpp` files inside this folder, there's a problem and your library won't work.

You need to place this folder and its contents where the Arduino IDE can find it — and where you place libraries depends on your operating system:

- ✔ If you are using Windows, this is usually in the folder: My Documents\Arduino\libraries

- ✔ If you are using a Mac, this is usually in the folder: Documents/Arduino/libraries

- ✔ If you are using Linux, its location will be similar to a Mac.

The `.h` and `.cpp` files must be inside a folder bearing the name of the library. They can't simply be copied into your Arduino directory or the library won't work.

You use code libraries to extend your Arduino's basic capabilities in Chapters 7, 8, 11, 13, and 14.

Powering your Arduino

For long-term applications, you need a constant DC power supply. You can get this from your computer via USB, but most likely you'll want to power up your Arduino whether or not there's a computer connected. If so, you need a power transformer to convert from common household alternating current (AC) to the direct current (DC) that your Arduino is expecting or a battery.

Selecting a power transformer

These power transformers (which I call *wall warts*) come in a huge variety of sizes and costs, but you really only need to keep an eye on two things — the voltage supplied and the current supplied. You can use a power transformer to supply anywhere from 6 to 20 volts to your Arduino, but the recommended range is 7 to 12 volts. Supplying more than 12 volts may cause the onboard voltage regulator to overheat.

If you are using that same transformer to power up other components that your Arduino is using, you need to make sure the voltages are matched. For example, a motor requiring 12 volts can use the same power supply as your Arduino, because both can use a 12-volt power supply. However, if you were to use, for example, a 24-volt transformer to power a motor, you would need to step down that voltage for your Arduino using another transformer or a voltage regulator.

You also need to pay attention to the amperage supplied by your transformer. The minimum requirement is about 250mA, but if you are connecting lots of LEDs, sensors, or other devices to your digital pins, you may need more current.

The best rule of thumb is to select a transformer that is matched to your Arduino's voltage requirement and exceeds your project's current requirement.

Selecting a battery power supply

If you want to go untethered, you need a battery power supply. Again you need to pay attention to both the voltage and amperage supplied by your battery. For an Arduino, you'll need a battery that can supply 7 to 12 volts, though you can be outside of these boundaries by a bit, because the onboard voltage regulator will condition the power so that your Arduino can use it.

The amperage supplied by a battery is measured in milliamp hours (mAh). The higher the rating, the longer your battery will last. However, the mAh rating doesn't exactly tell you how long your battery will last, because the current supplied will vary as your battery is depleted. Your Arduino needs about 250 milliamps (mA) to operate, and any additional components will increase the requirement.

Figuring out how long a battery will last is difficult to determine precisely. Battery design is a tradeoff between cost, performance life, and size. Battery depletion is a function of how much power the Arduino and any other components are using. Depletion is affected by other factors, too, including the number of external devices, variations in how your sensors operate, and ambient temperature. The best way to know is to perform some tests.

For a given voltage, the larger the battery, the longer its life.

Understanding Basic Electronics

Working with an Arduino means working with both software and hardware. If you are working with hardware, you'll be using electricity to either sense something or actuate something, or both. So understanding some of the basics of electrical circuits is a good idea.

Voltage (V)

Voltage (symbol: V) is a measure of potential energy to do work in a circuit — specifically to push around electrons. Because voltage is a measure of potential to move electrons from one point to another, its potential is measured as a reference between two points. Imagine you are dropping a ball to the ground. The ball will land harder if it is dropped from a higher point. The amount of energy released is related to where it is dropped from and where it lands. The potential for electron flow is expressed similarly, between its origin point and where the electron flow ends up. Thus voltage (or *volts*) is often expressed as a "drop" between two points in a circuit. A measurement of voltage at a particular point of a circuit is a way of expressing how much potential there is to move electrons around from that point to another point.

Current (I)

Current (symbol: I) is a measure of the flow of electrons through an electrical circuit. Electric current is composed of individual electrons flowing through a conductor by moving along and pushing on the electrons ahead. This is similar to water flowing through a pipe. Another analogy is marbles in a tube that push each other along. These analogies don't hold for all cases, but in general, they provide a good model for how current flows in a circuit. The amount of flow is the same everywhere in the circuit. If you could observe the electrons flowing in the wire of a circuit, you would see the same quantity at any point in the circuit. Current is measured in amperes (or *amps*), which is equivalent to 6,250,000,000,000,000,000 electrons passing by a given point per second. You will often see current expressed in milliamperes (mA).

Resistance (R)

Resistance (symbol: R) is a measure of the opposition to the flow of electrons in a circuit. It depends on a number of factors, including the medium — usually wire, its cross-sectional area, and its temperature. The resistance limits the flow of current in a circuit with a given amount of voltage supplied by the battery or power supply. The opposition to electron flow generates friction, similar to the way mechanical friction occurs and generates heat. If a lot of current is opposed by a resistor, it may get warm or even too hot to touch. This heat can be seen as inefficiency of a circuit. Resistance is measured in *ohms*, which is expressed with the Greek letter omega: Ω.

Ohm's Law

Voltage, current, and resistance are all interrelated in electrical circuits. The relationship between the movement of current in a circuit and the available voltage was first described by Georg Simon Ohm and is expressed by the simple algebraic equation, *voltage* equals *current* times *resistance*: V=IR. Using basic algebra, you can manipulate this equation into two variations, solving for I and for R: I=V/R and R=V/I.

So what?

Most of us would like to avoid math and just get on with building cool projects. The projects in this book have all been tested to work at the voltages and currents specified. The electronic parts you use in these projects are all engineered to use a certain voltage and current. However, you may want to use different components than those specified here, or you might also want to add components to make your projects even cooler.

If so, you need to make sure the voltages and current ratings for the parts you want to use are matched to those in your project. You don't want to end up frying your project or your Arduino or burning down the house. Always make sure additional components operate at the voltage of your project and they do not require more current than your project can supply. Some components will take as much current as you can give them. You need to use resistors to limit the current that encounters them.

For example, suppose you have an LED that you want to light up with a digital pin that requires a maximum of 30mA of current. Digital pins provide an output voltage of 5V. To provide no more than 30mA of current, you can calculate the value of the resistor you'd need to use in that circuit, using Ohm's Law:

Resistance = Voltage/Current (in Amps).

So the resistance in ohms equals 5 volts divided by 30 milliamps, which is 0.03 amps: 5/0.03=166. You'd need roughly 166 ohms of resistance to protect that LED from using too much current. In practice, people tend to use a greater value of resistance by 10 percent or 20 percent just to be on the safe side, and because resistors come in fixed values. So, a 180Ω or 200Ω resistor would provide the right amount of current limiting without reducing current flow so much that the LED fails to light up.

If you are adding additional components or electronic parts to your project, make sure you have used appropriate resistors so that you don't *overdrive* your components. Otherwise you may end up damaging the components or your Arduino.

If you want to take your electronics knowledge even further, you might want to check out *Electronics For Dummies* (by Gordon McComb and Earl Boysen) and *Electronics Projects For Dummies* (by Earl Boysen and Nancy C. Muir). They can give you a great start on understanding the fundamentals of how the circuits in this book work.

Identifying Electronic Components

To build the projects in this book, you connect your components according to *schematic diagrams* and *parts placement diagrams.* The former shows how things are connected in electronic circuits. The latter indicates how you place the parts into a breadboard so that the electrical connections indicated by the schematic are accomplished.

Details about how breadboards work and the different kinds available are in Chapter 2.

You can construct the projects by referring to the parts placement diagrams, but the schematics provide a second way of confirming that you've built your circuits correctly.

Reading schematic diagrams

As you work on the projects in this book, you can refer to diagrams that show you how to connect your Arduino and the electronic components. A basic schematic is an abstract representation of the parts that are connected in your circuit and the wires that join them. This schematic makes it easier to see how electricity is supposed to flow in the circuit and helps you to diagnose problems. It also helps you make sure you've got everything connected and haven't overlooked anything.

Check out the simple diagram in Figure 3-3. It shows an LED connected to an Arduino. The schematic representation of the Arduino has all its input and output pins organized for the sake of clarity, rather than showing physical positions of the pins on the Arduino. The LED is connected to Pin 13, and the Arduino *ground* pin is labeled GND. The breadboard used to connect the parts is not shown. The breadboard merely provides the physical connections shown by the wires in the schematic diagram.

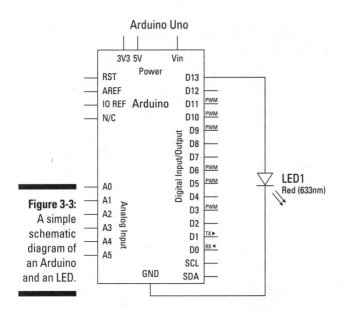

Figure 3-3: A simple schematic diagram of an Arduino and an LED.

To build the projects, you need to be able to identify a variety of parts in a schematic diagram. Figure 3-4 shows a summary of the parts you encounter and the symbols used to identify them.

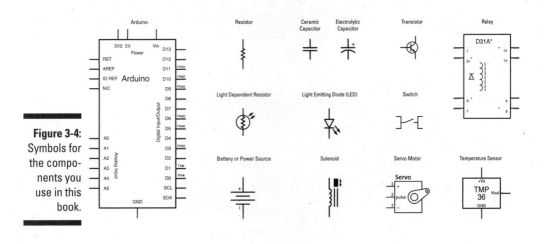

Figure 3-4: Symbols for the components you use in this book.

Reading parts placement diagrams

A lot of the work you do involves connecting your parts according to the schematic diagram. But to do this easily while you are getting a project going, you use a breadboard. You can simply connect parts on the breadboard without having to fire up your soldering iron. After you're satisfied the circuit is working on the breadboard, you can transfer it to a soldered circuit board.

The project chapters contain parts placement diagrams like the one in Figure 3-5 that show you how to put your components onto your breadboard. These have all been tested so that if you put your components in exactly the same holes, your project should work according to the electrical schematic diagram. You may choose to use different holes on your breadboard if you are using a different breadboard than the ones shown. In this case, you can refer to the schematic to make sure you've connected your parts properly.

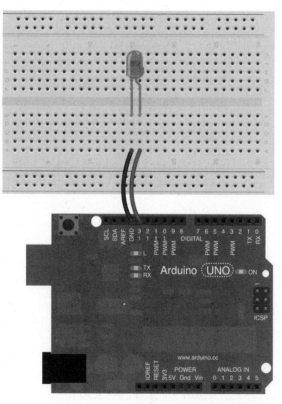

Figure 3-5:
A parts placement diagram of an Arduino and an LED on a breadboard.

Understanding Sensing and Actuating

You use your Arduino to do two main things: sense what's going on in the world and then respond to what's going on by moving or changing something, or *actuating*.

You can use a variety of sensors and actuators to build some of the projects in this book. Although you won't be using all the components in the list below, it's good to know about all the varieties of things you can sense and the many different ways you can actuate things.

Reading datasheets

If you are hunting for a sensor or actuator for a specific problem, you'll want to take a look at its datasheet. Supplied by the manufacturer, a product's datasheet tells you exactly what it can and can't do.

You can find datasheets for sensors and actuators on the suppliers' websites, or often you can locate them simply by doing a web search using the sensor's part number and the term *datasheet*.

Understanding and using sensors

Humans are pretty good general-purpose sensors. We can detect a wide range of sights, smells, and textures, but discerning something very precisely — an exact wavelength of light or a precise temperature — can be difficult. And some things we simply can't detect — like the presence of carbon monoxide. Electronic sensors can break down the five familiar senses that we humans are capable of: sight, sound, touch/vibration, smell, and to some extent, taste.

But electronic devices can be dramatically more sensitive. Electronic sensors are often tuned either to be good sensors for very precise quantities of things or are good for detecting things within a certain range. The myriad sensors and their capabilities can fill a catalog of hundreds of pages, so it's impossible to describe even a good chunk of what you'll find on the market.

In the following sections, I detail some of the sensors you use in this book, with a couple of extras you might find also interesting.

Seeing

These sensors detect light in either a general level of brightness, or on specific wavelengths. There are color sensors that will tell you the wavelengths they detect, sensors that detect luminous intensity, and Light-Dependent Resistors (LDRs) that respond to light levels more generally. Digital cameras are essentially complex light sensors, and you can find camera shields that you can use with your Arduino to take pictures. You use LDRs in Chapter 12 and an infrared light detector for the remote-controlled car in Chapter 14.

Vibration/Touch

With smartphones and tablets everywhere, we've become really used to interacting with touch-sensitive displays. But you can also think of the humble switch as a kind of touch sensor. Other sensors can detect bending and vibration. A piezoelectric sensor element can be used to detect vibrations. I place temperature sensors in this category, too. You use temperature sensors in Chapter 12 and switches in Chapters 7 and 8.

Hearing

The simplest kind of a hearing sensor is a microphone, which uses a thin membrane to detect vibrations in the air. You can connect a microphone to an Arduino to analyze low-frequency vibrations within the audio range. And although you can't use an Arduino Uno to record high-quality audio, you can record sounds nearing the quality of a recordable greeting card or child's toy. Detecting specific radio frequencies is also equivalent to hearing — just way above the range of human abilities. This is well within the capability of an Arduino if you use specialized hardware, such as a Radio Frequency ID (RFID) reader. The Radio Frequency ID (RFID) sensor in Chapter 9 is one of these kinds of sensors.

Smelling

Smell involves detecting sometimes-minute traces of molecules that float on currents of air. Common examples are smoke detectors or breath analyzers for detecting alcohol levels. There aren't any projects in this book that use this kind of sensor, but that shouldn't stop you from exploring what they can do. Why not connect a CO_2 sensor to your home sensing station in Chapter 12? With a little hacking and ingenuity, you could connect a commercial breath analyzer to your remote-controlled car in Chapter 14, taking safe driving to an absurd new level!

Tasting

In industry, highly specialized sensors are used to detect the chemicals in a variety of compounds by heating them up and detecting their molecular composition. This may be a bit of a stretch, but to my mind, moisture detection is also a sort of electronic equivalent of tasting. In Chapter 10, you build a moisture sensor from scratch to "taste" the humidity of soil so you can sense when to water houseplants.

Understanding and using actuators

When you want objects to do things, you need an actuator. Actuators emit light and sound, heat things up, cool them down, move them quickly, move them slowly, and move them precisely. Here's a rundown on the kinds of actuation and actuators you encounter in this book.

Visible indication

The simplest actuator is a visible indicator. This can be a simple incandescent lamp or more likely an LED. LEDs come in all shapes, sizes, and colors. You can find them in single-unit packages, and LEDs indicate letters and numbers in seven-segment displays and matrix displays. You use LEDs in several projects in this book. In Chapter 6, you use a matrix of them to create a scrolling sign like a stock market ticker or the signage on the front of a city bus. Chapter 15 describes how to combine them into an animated, programmable LED cube.

Audible indication

Another simple indicator is an audio actuator — a speaker or buzzer. These simply use electrical currents to cause vibrations in the air. Generating all but the most basic sounds with your Arduino requires additional components. If you want to play recorded sounds, you need to use special add-ons such as the Wave Shield from Adafruit Industries. But simple audio is possible. The alarm clock in Chapter 7 uses a piezoelectric sounder to really wake you up. You can add one to any project where you need an audible indication.

Movement

Many different devices turn electrical potential into movement. The most basic is a motor. Motors convert the current in an electric field to movement through the attraction and repulsion of magnetic fields. Specialized motors, such as *servo motors* and *stepper motors,* can be programmed to move things to precise positions. You use servo motors in Chapter 14 to drive a remote-controlled car.

Solenoids are special electromagnetic cylinders that can push or pull a piston. They relay a magnetic field to create attractive and repulsive linear force. You use a solenoid connected to a valve to turn on and off the flow of water to a houseplant in Chapter 10.

Relays are devices that rely on electromagnetic current to flip a switch. Inside relays a small metal contact is moved to close the gap between two wires, thereby allowing electricity to flow in a circuit. You use a relay in Chapter 8 to activate a door locking mechanism.

Making Projects Work

Most of the projects in this book use a breadboard, the perfect tool for proto-typing electronic circuits and projects. Your breadboard makes it super easy to wire up electronic parts to your Arduino so that you can use sensors and actuators in your projects. The whole purpose of a breadboard is to make it easy to build things, try out circuits, make mistakes, and change your plans quickly and easily without having to break out the soldering iron. For prototyping ideas, the breadboard is probably your most important tool. But sometimes, you want to make things a little more permanent. That's when you want to consider two things: soldering your components together and putting everything into an enclosure.

Moving from your breadboard to your project box

You prototype and build most of the projects in this book on a breadboard. But when and if you want to make one of them more permanent, you can easily do so by transferring your circuit to a piece of stripboard or making your own Arduino shield. If you want to try this out, the home sensing station in Chapter 12 is a good place to start because it shows you how to start your project on a breadboard and then move it to a piece of stripboard. After you've done it once, you'll be able to do it with all the other projects pretty easily.

You can also make a printed circuit board. I used the software program Fritzing to lay out all the circuits and diagrams for this book, and it also has the capability to create custom printed circuit boards (PCBs). You can use the artwork to fabricate your own, or you can send the design off to a PCB manufacturer, who will etch, drill, and silkscreen artwork onto your board for you. Although this used to be very expensive and really only practical for hundreds of copies, new services are now offering one-off boards, and the prices for this are really coming down. This topic is a bit out of the scope of this book, but there are plenty of resources online if you want to investigate how to do it.

To make your project more permanent, you also need to consider what kind of enclosure to put it into. Chapter 2 contains a guide to the kinds of enclosures you can use and some of the important considerations when choosing one.

Learning soldering basics

You can build all these projects on a breadboard, which is easy to use and change if you make a mistake. After you are satisfied with the results, you can connect the components more permanently using a perfboard or stripboard and by soldering them together.

You solder parts with a soldering iron, the tip of which heats up to a few hundred degrees — hot enough to melt the metal solder you use to join your components. The molten solder pools around the hot metal components and cools quite quickly when the heat from the soldering iron is removed. The result is an electrically conductive, strong joint that is permanent until you apply heat from a soldering iron again.

When you are first trying your hand at soldering, it's a good idea to practice on some throwaway stuff that you won't mind messing up. Practice makes perfect, as the saying goes. It takes a while to get the hang of how long it takes to heat up the solder, how to flow it onto components, and how to make a good solder joint. You can use a piece of stripboard to do a few test connections, without worrying about damaging things on your project.

You can practice soldering on resistors because they are cheap and easy to work with and it doesn't matter if you overheat them — you can just throw them away after you're finished practicing. If you have any electronics board lying around, you can practice your desoldering skills too, by using a desoldering wick mentioned in Chapter 2. Try to remove parts from the boards. You quickly see why it's a good idea to get your soldering skills up to speed — taking things off of a circuit board is a lot harder than soldering things on!

Figure 3-6 shows an example of soldering a component to a perfboard. When you are soldering, you apply the iron to the components and then flow the solder into the heated area. You need to ensure that the components are hot enough for the solder to adhere to them. You don't heat the solder and drip it onto the parts. Once you've heated the components, some solder will liquefy around the components and coat them. When they are coated, remove the solder and the iron and allow the parts to cool. The result should be a strong connection that you can't pull apart.

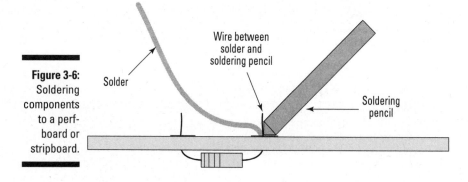

Figure 3-6:
Soldering
components
to a perf-
board or
stripboard.

Here are some soldering tips to keep in mind:

 ✔ Make sure your parts and surfaces are clean. In particular, make sure you clean your soldering iron tip with a damp sponge.

 ✔ Coat the tip of your iron with a little solder — just enough to make it shiny. This is called *tinning* and will make it easier to solder your connections.

 ✔ Don't overheat parts. You should only heat the components long enough to make a good connection. If you apply too much heat, some sensitive components could be damaged.

 ✔ Safety first. Make sure you are not soldering over your hands or another part of your body. If the solder drops off of your work you could be burned. Also, wear safety goggles; burning solder can sometimes spit and fly in unexpected directions.

 ✔ Be careful not to breathe the soldering fumes. Although solder containing lead (which is a neurotoxin) has been banned in many places, the fumes are not very nice. Make sure you are working in a well-ventilated area.

Part II
Basic Arduino Projects

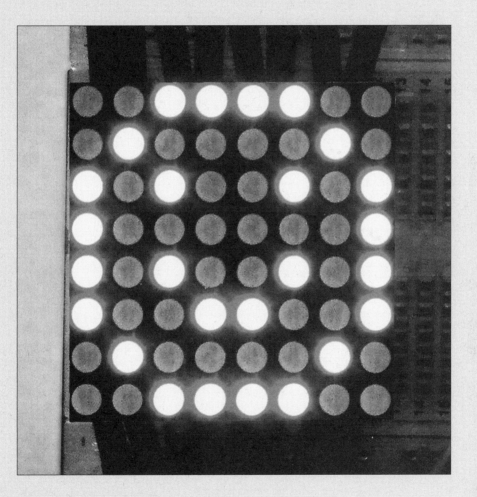

Learn how to add keyboard input to the all-seeing eye project from Chapter 2 at www.dummies.com/extras/arduinoprojects.

In this part . . .

✔ Find out the basics of programming your Arduino

✔ Program and control LEDs

✔ Create and program a scrolling sign

✔ Find out about keeping time with an Arduino

✔ Display text on an LCD

Chapter 4

The All-Seeing Eye

- -

In This Chapter

▶ Powering and controlling LEDs

▶ Using arrays and loops

▶ Counting time

▶ Using a potentiometer to control speed

- -

*1*f you've never made an Arduino project before, this is a good place to start. In this chapter, I go over the basic steps in building any Arduino project, writing the code, and spicing things up a bit once it's all working.

If you're reading this book, you likely have a soft spot for science fiction, like me. This project was inspired by long hours of reruns from 1980s science fiction on TV. I'm thinking of *Battlestar Galactica* — with its Cylon Warriors, and *Knight Rider* with KITT, the advanced car with a personality. For me, KITT was the star of the show, not David Hasselhoff! Both the Cylons and KITT had one thing in common — what passed for "eyes" more or less consisted of a horizontal band of lights that cycled back and forth — an electronic all-seeing eye. In this project, you build just that, using a series of light emitting diodes (LEDs). You can also change the behavior of the lights to emulate a cinema marquee or bouncing ball.

Along the way, you become familiar with several key Arduino concepts, including counting time, storing and retrieving lots of data values, and adding a dial to control the speed of your all-seeing eye. These are used in several of the other projects in this book and will be useful for your own projects.

If you haven't connected your Arduino yet, flip over to Chapter 2, which walks you through setting it up. It also covers the Arduino integrated development environment (IDE) where you write your programs. Review Chapter 3 if you need a refresher of the basics that are common to all Arduino code, the code structure, and an explanation of how your code gets processed by the *compiler* so that it will work when it is loaded onto your Arduino.

Selecting Your Parts

Start by getting together the parts you need to create the eye, as shown in Figure 4-1. This one is pretty simple. First, make sure that you have the following parts:

- ✔ Your Arduino Uno
- ✔ A breadboard
- ✔ Ten LEDs of the same kind and color. I'm using red LEDs, just like the Cylons and KITT.
- ✔ Ten 250 or 270 ohm resistors
- ✔ 4.7K ohm linear potentiometer
- ✔ Jumper wires of various lengths

When you are looking for parts, you don't have to get exactly the resistor values shown here. Arduino kits tend to have resistors ranging from 220 to 470 ohms, which will work fine. You may also use larger values, but they may reduce the flow of current so much that your LED will be dim or won't light up at all.

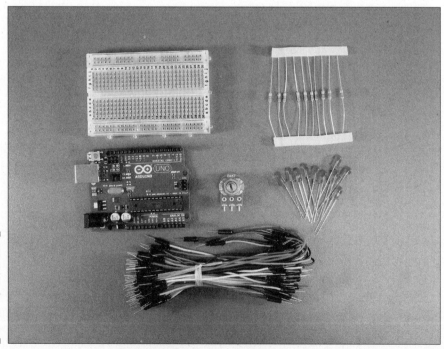

Figure 4-1:
Gather the parts you need for your all-seeing eye.

Parts of an LED

LEDs, LEDs everywhere! You see them all over the place, and they are now starting to become bright enough to be used in place of traditional lighting. But what makes an LED tick? Light emitting diodes are based on a special material called a *semiconductor* that only permits electric current to flow in one direction. Such a component is called a *diode*. All LEDs contain a bit of semiconductive material that forms the diode. This diode is surrounded by a tiny concave *shield* that focuses the light. The light is further focused by the *epoxy lens* that also provides protective encapsulation of the parts. All kinds of lenses are available to control the light they generate. Besides the electrical characteristics, the key things to be aware of when you are selecting an LED are brightness and viewing angle. The brightness, usually measured in microcandelas (mcd), can range from a few thousand to 25,000 or more mcd. The *viewing angle* refers to how broadly LED light is cast and can be as little as a few degrees — to 180 degrees. The longer leg is the *anode* and connects to a *positive* power supply (+). The shorter leg is the *cathode* and connects to the negative (-) or *ground* power supply connection. The epoxy enclosure has a flat side that corresponds to the cathode.

So if you ever are uncertain about which leg is which — or if the legs have been cut short — you can refer to this diagram.

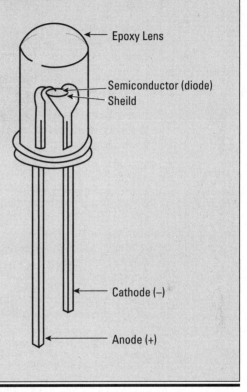

Building the Circuit

After you have the parts ready, start by connecting each of the components to the breadboard. There are 20 components, and it's easier to connect the Arduino last. After the other components are all in place, you connect the negative, also called the "ground" side of the circuit, to your Arduino, and finally connect the positive side of the circuit to each LED.

Follow these steps to build it, referring to Figure 4-2:

1. **Insert the ten 250 ohm resistors into the breadboard.**

   If you have a slightly higher resistance like 270 ohms, that's okay. One leg of each resistor should be on either side of the gutter in the center of your breadboard. Remember, no electricity flows across this gutter, so you can put both legs in the same row without connecting them electrically. Don't worry about whether the color bands face the same way — resistors work the same way in both directions.

2. **Insert the LEDs. Connect the long leg (called the anode) of your LEDs to the same row as a resistor and put the short leg into the adjacent row.**

   Unlike resistors, LEDs only work in one direction — they have a "polarity" — and the positive, longer leg must always be connected to the +5 volt side of your circuit. That will be coming from the digital pins on your Arduino.

   Power will only flow in one direction to light up the LED — from the anode to the cathode.

3. **Use a jumper wire to connect the negative leg of each LED to one of the long columns of holes on the side of your breadboard, to make a ground rail.**

   The negative leg of all your LEDs is going to the GND pin on your Arduino.

   The holes in each long column are all electrically connected. You could use either of these columns, but by convention, people use the column with a blue or black stripe next to it as the ground rail, and the other as a power rail. Some breadboards don't have a colored stripe at all, but it doesn't matter. The color coding is just to help you keep track of which is which.

4. **Use a jumper wire to connect one of the unused holes on your ground rail to the GND pin on the Arduino.**

5. **Connect the positive side of the circuit.**

   You'll be sending power to each of your LEDs by turning its digital pin on or off. Starting with Pin 4, connect the anode of each LED to one digital pin on your Arduino. Figure 4-2 shows what your breadboard should look like after you have completed the circuit.

You have now established an electrical connection that will allow electricity to flow from individual digital pins (4–13) through individual LEDs, and then to ground. You should be able to trace an imaginary pathway from Pin 4 through a resistor, across one LED and your ground rail, to the GND pin on the Arduino. The same goes for the other pins. Each LED has its own separate route, but the ground rail is shared by all of them.

On the resistors, the color bands indicate their resistance in ohms.

Check the illustration to make sure you've done it correctly. Don't worry about the potentiometer now. You add it later.

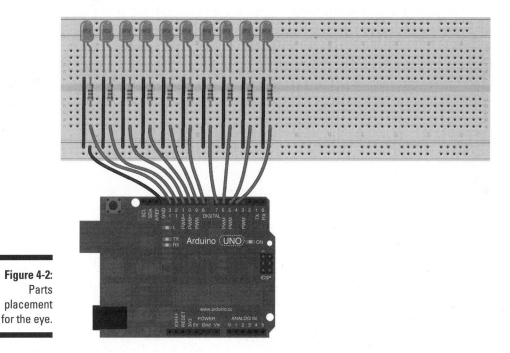

Figure 4-2:
Parts
placement
for the eye.

Understanding How the Code Works

Now that you've wired up, you can enter the code.

Flowcharts are useful for understanding what happens each step of the way, when the Arduino is processing your code. The flowchart in Figure 4-3 shows the series of events and decisions in this program.

All in good time

The Arduino's internal system clock plays a key role in this project. The Arduino keeps track of the time that has elapsed since your program started running in milliseconds. You can use this for all sorts of useful things, including building clocks and timing events. Here, it's used to create a delay between the lighting of each LED, just a little. You increase or decrease that delay to change the speed that the light emitted moves left and right.

You use a delay to adjust how long each LED is lit up. You step from each LED to the next one, turning off the previous LED and turning on the next one, pausing at each LED for the amount of the delay. When you get to the end of the line of LEDs, you switch directions and continue the process.

All the code used in this book can be copied from the Downloads tab of the companion website at `www.dummies.com/go/arduinoprojectsfor dummies` — unless you need to practice your typing!

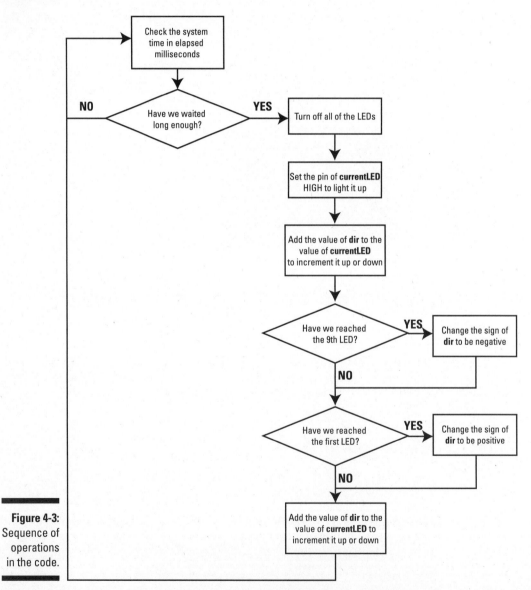

Figure 4-3:
Sequence of operations in the code.

To get a sense of what is going on, enter the following code into a new sketch. You can also download the code from the book's companion website at www. dummies.com/go/arduinoprojectsfordummies.

```
// Chapter 4: The All-Seeing Eye
// Sequentially lights up a series of LEDs
// A variable to set a delay time between each LED
int delayTime = 40;

// A variable to store which LED we are currently working on
int currentLED = 4;

// A variable to store the direction of travel
int dir = 1;

// A variable to store the last time we changed something
long timeChanged = 0;

// An array to hold the value for each LED pin
byte ledPin[] = {4, 5, 6, 7, 8, 9, 10, 11, 12, 13};

void setup() {
  // Set all pins for OUTPUT
  for (int i=0; i<10; i++) {
    pinMode(ledPin[i], OUTPUT);
  }

 // Record the time once the setup has completed
  timeChanged = millis();
}

void loop() {
  // Check whether it has been long enough
  if ((millis() - timeChanged) > delayTime) {

    //turn off all of the LEDs
    for (int i=0; i<10; i++) {
      digitalWrite(ledPin[i], LOW);
    }

    // Light the current LED
    digitalWrite(ledPin[currentLED], HIGH);

    // Increase the direction value (up or down)
    currentLED = currentLED + dir;

    // If we are at the end of a row, change direction
    if (currentLED == 9) {
      dir = -1;
    }
    if (currentLED == 0) {
      dir = 1;
```

```
    }
    // store the current time as the time we last changed LEDs
    timeChanged = millis();


  }

}
```

Setting up the code

At the beginning of the code, there are some comments describing what the code does. In a line of code, anything after a slash (/) will be ignored by the program compiler. Comments are a good place to describe what the code does so that you or others can tell what's going on. This is surprisingly useful months later, when you've forgotten the details of how a particular chunk of code works but want to reuse some parts of it for another project.

The code starts out by creating several *variables,* which are simply places in memory to store and recall values. Each variable has a meaningful name that makes it easy for humans to write and read the code.

Because there are many different kinds of variables, you have to tell the Arduino what kind you are using. The first one is an *integer* variable — which just stores a regular, whole number from -32,768 to 32,767. It's going to be called delayTime, because that's what it's used to store — the time in milliseconds that the Arduino waits before lighting up the next LED:

```
int delayTime = 40;
```

int is a *keyword* that creates the integer variable. All keywords are automatically highlighted in orange by the Arduino IDE, and you can't use them for anything else, or it will cause an error.

Next is the name of the variable, delayTime. Variable names are case sensitive, so make sure you always type the name correctly. In the second half of the variable name, the letter "T" is capitalized to make it easier to read the name. This is commonly used by programmers and is known as "camel case" because the capital letters create "humps" in the variable name!

The equal sign means that the following value will be stored in the memory location designated by delayTime. It might be easier to think about the equal sign meaning "assign the value of" rather than "equals." The value you're assigning to delayTime is 40. Later, the code determines whether 40 milliseconds have passed, to check whether it's time to light up the next LED. Assigning a variable a value when you create it is often called *initializing* the variable.

Next, you need to keep track of which LED is being lit up, and this is done with a sensibly named variable called currentLED. This stores the pin number of the current LED that you are dealing with. It's set to 4, because it's a good habit to initialize variables with a value of some kind, and the LED on Pin 4 is the first one that lights up.

```
int currentLED = 4;
```

Another integer variable controls the direction of the lights:

```
int dir = 1;
```

A clever trick increments currentLED up, until Pin 13 is reached, and then goes back down again. As you can see, dir is initialized to a value of 1. After the Arduino lights up its first LED on Pin 4, currentLED has a value of 4. Adding dir to currentLED will change its value to 5, so the next time around the program loop, the next LED will be illuminated, and so on through to Pin 13. After the program has reached Pin 13, you will change the value of dir −1 and continue to add it to the value of currentLED, making it 12. Each time you add dir to currentLED, it will decrement the value of currentLED by 1. This will continue down to Pin 4, and the whole cycle will start all over again. Nifty, huh? The details of how this works come a little bit later in the chapter.

Elegance, economy, simplicity

There are many methods to increment up and down a line of LEDs. For example, you could write code that uses a loop to count from 4 to 13, followed by another loop to count from 13 to 4, and so on. This would have the same effect, but would use two loops instead of one. Whether to use one approach or the other is a question of elegance and economy of memory. Many discussion forums have been filled to the brim with debates about how and whether to make code more elegant and compact, and the merits of both. Often, it's a question of style.

But with microcontrollers, the available RAM is at a premium. If you can write something a little more efficient and a little bit shorter, it's usually a good idea to do so. For example, the data type "byte" can store a number from 0 to 255, whereas the data type int can store a number from -32,768 to 32,767. A byte variable uses only one byte of RAM, but an int variable uses two bytes of RAM. This may not seem like much, but when your programs get larger, memory space can become tight. So it makes sense to choose the right kind of variable for the data you want to store. With long programs that are running short on memory, you will figure out all kinds of clever ways to economize on every last byte!

Next, you have an integer to keep track of the last time a change was made. This is used to determine whether it is time to move on to the next LED. It's initialized to 0:

```
long timeChanged = 0;
```

The variable type `long` is similar to `int`, but it can store values from –2,147,483,648 to 2,147,483,647. Because the value of `changeTime` increases by 1000 every second, an `int` would reach its maximum value after 32,767 seconds, and the timer would stop working properly.

The last item is a new data type, an *array*. Arrays are extremely handy because they can be used to store many variables. In this program, you use the array to store the pin number for each of the ten digital pins connected to your LEDs. Arrays have to have a name, and the name of this array of bytes is `ledPin`.

Each value stored in an array has an address, called the *index*. You can request the value that has been stored at that address, or can store a value in that address. You can think of an array like a wall of sequentially numbered cubbyholes in which you put chunks of data. Each cubbyhole is called an array *element*. To access the contents of an element in an array, all you need to know is its index number.

In addition to the name `ledPin`, you also need to tell the compiler what kind of data you are going to be putting in this array. This array will be used to store bytes:

```
byte ledPin[] = {4, 5, 6, 7, 8, 9, 10, 11, 12, 13};
```

You've initialized this array with ten elements in the curly brackets, which are the pin numbers that correspond to the digital pins on the Arduino. So the compiler can count how many elements there are.

In some cases you will want to create an array without initializing any elements in it. In this case, you just specify how many elements there are, in the square brackets: `byte ledPin[10];`

An array index starts at zero. So, the first value in this array, 4, is at index 0. To access the value of one of the elements of an array, you simply refer to its index in the square brackets: `ledPin[0]` has a value of 4. `ledPin[1]` has a value of 5, and so on.

To use the value of one of the elements of your array, you specify which one you want to use, like this:

```
i = ledPin[3];
```

`ledPin[3]` has a value of 7, so your program would assign the value 7 to a
variable named `i`.

With all the variables specified, it's time to move on to setting up the
initial conditions that your code will start with, which is done in the `setup()`
function:

```
void setup() {
  // Set all pins for OUTPUT
  for (int i=0; i<10; i++) {
    pinMode(ledPin[i], OUTPUT);
  }

  // Set up the current timeChanged
  timeChanged = millis();
}
```

As you might remember, functions are chunks of code that execute everything between two curly brackets. All Arduino programs must have a
`setup()` function and a `loop()` function. Everything in the `setup()` function is executed once, before the main loop starts. Everything in the `loop()`
function is executed as long as the Arduino is running.

The compiler needs to know which digital pins are going to be used and what
they are going to be used for — either sending a signal or receiving a signal.
This is done with the built-in function `pinMode()`. If you were going to set up
a single digital pin, say 13, for digital output (as in the Blink program example), you would simply specify which pin number, and output, like this:

```
pinMode(13, OUTPUT);
```

However, there are ten pins to set up. You could simply write this statement
ten times, using a different pin number each time, but there is a shorter way
to do it by using a technique called a *for loop*. In programming, you encounter
many situations in which you need to do something repeatedly, and a `for`
loop is one of the most common ways of doing so.

A `for` loop needs three things: an *initialization* variable to count with, a
test *condition* to see how far it has counted, and an amount to *increment* by.
These *parameters* set up the conditions the loop is to be executed with and
are specified within parentheses. The loop continues to execute the code
within the curly brackets and to increment until the test condition is no
longer true.

Here, you are creating a variable that is only used for this loop (called a *local* variable). It's an integer to increment with and for brevity, is called i, and set at a value of 0:

```
for (int i=0; i<10; i++) {
    pinMode(ledPin[i], OUTPUT);
 }
```

You've initialized the integer i to 0 with: int i=0. The semicolon indicates that you've finished setting up the integer variable and now the loop needs to know how high to count. The test condition is specified next:

```
i<10;
```

Every time the loop iterates through the code between the curly brackets, it tests whether the condition is true: "Is i less than 10?" The < is called a comparison operator.

If the comparison is true, the loop increments the value of i by 1:

```
i++
```

You don't need a semicolon after this statement. If the comparison is false, because i becomes 10 or more, the loop quits and the Arduino goes to the next code in the program.

You're using this loop to count up from 0 to 9. Each time the loop increments, you are setting up a digital pin to be used for output, using a value from the array ledPin[]. Which value you use is specified by the number of the array index, which is the integer i that is used by the for loop to count with:

```
pinMode(ledPin[i], OUTPUT);
```

When i is 0, the value of 4 is retrieved from the ledPin[] array. When i is 1, the value 5 is retrieved, and so on.

Using a loop is perhaps a little more complicated than explicitly writing out all ten pinMode() declarations, but it saves on memory. This is a bit of code that people often cut and paste from project to project, modifying the parameters as needed.

The last part of setup() is making a note of the current time in milliseconds, which you'll use to determine whether it's time to light up the next LED. The current time is retrieved from the CPU with the built-in function millis(). This value is then saved to the integer timeChanged (even though nothing has been changed yet!).

Comparison operators

There are lots of comparisons you can test, such as:

- == is equal to
- != is not equal to
- < is less than
- <= is less than or equal to

- \> is greater than
- \>= is greater than or equal to

Pay close attention to the first comparison ==. A single = sign is used to assign a value. A double == sign is used to make a comparison. Using a single = for a double == is a common error made by beginners. Luckily, the compiler usually tells you if you've made this kind of goof.

The main event

The show really begins in the main loop() function. Everything is contingent upon one question: "Has 40 milliseconds passed since the last time we checked?" This question is expressed as a special statement called an *if statement*. An if statement is a type of *control structure* that tests whether a question is true and if so, executes the code in the curly brackets. As you can see, the entire code of the program is contained within the curly brackets of the if statement:

```
if ((millis() - timeChanged) > delayTime) {
}
```

As with loops, the question is tested within the parentheses.

Here, you are using the millis() function to obtain the amount of time (in milliseconds) that has elapsed since the program started running.

```
if ((millis() - timeChanged) > delayTime) {
```

By subtracting the current time from timeChanged, you obtain a value, and if that value is greater than the value of delayTime (which you initialized to 40), then the code is executed that changes which LED is illuminated. No matter how long the Arduino has been running, and how high a number millis() becomes, the test will evaluate whether the last time an LED was changed was more than 40 milliseconds prior to the current time. Every time an LED changes, the value of timeChanged is updated, ready for the next test. The effect of this is to create a "heartbeat" in which the test will be true every 40ms, and the LED changing code will then be executed. Let's see how that works.

Stepping up and stepping down

The LED changing code starts by turning off any LEDs that might have been on from the previous iteration of the loop:

```
//turn off all of the LEDs
    for (int i=0; i<10; i++) {
        digitalWrite(ledPin[i], LOW);
    }
```

Here you are using a for loop again, this time with the digitalWrite() function, which is used to change the voltage on digital pins. HIGH applies 5 volts to the pin and LOW applies 0 volts. For example, to write Pin 13 to LOW (as you may recall from the Blink program code) you'd use this statement:

```
digitalWrite(13, LOW);
```

But in this case, you are using the index of the loop also as the index of the ledPin[] array, just as you did with the pinMode() function, in setup().

Now that the LEDs are all off, you can turn on the next one:

```
digitalWrite(ledPin[currentLED], HIGH);
```

In setup(), you initialized currentLED to be 4, so the first time around, the Arduino will raise the voltage on Pin 4 to HIGH, and the LED will go on. Hooray! There are just a few more things to take care of now.

First, use that clever trick with the variable dir, to increment up (or down) to the next LED, by adding either +1 or -1 to the value for currentLED:

```
currentLED = currentLED + dir;
```

Next, you need to check whether you've reached either end of the row of LEDs and if so, change the sign of dir. Note that in this if statement, you are testing whether one value is equal to another, so you use two equal signs to perform this evaluation:

```
if (currentLED == 9) {
        dir.= -1;
    }
    if (currentLED == 0) {
        dir = 1;
    }
```

With that bit of housekeeping out of the way, there's one final thing to do, and that's to make a note of the time this change was made:

```
timeChanged = millis();
```

The program is now ready to test again whether 40ms has passed, and the whole cycle starts all over again at the beginning of loop().

Understanding How the Hardware Works

From an electronic point of view, this project is pretty simple. You are merely using the Arduino to provide a voltage from its digital pins to light up each of the LEDs, in turn. You are only lighting up one LED at a time, and they all share the same pathway to ground. The schematic for this project is shown in Figure 4-4.

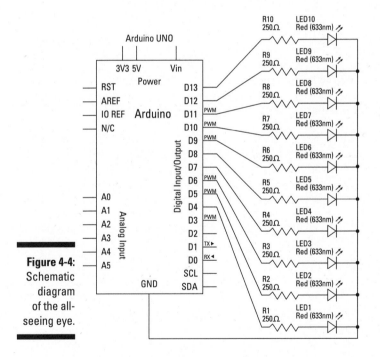

Figure 4-4: Schematic diagram of the all-seeing eye.

The main consideration is providing the right amount of current to your LEDs. The resistors are there to prevent too much current from flowing from the digital pins to the LEDs, which could harm the LEDs, the Arduino, or both. For most garden-variety 5 millimeter LEDs, the operating current is somewhere between 15 and 30 milliamps.

To determine the right resistors to use, you use Ohm's Law. The digital pins put out 5 volts. So you simply divide 5 volts by the amount of current the LEDs are rated at. The ones I used are rated at 20 milliamps. A milliamp is one thousandth of an amp. So to get an amp value of 20mA, move the decimal place over three places to the left, for 0.02 amps:

5 volts / 0.02 amps = 250 ohms.

The result is 250 ohms. If you don't have a 250 ohm resistor handy, use one with a slightly higher value, such as 270 ohms. You can safely use even higher values, but the higher the value, the dimmer your LEDs will be, because less current will flow through them.

The Potential of a Potentiometer

Now that your eye sees all, it's time to perk things up a bit. The simplest thing to do is to change the variable `delayTime` to a larger or smaller value. The smaller the value, the faster your LEDs will change. Setting the value to 20 will make them go twice as fast. Eventually, it will change so fast that you won't be able to perceive the back-and-forth effect. The LEDs will just appear to be constantly on, though a bit dimmer.

You can tweak the numbers in the code to see this effect. However, it's a drag to have to change the value, upload the code, test the result, and then tweak the value again. It would be much easier to simply add a dial to the project, so that you can quickly change the speed of the LEDs. Is there an easier way to do this? Of course there is!

Up until this point, you've been using the Arduino to control *output,* using the digital pins, using the `digitalWrite()` function. As you might expect, the digital pins can also sense *input.* However, because they are *digital* pins, they can only be used for digital input and output — that is to say, 1 or 0, on or off, +5 volts or 0 volts.

To continuously change the speed of the LEDs until you get it to where you want it, you need a way for the Arduino to sense a continuous change between a HIGH value and a LOW value — an analog input. There are six pins for just this purpose on the lower right of the board, labeled ANALOG 0-5. You can use them to read a voltage that's somewhere between 0 and 5 volts.

You do this with a function called `analogRead()`, specifying the pin you want to read in the parentheses. For example, to read Pin 0, you'd do this:

```
analogRead(0);
```

When you use this function in your code, you will get back a numerical value that corresponds to the voltage that the Arduino detects on that pin. A voltage value of merely 0 to 5 wouldn't be very helpful, so the Arduino is designed to return a value within a more precise range, from 0 to 1023. You then use this number in your code to change how the code behaves.

In this case, you want to change the speed of the delay between each change of LED by modifying the value of `delayTime`. I added this to the end of the code, just before the last line of code that ends the main `loop()`:

```
delayTime = analogRead(0);
delay(5);
}
```

All you need now is a way to provide a voltage between 0 and 5 volts to analog Pin 0. This is where the potentiometer comes in.

There is a proportional relationship between voltage and resistance. The greater the resistance at a given point in a circuit, the less voltage can be measured after it. Varying the proportion of resistance in a circuit will therefore vary the measureable voltage.

A potentiometer is simply a variable resistor. It has three connection points, or *legs*. Inside, there is a resistive material between the left and right legs. The center leg is connected to the dial and an internal wiper that traces along the resistive material. Rotating the dial changes the position of the wiper. If a voltage is placed across the left and right legs, the center leg will provide a variable voltage, because the resistance of the center leg depends on where it is positioned. It is the variable voltage of the center leg that is provided to analog Pin 0.

The 5V pin in the POWER section of the Arduino supplies the source voltage to the left leg of the potentiometer. Any circuit has to have a continuous path from power supply to ground, which is why the right leg is connected to ground. The center leg is connected to Pin 0, where the Arduino will read the variable voltage with the `analogRead(0)` function.

Make sure to disconnect the USB connection before you add or remove any components!

Add the potentiometer and jumper wires to your breadboard. Figure 4-5 shows how a potentiometer is connected, and Figure 4-6 shows the entire circuit with LEDs and potentiometer. The spacing of the holes, or *pitch,* of most breadboards is typically 0.1" (2.54 mm). Depending on the spacing or thickness of its legs, you might not be able to insert the potentiometer directly into the breadboard. If your legs won't fit, you can use alligator clips to connect the potentiometer to wires leading to your Arduino and breadboard, or solder wires to your potentiometer. Soldering tips are in Chapter 3.

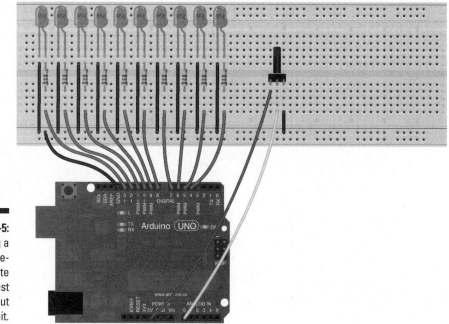

Figure 4-5:
Using a potentiometer to create the simplest analog input circuit.

Now that you have all your components connected, attach your USB cable to power up the Arduino. If you haven't uploaded the modified code to your Arduino board, do so now. If everything is working correctly, you should be able to change the speed of the LEDs by turning the potentiometer. If it doesn't seem to be working, disconnect the power and check all your connections.

You can play around with different resistor values and potentiometers to get a sense of the relationship of the resistance in the input circuit to the speed of the all-seeing eye. You can also get slider potentiometers that you might see on a mixing board.

Figure 4-6:
Adding
a poten-
tiometer
to control
speed.

Now that you can control the speed of the eye, you can try some other ideas. See if you can create other effects, like colliding two lights from opposite ends, or creating a bouncing effect. After understanding some of the basics of building the circuit and programming, you can tackle a lot of different visual effects. The eye's the limit, you might say!

Chapter 5

Making a Light Pet

*L*ight can certainly be warm and emotional. As light changes or shifts, you may find that it takes on a personality all its own. Perhaps you never thought of light as a pet, but by using a little creativity, and the information in this chapter, you can create one. You can build a critter with colors and moods. The light pet cycles through a random series of colors by mixing red, green, and blue light from LEDs. You can make just about any color by varying the combinations of the brightness of these three LEDs.

In this chapter, I detail how to get together the necessary parts. I explain how to wire up the parts, build the circuit, and check that you have connected everything properly. After you upload the code to the Arduino, you can tweak it to give your pet a fun personality. The final step is putting it all into an appealing enclosure.

My version of this project is a pet I've named Lux. I chose this name because it is the international standard (SI) unit of measurement of illuminance. Also, it sounds kind of cute. All pets have their moods, and Lux is no different. To make it seem more like a real pet, it occasionally purrs by slowly pulsating. Lux also randomly goes into a happy mood, indicated by a green glow, and a sad mood, indicated by a red glow. What's cool is that when you understand how the code for Lux works, it's easy to change it to create new moods for your own light pet.

Selecting Your Parts

The first step of the project is getting the parts you need to build your light pet. If you have not set up your workspace or Arduino yet, check out Chapter 2 for more details on how to connect Arduino to your computer and how to use the Arduino integrated development environment (IDE) to upload programs.

Getting together parts for your light pet is pretty simple. As shown in Figure 5-1, you need the following:

✔ Your Arduino

✔ A breadboard

✔ Three 5mm super bright LEDs (one red, one green, one blue)

✔ Three 250 ohm resistors

✔ Jumper wires of various lengths

✔ A 7 to 12 volt DC power supply

✔ An enclosure — something translucent to put it in

Figure 5-1: All the parts you need for the light pet. Get creative with your enclosure!

The enclosure you choose is important, because it gives your project some personality and hides all the innards. The enclosure could be anything that's frosted and allows light to glow through. Perhaps something as simple as a small plastic box, a food container, or an origami cube? Use your imagination, because the enclosure is what gives your pet some style.

Create your own enclosure or hunt for something that's large enough to put the Arduino and breadboard inside. If the enclosure you want to use is too small, you can house these separately and solder longer wires to your LEDs. After you start thinking about general consumer products this way, you may start seeing potential enclosures whenever you go shopping!

Building the Circuit

Make sure that the power supply is turned off when you are building your circuit. Safety is important, and you could damage your Arduino, your computer, or yourself if you are working on circuits that are powered up! So make sure your Arduino is not connected to your computer or plugged in to the power supply.

When you are sure that it's not powered up, start out by connecting the Arduino to your breadboard. Use your jumper wires to do the following:

1. **Connect a jumper wire to the pin labeled GND that is in the row of digital pins at the top of your Arduino.**

   You can also use the Arduino pin(s) labeled GND, in the POWER pins area on the bottom of the Arduino. The Arduino Uno has two of them, so you can use either one.

2. **Connect the other side of the jumper wire to the first hole in one of the long columns on the side of your breadboard.**

   This wire is your ground rail, which provides a shared connection for many components to connect to ground. On some breadboards, the rails on the side are color-coded. By convention, people use the black (sometimes blue) column for their ground rail and red for the power rail. (For clarity, the breadboard is shown rotated 90 degrees, so the columns are running left to right and the rows are running top to bottom. See Figure 5-2.)

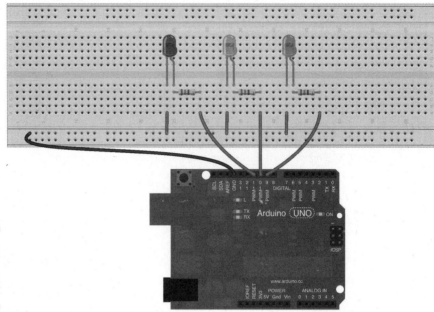

Figure 5-2:
Parts place-
ment on the
breadboard.

Next, you add the resistors and the LEDs to the circuit. Follow these steps:

1. **Connect the three resistors to the breadboard.**

   Each of the legs of the resistors should be in a different row on the breadboard, as shown in the Figure 5-2. Arrange the resistors neatly. None of
   the legs should be connected to any other holes in the same row.

2. **Insert the three LEDs so that the long leg is in the same row as the
   other side of each resistor and the short leg is in an unused row of
   holes.**

3. **Use some short jumper wires to connect the leg of each resistor that
   is not connected to the LED to the Arduino digital Pins 9, 10, and 11,
   respectively.**

4. **Use some short jumper wires to connect the short leg of each LED to
   the ground rail you made in Step 2.**

You have now established an electrical connection that allows current to
flow from Pin 9 through one of the resistors, through the red LED, and to the
ground rail. You should be able to trace an imaginary pathway from Pin 9

continuously to the GND pin on the Arduino. The same applies for Pin 10 and
Pin 11.

The long leg of the LED is called the *anode,* and the short leg is the *cathode.*
Power only flows through in one direction to light up the LED: from the anode
to the cathode.

Review Figure 5-2 to make sure that you've done it correctly. Pay particular
attention to the orientation of the LEDs. If you've got one backward, it won't
light up. Fortunately, it won't be damaged, but it's good to get it right before
powering up.

Now that you've built the circuit, you can enter the code, take a look at how
it works, and then upload it.

Understanding How the Code Works

The code directly defines your light pet's behavior, so it's important to understand the decisions that are made in the code and the resulting behavior.

I find it handy to make flowcharts when I'm trying to decide how code will
work and to map out what happens when certain events occur. The flowchart
in Figure 5-3 explains the sequence of decisions that the light pet will make.

Making moods

For Lux, selecting its (his?) mood is the first decision. There are four moods
to choose from: purring, happy, sad, or regular light blending mood, which
he does most of the time. To select a mood, the Arduino picks a random
number from 0 to 20. If the number is 0, that's purring mood, in which Lux
will slowly fade the current color on and off 10 times. If the number is 1,
that's happiness. Lux will glow green for 10 seconds and then start all over
again. If the number picked is 2, that's sadness. Lux will glow red for 10 seconds and then return to normal. If the number is anything over 2, then that's
the normal mood in which Lux slowly shifts and blends his three colors.

As you can see in Figure 5-3, 85 percent of selections will be the normal mood.
Lux will only do something special now and then. You could change this behavior by changing any of these values, as I describe later in this chapter.

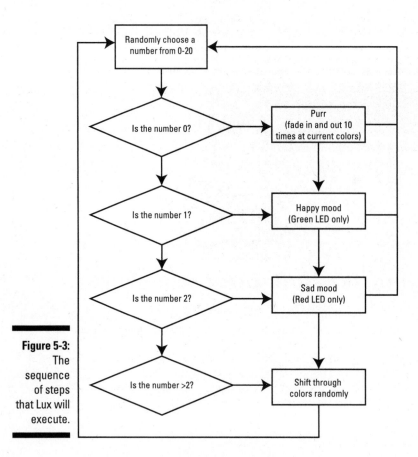

Figure 5-3:
The
sequence
of steps
that Lux will
execute.

Cranking out the code

You can enter the code that sets up the Arduino to run the light pet and control the light pet's normal behavior — gently blending colors. Later, you can add the extra functions to control its moods. Start by entering the following code into a new sketch. You can also download the sketch from the book's website, www.dummies.com/go/arduinoprojectsfordummies, or cut and paste it into your sketch from the website.

```
// The Light Pet - A Color Changing Mood Light
// Randomly selects and fades through colors of three LEDs

// Set which pins will use each color
const int redLED = 9;
const int greenLED = 10;
const int blueLED = 11;
```

```
// Assign variables for the LEDs
int redValue = 0;    // the current value of brightness
int newRedValue = 0; // the new value of brightness

int blueValue = 0;
int newBlueValue = 0;

int greenValue = 0;
int newGreenValue = 0;

// Assign "utility" variables for the random number, and the fading speed
int randomValue = 0;
int fadeSpeed = 50;

// Setup the three LED pins for OUTPUT
void setup(){
  pinMode(redLED, OUTPUT);
  pinMode(blueLED, OUTPUT);
  pinMode(greenLED, OUTPUT);
}

// The main loop of the program
void loop() {
  mood = random(20); // pick a number from 0-19 to set the mood of the pet
  if (mood > 2){   // if the number picked was anything higher than 2, run the
                color blending function
    blendColors();
  }
}
```

Take a moment to look at what's going on here.

At the beginning are some variable declarations. The three integer variables hold the numbers for the pins that Arduino will turn on and off to control the LEDs (Pins 9, 10, and 11).

The integers are named, sensibly, after the color of each LED:

```
const int redLED = 9;
const int greenLED = 10;
const int blueLED = 11;
```

These integers are *constants,* which means that they keep the same value throughout the whole program. Using constants saves on the limited memory available for your program. Although it's not vital for the light pet, which is a small program, it's a good idea to get into the habit of using constants, if you won't be changing a variable's value while your code runs. In this case, you'll always be using Pins 9, 10, and 11 for the red, green, and blue LEDs, so you can use a constant.

Next, the code creates more variables for each of the LEDs. To mix the colors at different levels of brightness, you'll be changing each LED successively from its current value of brightness to a new level. The first variable is red-Value, which holds the brightness value the red LED is currently at. It's good practice to assign a value to newly created variables, so this is set to 0, but will be changed as soon as the program runs.

The variable newRedValue holds the new brightness value that the LED will change to. This new value is set to 0, but once the program starts running, it will be chosen randomly to be somewhere between completely off (a value of 0) and full brightness (a value of 255):

```
int redValue = 0;     // the current value of brightness
int newRedValue = 0; // the new level of brightness
```

Finally, there are two *utility variables* that control how the program operates. The behavior of the light pet is that it will shift colors slowly. Every time the program loops, each LED will change to a new level of brightness. The first variable is randomValue. As the name implies, the code will use this variable to hold a random value, which is chosen later, in the main loop. The second variable is fadeSpeed. You use this later to control how quickly the lights fade:

```
int randomValue = 0;
int fadeSpeed = 50;
```

Moving on, the setup code defines the how the Arduino uses its digital pins. Here, you are declaring which three digital pins are used and that they are used for output. Because you specified above that redLED is a variable with a value of 9, the first statement sets up Pin 9 for output. BlueLED and greenLED do the same thing for Pins 10 and 11, respectively:

```
pinMode(redLED, OUTPUT);
pinMode(blueLED, OUTPUT);
pinMode(greenLED, OUTPUT);
```

Now take a look at the main body of the code, which is in the main loop. It's pretty simple. Two things are going on here: generating a random number and then blending colors if that number is over 2 but below 20:

```
void loop() {
  mood = random(20);
  if (mood > 2){
    blendColors();
  }
}
```

Defining your code's functions

You might notice something interesting about the way this code is organized. Often, within the main loop you would put all the instructions that you want the Arduino to do between the loop function's two curly brackets. However, if you have a lot of different things going on in your code, this can get a bit hard to read. It's a good idea to modularize your code, so that discrete sequences of events are self contained as their own functions. This makes it easier to read and change your code. It also means that in more complicated programs, in which a function is executed many times in different places, you only have to modify the function once to change its behavior in all parts of the code where that function is executed.

The important part is assigning the variable "mood" a random number that will be used to change the colors of the lights. Do this by using the `random()` function, which will choose a random number between 0 and whatever you put within the parentheses, not including that number. So in this code, you are telling the Arduino to pick a random number between 0 and 19. You can also use a range between two numbers, in which case the first number sets the lower limit and the second number the upper limit, not inclusive of the upper limit. For example `random(5,10)` will choose a number from 5 to 9.

 The equal sign tells the Arduino to assign to the variable `mood` the value that was chosen by the `random()` function. It doesn't really mean "equals" but more precisely "assign to." If you want to evaluate whether two things are equal, you need to use a double equal sign `==`.

The next statement is an `if` statement that tests whether the value for mood that was just chosen is greater than 2, which it will be most of the time. If it is greater, then the `blendColors()` function is executed. Later, you deal with what happens if the number is 2 or less, but first let's take a look at blending colors, which is what your pet will be doing most of the time.

The `blendColors()` function is a user-defined function that changes the brightness of each of the LEDs. Your Arduino comes with many predefined functions you already know about, such as `setup()`, `loop()`, and `random()`. But you can also create your own functions to organize your code and make it easier to change.

The description of what your function does is located in its own section of the code, after the main loop. So, you don't include these functions within the main loop — you only call them *from* the main loop. You can see in this code that once the `blendColors()` function is executed, the main loop is finished, and the Arduino will start back at the top of the loop by choosing the next random number.

Blending light

Now that you've specified the main loop, you're ready to add what that user-defined function does. It's a lot of code, but it just does two things. It chooses a new brightness level and changes an LED to that level — and it does this for each LED. Take a moment to enter or cut and paste the following code into your sketch:

```
void blendColors(){
newRedValue= random(255); // Pick a random value for the red LED

  if (redValue < newRedValue){
    for (int x=redValue; x<newRedValue; x++) {
      analogWrite(redLED, x);
      delay(fadeSpeed);
    }
  }
  else {
    for (int x=redValue; x>newRedValue; x--) {
      analogWrite(redLED, x);
      delay(fadeSpeed);
    }
  }
  redValue=newRedValue;

  // set the value for the green LED
  newGreenValue= random(255);
  if (greenValue < newGreenValue){
    for (int x=greenValue; x<newGreenValue; x++) {
      analogWrite(greenLED, x);
      delay(fadeSpeed);
    }
  }
  else {
    for (int x=greenValue; x>newGreenValue; x--) {
      analogWrite(greenLED, x);
      delay(fadeSpeed);
    }
  }
  greenValue=newGreenValue;

  // set the value for the blue LED
  newBlueValue= random(255);
  if (blueValue < newBlueValue){
    for (int x=blueValue; x<newBlueValue; x++) {
      analogWrite(blueLED, x);
      delay(fadeSpeed);
    }
  }
```

```
  else {
    for (int x=blueValue; x>newBlueValue; x--) {
      analogWrite(blueLED, x);
      delay(fadeSpeed);
    }
  }
  blueValue=newBlueValue;
}
```

Here's how this user-defined function works. You create a user-defined function by giving it a name, in this case, blendColors. The word *void* means that the function is just going to do what's specified within the curly brackets and that's all it will do. It returns no data, so it's void. Then you place some useful things to do within the two curly brackets:

```
void blendColors(){

  something useful gets done here!

}
```

It is often convenient to write a function that will take some data, do something to it, and then send the result back to the main loop. But blendColors() does not need any specific input and will not be returning any data back to the rest of the program — it's just changing the brightness of the LEDs. The empty parentheses () mean that this function will not be expecting to receive any data to do something with. Using blendColors() just changes each LED to a new level of brightness.

The first useful thing blendColors() does is choose a random value to set the new level of brightness to, and assign this to the variable newRedValue. This is the same method you used earlier to choose a random mood:

```
newRedValue = random(255);
```

You don't want the brightness to simply jump to this new value. You want to fade from the current value, through all the intervening values until you arrive at the newRedValue(). To do this, you need to know whether the new number is higher or lower than the current one. So the code tests whether the random value is higher or lower than the current value, by using an if statement:

```
if (redValue < newRedValue){
    for (int x=redValue; x<newRedValue; x++) {
      analogWrite(redLED, x);
      delay(fadeSpeed);
    }
```

```
} else {
    for (int x=redValue; x>newRedValue; x--) {
    analogWrite(redLED, x);
    delay(fadeSpeed);
}
```

If the test is true, and `redValue` is lower than `newRedValue`, then the code within the first set of curly braces gets executed. Otherwise (indicated by `else`), the test is false, and the code that comes after the word `else` is executed.

Now for the tricky part. The dimming is accomplished within a `for` loop, which you might recognize from Chapter 4, and a special method called `analogWrite()`. The `for` loop starts by assigning the current `redValue` to the local variable `x`:

```
for (int x=redValue; x<newRedValue; x++) {
    analogWrite(redLED, x);
    delay(fadeSpeed);
}
```

As long as `x` is less than `newRedValue`, each cycle of the loop increases the value of `x` by 1 (`x++`) until it reaches the `newRedValue`. You are simply increasing the value of `x` between the current `redValue` and the `newRed-Value`. You'll use this increasing value of `x` to set the level of brightness on your LED. The level is set with the `analogWrite()` method.

Fooling your eyes with pulse-width modulation

You change the brightness of each of the three LEDs with a technique called pulse-width modulation (PWM). Chapter 4 describes how to simply turn LEDs on and off, and if you've tried out the Blink example, you can see that it's pretty straightforward. What's trickier is getting the Arduino to make light fade in and out. LEDs are digital devices with only two possible states. By its nature, an LED can only be either fully on or fully off — there's no in between. But you can simulate fading an LED by fooling your eyes. You do this by rapidly turning the LED on and off so fast that it appears to be fading. This is done with pulse-width modulation.

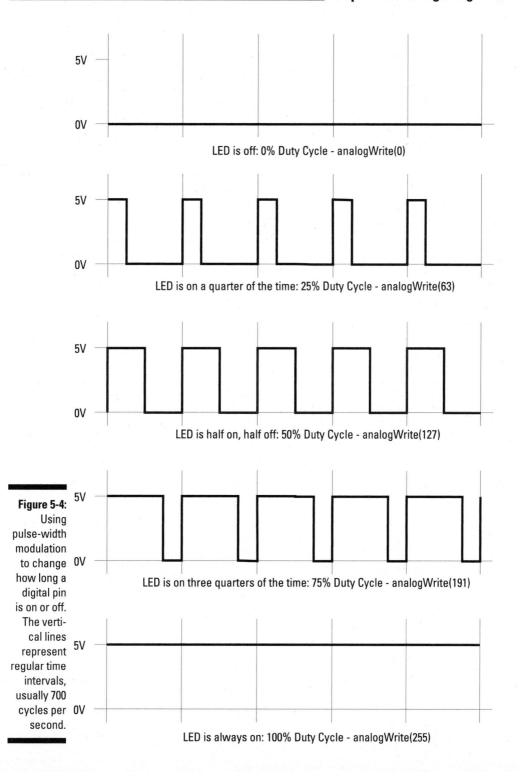

LED is off: 0% Duty Cycle - analogWrite(0)

LED is on a quarter of the time: 25% Duty Cycle - analogWrite(63)

LED is half on, half off: 50% Duty Cycle - analogWrite(127)

Figure 5-4:
Using
pulse-width
modulation
to change
how long a
digital pin
is on or off.
The verti-
cal lines
represent
regular time
intervals,
usually 700
cycles per
second.

LED is on three quarters of the time: 75% Duty Cycle - analogWrite(191)

LED is always on: 100% Duty Cycle - analogWrite(255)

Normally to turn an LED on or off, you would use the `digitalWrite()` function using one of the digital pins (0–13). However, the speed at which you can do this is limited, especially if you are controlling many digital pins. Also, if the processor has to take care of other operations, it can't also keep switching LEDs on and off really fast, which will cause the LEDs to jitter rather than fade smoothly. PWM is a special feature of the processor that solves this problem. You are using Pins 9, 10, and 11 for a good reason — they are three of the six pins available for pulse-width modulation.

You use PWM to generate analog output from a digital pin. PWM changes the proportion of time that a digital pin remains on or off, whether it's at 5 volts or 0 volts. This proportion of time is called the *duty cycle*. By varying the duration of the duty cycle, or modulating it, you can vary the duration that the digital pulse is on or off, which is called the *pulse width*. A 50 percent duty cycle means that the digital pin is powered at 5 volts for half the time, and so on. A 100 percent duty cycle means the digital pin is always on.

To use PWM, you use the `analogWrite()` method on a digital pin. It's called `analogWrite()` because the digital pins are being used to simulate continuously changing (that is to say, analog) values, although you are still only ever turning the LED on or off. Using `analogWrite`, you specify which pin is to be turned on and the duty cycle (0%–100%), using a value from 0 to 255. This can be a bit confusing.

For example, to turn on Pin 3 for a 50% duty cycle you would use:

```
analogWrite(3,127);
```

That's because 127 is 255/2, or 50%. A duty cycle of 80% would require a value of 204 (which is 255*.80). To fade each of the three LEDs on the light pet, you use PWM to change the duty cycle of its digital pin. Setting the red LED's digital pin to a 100% duty cycle means it will be at full brightness and at a 0% duty cycle, it will be off.

A bit confusingly again, the apparent brightness of the LED does not match the strictly linear output of PWM. Your eyes do not perceive brightness in a linear manner. In fact, your eyes perceive different colors with varying levels of sensitivity. So a 50% duty cycle doesn't appear to be "half as bright" as 100%, but for this project, it's not a big problem. You just want the brightness of the colors to appear to change in relation to one another.

The Arduino UNO processor architecture limits the number of PWM pins to six. On an Arduino UNO, Pins 3, 5, 6, 9, 10, and 11 can handle PWM. The Arduino Mega has 15 PWM pins, if you need more of them. Now that you understand when to use PWM, you can see how this is done in the code. See Figure 5-4.

In this code, you use `analogWrite` to change the value of each of the LEDs. The value x comes from the `for` loop that the `analogWrite` function is embedded in:

```
for (int x=redValue; x<newRedValue; x++) {
    analogWrite(redLED, x);
  delay(fadeSpeed);
}
```

The last thing that's going on here is the `delay()` function. This is used to control how fast the `for` loop is executed. You change the speed of the fading by changing the value of the variable `fadeSpeed`, which you set at the beginning of the program to 30 milliseconds. Each time the loop cycles, the processor waits 30 milliseconds. That way you can actually see the fading effect. Without this delay, the fading would occur, but it would happen too quickly to be seen.

Okay, that was a lot to get through. Now you can see the fruits of your labors!

Testing the code

After you get this code into the Arduino IDE, make sure to test it out by clicking on the compile button. The compiler tells you if your code has any errors and displays the results in the status window at the bottom of the Arduino IDE. It highlights the problem at the first place in your code that it encounters trouble.

At first, it can be a little confusing to understand what the compiler is telling you. The most common problems are forgotten (or extra) semicolons or curly brackets. If you have trouble immediately identifying the problem, a quick search of the Arduino forums usually solves the problem.

Save time and find typos in your code by compiling it first, before uploading.

Upload and go

Time to hit the launch button! If the compiler is happy, connect your Arduino to your computer with a USB cable, click the upload, and watch for the flickering TX and RX lights on your Arduino. After they stop, your three LEDs should light up with different levels of brightness and should slowly shift their intensities. Your light pet has come to life!

Hang out with it for a while. Get to know how it shifts and changes. Next, you can add a little personality by defining some behaviors through functions in your code.

Tweaking it!

After you are satisfied with the gently blending colors, you can make your pet come to life by adding moods. You do this by creating a variable for the duration of the mood and a user-defined function for each new mood. Adding new functions is pretty simple. They follow the same format as the `blendColors()` function. First, add your global variable for the duration of the mood:

```
// Assign variables to select the mood and the time to wait in a mood
int mood = 0;
const int moodTime = 10000; // time to wait in milliseconds, 10000 = 10 seconds
```

All that remains is to specify when the mood should occur, back in the main loop.

```
// The main loop of the program
void loop() {
  mood = random(20); // pick a number from 0-20 to set the mood of the pet
  if (mood == 0){     // if the number picked was 0, run the purr function
    purr();
  }
  if (mood == 1){     // if the number picked was 1, run the happy function
    happy();
  }
  if (mood == 2){     // if the number picked was 2, run the sad function
    sad();
  }
  if (mood > 2){      // if the number picked was anything higher than 2,
                      // run the color blending function
    blendColors();
  }
}
```

Depending on which random number was assigned to `mood`, the program executes a different function. If the random number is 0, the `purr()` function is executed. If the random number is 1, the `happy()` function is executed. If the random number is 2, the `sad()` function is executed. Note that the test to see whether two values are equivalent is accomplished by using two equal signs — not one!

Now you can add the functions that change the lights depending on the mood. Add these at the end of the program, after the `blendColors()` function. They use the same techniques as the `blendColors()` function. The `purr()` function is unique. It has two `for` loops — an inner loop to control the fading of colors with PWM and an outer loop to make this happen ten times.

The `purr()` function changes the duty cycle of all the LEDs, from 0 to 255 and back again. The outer loop uses the `count` variable to keep track of how many times this happens. Want a happier, more purr-fect pet? Just increase the number of counts. The `delay(10)` function slows things down just slightly, so you can see the fading occur:

```
void purr(){
  for (int count=0;count<10;count++){
    for(int x=0;x<255;x++){
      analogWrite(redLED, x);
      analogWrite(greenLED, x);
      analogWrite(blueLED, x);
      delay(10);
    }
    for(int x=255;x>0;x--){
      analogWrite(redLED, x);
      analogWrite(greenLED, x);
      analogWrite(blueLED, x);
      delay(10);
    }
  }
}
```

Finally, you describe the last two moods, `happy()` and `sad()`. By now, it should be pretty clear how these are working. Both use PWM to fade the LEDs from their current level to a new level. For `happy()`, the green LED is brought up from its current level, `greenValue`, to full brightness — a duty cycle of 100%, while the other two LEDs are brought to a 0% duty cycle. The `sad()` does the same thing, but makes the red LED brightest.

The pet then waits in this mood for the `moodTime` you set at the top of the code, which was 10000 milliseconds, or 10 seconds. There's one last loop at the end of each function that fades to black, before the function is finished and everything starts all over again in the main program loop:

```
void happy(){
  for(int x=greenValue;x<255;x++){
    analogWrite(greenLED, x);
    delay(fadeSpeed);
  }
  for(int x=redValue;x>0;x--){
    analogWrite(redLED, x);
    delay(fadeSpeed);
  }
  for(int x=blueValue;x>0;x--){
    analogWrite(blueLED, x);
    delay(fadeSpeed);
  }
  delay(moodTime);          // sets how long the pet will wait in this mood
```

```
    for(int x=255;x>0;x--){  // fade to black
      analogWrite(greenLED, x);
      delay(fadeSpeed);
    }
  }


    // the sad function turns on only the red LED for the mood time
  void sad(){
    for(int x=redValue;x<255;x++){
      analogWrite(redLED, x);
      delay(fadeSpeed);
    }
    for(int x=greenValue;x>0;x--){
      analogWrite(greenLED, x);
      delay(fadeSpeed);
    }
    for(int x=blueValue;x>0;x--){
      analogWrite(blueLED, x);
      delay(fadeSpeed);
    }
    delay(moodTime);            // sets how long the pet will wait in this mood
    for(int x=255;x>0;x--){  // fade to black

      analogWrite(redLED, x);
      delay(fadeSpeed);
    }
  }
```

Notice that you're using the `fadeSpeed` variable again to make the transition gradual.

Try using different values for these variables to alter your pet's moods. Get creative! You'll quickly find that you want to give your pet a personality all its own.

Understanding How the Hardware Works

Now that your code is in the Arduino, and hopefully you have seen some new moods and colors, it's a good idea to review what's going on with the hardware from an electronic perspective. That way, when you take on more advanced projects, it will be clearer what's going on. Putting all this into the enclosure keeps everything nice and neat, and gives your pet an identity.

You don't have worry too much about getting exactly the same LEDs as those in the parts list. But ideally, use super bright LEDs. LED brightness is measured in microcandelas (mcd). Choose LEDs with high mcd values. The higher they are, the brighter they are and the brighter your pet glows.

The schematic in Figure 5-5 shows the light frequency of each LED in nanometers. Very often, you'll find these ratings on the datasheet for LEDs, along with other specifications. The main thing to pay attention to is the maximum forward current rating of the LEDs, which is measured in milliamps (mA). If you don't know the maximum, you can look for a datasheet for most electronic parts on the Internet. For garden-variety LEDs, it's usually 20mA or less.

The resistors limit the amount of current that is flowing from each of the Arduino digital pins to ground. Because the digital pins provide output at 5 volts, you can work out what resistors are needed using Ohm's Law, which states that the voltage in a circuit is equal to the current times the resistance (or V=I*R):

5 volts / 0.02 amps = 250 ohms.

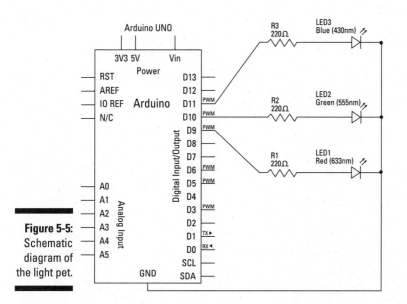

Figure 5-5: Schematic diagram of the light pet.

Divide 5 volts by the maximum amount of current the LEDs are rated at, which is 20 milliamps. A milliamp is one thousandth of an amp, so to get a milliamp value of 20mA, move the decimal place over three places to the left: 0.020 amps. The result is 250 ohms. If you don't have a 250 ohm resistor handy, use one with a slightly higher value, like 270 ohms. The higher the value, the dimmer your LEDs will be, because less current will flow through them.

Of course, you don't have to use three individual LEDs to blend colors. There are three-color LEDs for exactly this purpose that incorporate red, green, and blue LEDs within a single package with four wires — three anodes and one cathode. This package is often referred to as a *common cathode design* because the LEDs share the cathode, which is connected to ground in your circuit.

Once you've put all of your parts onto a breadboard and programmed your Arduino, you can get rid of the computer altogether! Disconnect your USB cable and connect the power transformer to the Arduino. Your Arduino should start running the code in just a moment or two.

Once you are satisfied with it, hide the Arduino and breadboard inside your light pet's enclosure. For Lux, I used the little space alien toy from IKEA (see Figure 5-6). This guy has some pretty nice electronics inside already, including an LED, microcontroller, and a switch, which I've saved for another day. The enclosure is made of translucent, stretchy rubber, and even has a convenient little hole in the back for a power adaptor. Squeezing the hardware inside was a little tricky, so I used longer wires to connect the Arduino to the breadboard, and folded the breadboard onto the back of the Arduino, like a little sandwich.

Figure 5-6:
You can use existing toys or products for your enclosure.

If your enclosure is not big enough, brush up on your soldering skills in Chapter 3, and solder long wires to your three LEDs. That way you can hide the Arduino and breadboard out of sight.

All that remains is to find a nice cozy place for your pet to keep you company!

Chapter 6

Making a Scrolling Sign

*B*ecause the cost of LEDs is really negligible and their range of colors and brightness have increased, LED signs have become gigantic. It's pretty much impossible to walk out your door and not be accosted by animated signs these days. We're surrounded by them, even in small towns. The animated LED signs in New York's Times Square and London's Piccadilly Circus use millions of LEDs. With an Arduino, and only a few components, you can easily create and send a message of your own.

This chapter gives you a project in which you will build an 8 x 8 LED matrix of 64 LEDs on your Arduino. You create a custom image on the display by using a *sprite*. You can create custom fonts and custom characters with sprites. You then discover how to swap out different sprites to create animations and change their speed. When you've mastered control of sprites, you can then string together a sequence of them to spell out the characters of any message you like.

Selecting Parts

This project is light on parts, but has a lot of wires. Before you start, get hold of these items, shown in Figure 6-1:

✔ Your Arduino

✔ A breadboard

✔ An 8 x 8 LED matrix display with a common cathode (such as Jameco 2132349, BetLux BL-M23B881UHR-11, or Sure LE-MM103, available from Oomlout.com), or similar.

✔ Eight 1K ohm resistors

✔ Thirty-two jumper wires

✔ Pin headers, stackable headers (such as SparkFun PRT-09280), or ribbon cable (optional)

You won't be building a million-LED display, but you will need 64 of them. Laying out that many LEDs in a tiny space can be tricky, and that's why manufacturers have created LED matrix displays. These are single blocks of plastic that have all the LEDs and lenses encased inside. Having 64 LEDs means having 128 pins — one for each LED's power supply and ground. Having 128 pins is a bit impractical, so to reduce the number of pins in an LED matrix, they usually share either the pin that's connected to ground (a *common cathode*) or the pin that's connected to the power source (a *common anode*). The matrix used in this project is a common cathode display.

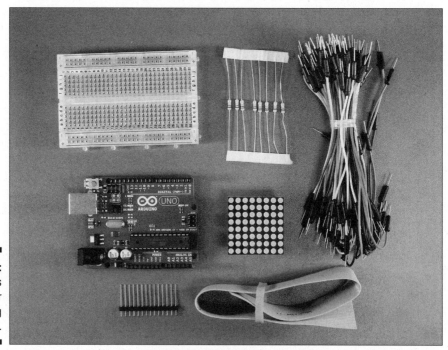

Figure 6-1:
Parts needed for the scrolling sign.

You can also use an LED matrix with the same pinouts but using a common anode (such as the SparkFun COM-00681 or NKC Electronics COM-0018). If you do, you will need to change the code so that it is driving them in the opposite way, with power applied to the columns by driving them HIGH, and the rows connected to ground by driving them LOW.

You'll be providing a supply voltage from the digital pins on your Arduino. The resistors are used to limit current through your LEDs and are calculated to provide less than the maximum forward current that is allowed. According to the datasheet, that's 20 milliamps. Using 1K ohm resistors provides a substantial leeway, and you could use smaller resistors, ones down to about 150 ohms, if need be. The lower the value of the resistors, the brighter your matrix will be because more current will flow to the LEDs to light them up.

The pin headers and ribbon cable are optional. The pin headers are merely a way of extending your matrix above the breadboard a little bit, thereby making it easier to fit your wires into the holes. If you'd like to place the matrix some distance away from the breadboard and Arduino, you just need to extend the 24 wires from your Arduino to the display. Connecting 24 individual extension wires would be a big mess, so using ribbon cable is a tidy way to make all the connections. If you do this, you need to solder pin headers onto each of the wires of the ribbon cable, so that you can fit them into your breadboard and Arduino.

Building the Circuit

This project uses an LED matrix with a common cathode. Figure 6-2 shows the display and how the pins are connected, its *pinouts.* The Sure LE-MM103 matrix is a two-color display with both red and green LEDs. Each of the dots on the front of the matrix actually has two LEDs behind it. You can choose one or the other because there aren't enough output pins on an Arduino Uno to do both colors. Because this project uses only the red LEDs, Figure 6-2 only shows the LED matrix pin numbers you need to use for the red LEDs.

If you use the Jameco display, there are only red LEDs, so there are fewer pins on the bottom.

Take a closer look at Figure 6-2. There are a lot of pin numbers here. Notice that the Arduino Pins 2 through 9 are indicated on the left. Each of these is connected to your Arduino's digital outputs through a 1K ohm resistor. In each of the rows, all the cathodes of the LEDs are connected to the same digital output. This is why the display is referred to as a *common cathode* display.

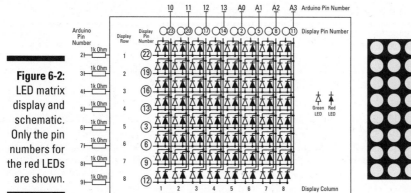

Figure 6-2:
LED matrix
display and
schematic.
Only the pin
numbers for
the red LEDs
are shown.

Each of the columns is also connected to your Arduino digital output pins. The top row of labels (10 through A3) indicates which Arduino pin each of the columns is connected to. The Display Pin Number tells you which of the pins on the back side of the matrix is connected to each LED (only the pin numbers for red LEDs are shown).

Your code will be turning on and off individual LEDs by providing current to the columns and providing a path to ground on the rows. For example, setting Arduino digital output in number 2 to LOW and output Pin 10 to HIGH provides a pathway for electricity to flow through the LED and it would light up. If you set the pins the other way around, however, the LED would not light up.

There are two LEDs for each of the 64 positions on your matrix. In this project, your code goes through each of the red LEDs at each position to light it or turn it off. When you wire up columns on a two-color LED matrix, you connect the red LED pins (for example, 23, 20, 17, 14, 2, 5, 8, and 11). In the illustrations, I show how to connect the red ones. If you prefer, you can connect to the green LEDs (for example, 24, 21, 18, 15, 1, 4, 7, and 10).

If you want to use both colors of LED, you could use an Arduino Mega, which has 54 digital I/O pins, but you'd need to modify the code accordingly.

Pay close attention to the difference between the Arduino pin number, the LED matrix row and column numbers, and the LED matrix pin numbers. If you are using a different LED matrix than the example, then you need to identify which LED pin corresponds to a labeled row or column, and then connect that LED pin (not the LED pin number in the diagram) to the indicated Arduino pin number.

Looking on the underside of the matrix, notice that the pins are in two columns. Each of the LEDs is connected to a pin for its anode and a shared pin for the cathode. Look closely and you may see that Pin 1 is labeled at the lower-right side of the display, underneath the clear resin. If your matrix isn't labeled, check your data sheet to identify which is Pin 1.

Table 6-1 shows how the pins on the bottom of the Sure LE-MM103 display are connected to the LEDs on the top.

Table 6-1	Pinouts of the Sure LE-MM103 Matrix LED		
LED Matrix Pin	_Connection_	_LED Matrix Pin_	_Connection_
1	Column 5 (-) Green	13	Row 4 (+) Red & Green
2	Column 5 (-) Red	14	Column 4 (-) Red
3	Row 5 (+) Red & Green	15	Column 4
4	Column 6 (-) Green	16	Row 3 (+) Red & Green
5	Column 6 (-) Red	17	Column 3 (-) Red
6	Row 6 (+) Red & Green	18	Column 3 (-) Green
7	Column 7 (-) Green	19	Row 2 (+) Red & Green
8	Column 7 (-) Red	20	Column 2 (-) Red
9	Row 7 (+) Red & Green	21	Column 2 (-) Green
10	Column 8 (-) Green	22	Row 1 (+) Red & Green
11	Column 8 (-) Red	23	Column 1 (-) Red
12	Row 8 (+) Red & Green	24	Column 1 (-) Green

There is no standard pinout for LED matrix displays. You might find that on your display (even if it's a common cathode display), the pins do not match the one in this project, in which case the code will not work. Refer to the data sheet for your matrix to determine which pins to connect. If you don't have the datasheet, a PDF of it should be available from the website of your supplier.

Often you can find your product's datasheet simply by using the term "datasheet" and the part number in your search.

You might find that the matrix display doesn't quite fit onto your breadboard. In that case, you can use *stackable headers* that have holes on one end and pins on the other. You simply insert your display into the holes. If you don't have any stackable headers, you can solder longer *pin headers* onto the matrix, as shown in Figure 6-3. Or perhaps you'd like to separate the matrix and the breadboard. You can solder ribbon cable to the pins so that you can tuck the Arduino out of sight.

If you are using the specific matrix display in the example, follow the layout in Figure 6-4. Otherwise, refer to your datasheet to figure out which LED pins to connect to which Arduino pins.

Follow the layout in Figure 6-4 to connect your Arduino pins to your resistors and LED matrix. It's good to be very detail oriented at this stage and to double-check your connections! You're not likely to damage anything if you wire it up incorrectly, but the matrix won't display correctly if you get something wrong.

Figure 6-3:
LED Matrix
Display with
extension
pin headers
soldered on.

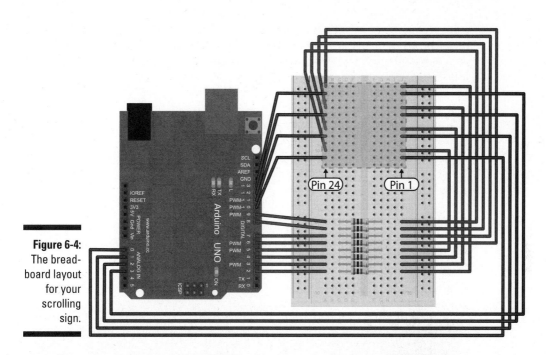

Figure 6-4:
The bread-
board layout
for your
scrolling
sign.

Understanding How the Code Works

Your matrix is now wired up and ready to go, but what will you display? Each LED is essentially a *pixel* of the display. You can create static drawings or icons using the pixels of your matrix. You can also create animations, which are merely static images displayed rapidly. There are two ways that people tend to display things on matrices, as an algorithm or as a *bitmap*.

This first involves mathematically calculating which LEDs to light up and then turning them on. This is the approach that's used for things like peak level audio meters, or bouncing balls. If you built the All-Seeing Eye project in Chapter 4, you used an algorithm to calculate which LED to illuminate. You could use the same principle for your LED matrix.

The second way of doing this is to store a map of all the LEDs that specifies which ones are on or off. Because each LED can be only on or off, its condition can be stored as a bit, a 1, or 0. Hence the term *bitmap,* which you've no doubt heard before. When you want to display something, you look up its bitmap in memory and then send it to the LED matrix, which you could think of as a sort of tiny screen.

By cycling through the bitmaps stored in memory, you can create animations, and that's what you'll do to create your scrolling text, using bitmaps of the letters of the alphabet. But first, you need to write the code to create a bitmap and display it on the matrix.

Summoning a sprite

No, you're not summoning up a supernatural legendary creature — you're just painting with light! In computer graphics, *sprites* are bitmaps that store predefined images that can be integrated into a larger scene. Although that's not exactly what's going on with your LED matrix, people often refer to bitmaps as sprites.

To display something interesting on the LED matrix, you will probably want to draw some characters and icons. You store these as bitmaps as an array of values, 1 to turn an LED on, and 0 to turn an LED off. Figure 6-5 shows a sprite displayed on the LED matrix.

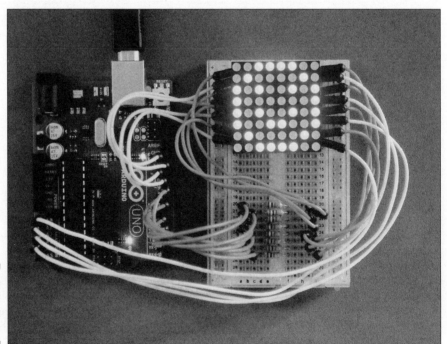

Figure 6-5:
Displaying a sprite on the matrix.

Enter the code to create your sprite. This example creates a smiley face:

```
/*
 * Chapter 6: Making a Scrolling Sign (a Sprite)
 * Adapted from Oomlout.com http://www.tinyurl.com/yhwxv6h
 * Displays a smiley face
 */

// Arduino Pin Definitions
int rowPin[] = {2,3,4,5,6,7,8,9};          //An Array defining which Arduino pin
            each row is attached to
                                          //(The rows are common anode (driven
            HIGH))
int colPin[] = {17,16,15,14,13,12,11,10};  //An Array defining which pin each
            column is attached to
                                          //(The columns are common cathode
            (driven LOW))
byte smile[] = {                           //The array used to hold a bitmap of
            the display
  B00111100,
  B01000010,
  B10100101,
  B10000001,
  B10100101,
  B10011001,
  B01000010,
  B00111100};

void setup()
{
  for(int i = 0; i <8; i++){  //Set the Arduino pins to be OUTPUTs
    pinMode(rowPin[i], OUTPUT); //These refer to the Arduino pins in the arrays
    pinMode(colPin[i], OUTPUT);
  }
}

void loop()
{
  displaySprite();                         // display the Sprite
}

void displaySprite(){
  for(int count = 0; count < 8; count ++){    //A utility counter
    for(int i = 0; i < 8; i++){
      digitalWrite(rowPin[i], LOW);                //Turn off all row pins
    }
    for(int i = 0; i < 8; i++){                    //Activate only the Arduino pin
            of the column to light up
      if(i == count){
        digitalWrite(colPin[i], LOW);
```

```
      }
     else{
        digitalWrite(colPin[i], HIGH);            //Turns all the other rows off
     }
   }
   for(int row = 0; row < 8; row++){              //Iterate through each pixel in
            the current column
     int bit = (smile[count] >> row) & 1;         //Use a bit shift in the smile[]
            array to do a bitwise comparison
                                                  //And assign the result of the
            comparison to the bit
     if(bit == 1){                                //If the bitwise comparison is 1,
        digitalWrite(rowPin[row], HIGH);           //Then light up the LED
     }
   }
  }
 }
}
```

Getting the LEDs to light up requires supplying them with power and a connection to ground for the current to flow. Therefore, you have to specify which rows and columns are being used for each LED and select the appropriate row and column in the code. The pins used for the rows and columns are defined in the two integer arrays at the top of the code:

```
int rowPin[] = { 2, 3, 4, 5, 6, 7, 8, 9};
int colPin[] = {17,16,15,14,13,12,11,10};
```

The Arduino Uno does not have digital pins labeled 14 through 17. To get the extra four pins you need, you can use the analog 0 through 3 pins as digital outputs.

The two key parts of this code are the data, stored as a bitmap, and the function that displays it. It's also important to specify which pins are used for supplying voltage to the LEDs and which pins are used for providing a path to ground. On this display, the rows are connected to the LED anodes, so you supply them with power by driving them HIGH, and the columns are connected to ground by driving them LOW. The number sequences are in reverse order because of the way that they are addressed in the display-sprite() function.

Here's where the fun begins. The bitmap is simply an array of data which encodes a 1 or a 0 value for every LED. Because each value is a bit, and there are 8 bits in a byte, you can store the entire smiley face in 8 bytes. That's 64 bits — one for each pixel that corresponds to a single LED. I've made the "1's" boldface in the following code, so it's easier to see the smiley face:

```
byte smile[] = {
  B00111100,
  B01000010,
  B10100101,
  B10000001,
  B10100101,
  B10011001,
  B01000010,
  B00111100};
```

This code creates an array of the type *byte,* with the name "data." The values for each of the eight bytes in this *byte array* are stored within the curly brackets. The capital letter "B" indicates that this data is stored in binary format. However, putting each byte on a separate line makes it easier to read. The following would also work, but is harder to read:

```
byte smile[] = {B00111100, B01000010, B10100101,
        B10000001, B10100101, B10011001, B01000010,
        B00111100};
```

Having defined all the variables, the `setup()` function uses the integer arrays you just created to set all the LED pins for output using a simple `for` loop.

Now for the main attraction! Displaying the smiley is accomplished in the `displaySprite()` function, which is the only thing that is done in the main `loop()` of the program. It's good to organize your code this way, writing a separate user-defined function to display the sprite, because you may want to add other functions later.

If you examine the code closely, you see that only one LED is lit up at a time. (That's how you can get away with using only eight resistors.).You are never driving more than one LED, but it is happening so fast that the LEDs appear to be continuously illuminated.

To do this rapid-fire illumination, the `displaySprite()` function is composed of four loops that set the pins to turn off and which single pin to turn on, like this:

1. The first loop is a counter called "count" to keep track of where you are from 0 to 7. This utility counter keeps track of which byte of the `smile[]` array you are on.

   Array numbering starts from zero, so the numbers from zero through seven keep track of eight iterations of the loop.

2. The second loop goes through each of the row pins and sets them LOW. Setting them LOW turns off the supply voltage for all eight of the LEDs in each ROW. Because the supply voltage to all the pins is turned off, anything that might have been turned on previously is turned off, which will be important for making animations later.

3. Now, the next loop sets the LED anodes of the column you are working on to LOW. However, you set all the other columns to HIGH, which means no power will flow through them. This isolates the current row to be the only one that can actually be active.

4. The final loop lights up the LED you are working on. Starting with the first LED in this current column, at ROW 0, compare it to the data in the bitmap (smile[count]). If the data at that point is 1, then set the current row to HIGH.

The trickiest part of this is the last loop, where the smile[] array is used to determine whether to light up the current LED. This is done with two operations, a *bit shift* and a *bitwise comparison*. Here's how:

```
int bit = (smile[count] >> row) & 1;
```

A temporary integer variable called bit is created to store the results of these operations. The >> is a bit shift operation, which selects which of the eight bits in the current byte are being compared, starting with bit 0 (ROW 0) and continuing through (ROW 7). The byte is shifted to the right by the number of bits that corresponds to the current ROW.

A bitwise comparison is simply a way of comparing 1's and 0's. In this comparison, you are checking whether the byte in your data is a 1 and if it is, lighting up an LED. This is done with a bitwise "and" comparison using the ampersand (&). If your data bit is a 1, it will match the test data bit that is a 1, with the resulting value of 1. You can do four bitwise comparisons: AND, OR, NOT, and exclusive or XOR. Using bitwise AND will ensure that a value of 1 is returned only when the data bit in your bitmap is also a 1.

For example, imagine that you are examining the very first byte of data (which confusingly, starts at 0), smile[0]. This first byte of the smiley face is B00111100, which corresponds to the first row of the display. The first bit is a 0. This is compared to the value of 1 using a bitwise comparison to the value 1. If the bit stored in the bitmap were 1, the test would be true and the LED could be lit. Because it is 0, though, the test is false and the LED is not lit. In the next iteration, the byte is shifted to the right, meaning the next value in the byte can be examined. It is also a 0. This bit shift is continued for each of the eight bits in the byte, and each time the bitwise comparison is made, so the LED can be lit, if necessary. This is done in the next operation:

```
if(bit == 1){                          //If the bitwise comparison is 1,
    digitalWrite(rowPin[row], HIGH);   //Then light up the LED
}
```

Remember, the "is equal to" comparison requires a double equal sign. If the comparison is true, the Arduino pin for the current row can be set to HIGH. Because the column was already set LOW earlier, the selected LED will light up. Remember, you are only ever lighting up one LED at a time. It will be turned off during the next iteration.

Animating sprites

Now that you've displayed a single image, you can try swapping between two images. You will add another bitmap to the data and modify the `display-Sprite` function to switch between them. Add the following code after the `smile[]` array and before the `setup()` loop:

```
byte frown[] = {
    B00111100,
    B01000010,
    B10100101,
    B10000001,
    B10011001,
    B10111101,
    B01000010,
    B00111100};
```

This creates a second array of bytes to store a bitmap of a frown. Now you can add the code that determines which bitmap to show and how long to display it:

```
void loop()
{
    displaySprite(smile, 1000); // display the Smile for 1 second
    displaySprite(frown, 1000); // display the Frown for 1 second
}
```

The loop function now contains two requests to `displaySprite()`, which use two parameters, the byte to display, and the duration to display it. The function is modified to accept these parameters:

```
void displaySprite(byte * data, unsigned long duration){
    unsigned long start = millis();
    while (start+duration>millis()){
...
    }
}
```

Make sure that you've also changed the name of the array that you are using for the bitmap:

```
int bit = (data[count] >> row) & 1;
```

After you've entered the code, try it out and watch the frown turn upside down! Now, you've got the basics down to do a scrolling sign display.

Make sure to add the closing curly bracket for the *while loop* at the end of this function or the function won't work and the compiler will complain!

The displaySprite() function now takes two parameters. The first is the byte of data to display, which corresponds to the byte in the data array containing the bitmap. The second parameter is the duration to display it:

```
void displaySprite(byte * data, unsigned long duration){
```

The asterisk is a *pointer, a dereference operator* in the C programming language, which is the native language that the ATmega328 processor runs. It's outside the scope of this book to explain pointers in depth, and they are actually one of the more challenging programming topics. What's important here is that this parameter enables you to easily specify the current bitmap to the displaySprite() function. The unsigned long is an integer value that cannot be negative, but which is an extended size variable for storing larger numbers. It is commonly used to store time in milliseconds.

The length of time to display a sprite is handled in the next two lines of code. The first line takes a time stamp in milliseconds of the current system time and saves it in a variable called start:

```
unsigned long start = millis();
```

Next, a while loop keeps track of how long to keep executing the display-Sprite() function. It adds the value of start and duration and compares this to the current time. If the current time is a larger value, the function stops and the program returns to the main loop. For example, if the duration specified was 80 (milliseconds) and the start time was 2000, the while loop will continue operating until the current system time exceeds 2080 milliseconds.

Displaying scrolling text

With the key elements built, all you need to do is put the pieces together, define bitmaps for the characters, and add the scrolling feature. You can think of the scrolling text as a sequence of frames of animation. All 64 LEDs of each letter, whether on or off, are loaded to memory and then sent to the animation frame. Then, in memory, the bitmap of the character is moved one pixel to the left. At the same time, the next character is moved into view in memory and if necessary, any visible pixels are lit up on the display. The frame is cleared and is ready for the next iteration. Only one whole character can be displayed at a time, and as the letters scroll by, the necessary parts of two characters are shown.

The following code is very lengthy, so you might want to download the code for this chapter from the book's companion website at www.dummies.com/go/arduinoprojectsfordummies and copy it into your Arduino sketch. This sketch is called: APFD_Chapter6_Text_Scrolling.

Creating the variables

When you are drawing scrolling text on the display, you use several more variables. You need to keep track of the message to be displayed, which letter you are currently displaying, which LEDs are lit to create each character, and so on.

To accomplish this, you create several variables, as shown in Table 6-2:

Table 6-2   Global Variables Needed for the Scrolling Text

Purpose	Variable Type and Name
char message[]	Stores the message text to be displayed
int index	Stores the current letter to be displayed
int offset	Stores the number of LED columns that the letters are to be offset (this allows the scrolling to occur)
const int _A[] through _Z[]	Stores the bitmaps of all the characters
const int letters[]	Stores the bitmaps of all the letters in one array
const int A through Z	Stores the position of each letter in the array of all the letters
byte data[]	Stores the bitmaps of the characters while they are being displayed
powers[]	Stores the powers of 2, providing an easy way to determine which LED to light

First, you need a number of *global variables* to store the message and control which letter is being displayed and where it is on the matrix in the current frame. Because it is sliding into and out of view, often only part of the letter will be displayed. So, you also need a variable to store the position of the character in the matrix, its *offset:*

```
char message[] = "HELLO WORLD"
int index = 0;
int offset = 0;
...
```

Following these variables, you create an integer variable for each letter of the alphabet to be displayed:

```
const int A = 0;   const int B = 1;   const int C = 2;

... through to letter Z and including some punctuation
```

The number corresponds to the position of each character in an array called `letters[]` that holds all the characters of the message that needs to be displayed. Each character is, itself, an array of the bytes that make up the bit-mapped characters:

You also create an array of bytes called `data[]` to hold the bitmaps while they are being processed. However, the data will be loaded into this array, as needed, depending on the message to be displayed, so the array is initialized with values of 0:

```
byte data[] = {0,0,0,0,0,0,0,0};
```

The next part of the code adds all the characters of the alphabet as bitmaps, plus a few extra symbols, like punctuation, space, and a checkerboard. Each character's bitmap is specified and stored as an integer array. This is where the code gets really long, because each pixel of each letter has to be defined. But you can also get creative here. Ever longed to be a font designer? Here's your chance! You could even put the smiley faces in. The following code shows the bitmaps for letters A and B:

```
const int _A[] = {B0001000,
                  B0010100,
                  B0100010,
                  B1000001,
                  B1111111,
                  B1000001,
                  B1000001,
                  B0000000};

const int _B[] = {B1111110,
                  B0100001,
                  B0100001,
                  B0111110,

                  B0100001,
                  B0100001,
                  B1111110,
                  B0000000};
...
```

To keep the code short, only capital letters are used (though you could add them with plenty of room to spare on the Arduino). When the message is stored, any lowercase characters are capitalized and unknown characters are rendered as a checkerboard pattern.

The last bit of setup is creating the array to hold all the bitmap characters. This will be used to look up each of the bitmaps, when the message to be displayed is stored in the variable `message[]`:

```
const int * letters[] = {_A,_B,_C,_D,_E,_F,_G,_H,_I,_J,_K,_L,_M,_N,_O,_P,_Q,_R,
         _S,_T,_U,_V,_W,_X,_Y,_Z,_COL,_DASH,_BRA2,__, _FULL, _CHECK, _B2,
         _TEMP, _LINE, _SMILE, _DOT, _COLDOT};
```

Finally, a utility variable is used to hold the powers of 2. This is used for bit shifting, when the sprite for the current frame is loaded into the `data[]` array.

```
const int powers[] = {1,2,4,8,16,32,64,128};
```

Loading and displaying the letters

The main loop does only two things. It loads the current frame as a sprite and then it displays that frame. To load the sprite, you use the `loadSprite()` function:

```
void loadSprite(){
  int currentChar = getChar(message[index]);
  int nextChar = getChar(message[index+1]);

  for(int row=0; row < 8; row++){              //iterate through each row
    data[row] = 0;                             //reset the row we're working on
    for(int column=0; column < 8; column++){   //iterate through each column
      data[row] = data[row] + ((powers[column] & (letters[currentChar][row] <<
              offset)));   //loads the current character (offset)
      data[row] = data[row] + (powers[column] & (letters[nextChar][row] >>
              (8-offset) ));   //loads the next character (offset)
    }
  }
  offset++;        //increment the offset by one row
  if(offset==8){offset = 0; index++; if(index==sizeof(message)-2){index=0;}}
              //if offset is 8 load the next character pair for the next time
              through
}
```

The `loadSprite` function puts the appropriate pixels to display into the current frame working with two characters at a time. The whole message is stored in the `message[]` array and so the index can be used to look up the current character and the next one in the message (`index+1`). When these two characters are loaded, they are processed in the same way as the smiley faces. The row and column for loops iterate through each pixel and load them into the `data[]` array for the current row.

The key part of this code is the bit shifting operation, using <<, which selects the appropriate pixel to display by looking up the power of two for the current column to be displayed from the character's bitmap. The powers[] array simply provides a convenient way to set the next position of the bytes to start at for painting its LEDs:

```
data[row] = data[row] + ((powers[column] & (letters[currentChar][row] <<
            offset)))
```

Finally, the offset of the characters is incremented and if 8 pixels have been offset, it's time to start over from 0, since the next character is ready to be loaded.

With the current frame of the sprite loaded, it's time to display it. This uses the same displaySprite() function that you've already used. The only change that needs to be made is to use the data[] array, instead of the smiley[] array from the first code:

```
int bit = (data[column] >> row) & 1;
```

You can set the speed of the scrolling text when you use the displaySprite function, by changing the duration parameter of displaySprite(), as you did with the smileys. When you run the code, you should see the text characters you have stored in the message[] char array. In the example you can download from the book's companion website (www.dummies.com/go/arduinoprojectsfordummies), the code says HELLO WORLD! Figure 6-6 shows what the letter A looks like.

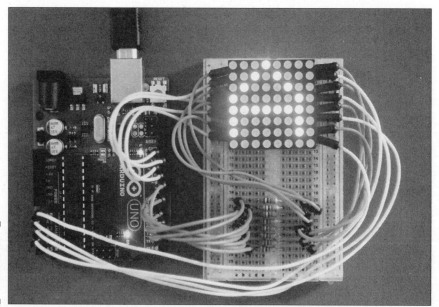

Figure 6-6:
Displaying
scrolling
text.

Understanding How the Hardware Works

From an electronics perspective, the project is pretty simple. The resistors are determined by the maximum forward current that's allowed by any given LED. For the Sure LE-MM103, the maximum current that should flow through an LED is 20mA. Because only one LED is lit, you could use a fairly low resistor of about 180 ohms to give a forward voltage of 1.8 volts. However, erring on the conservative side, and because I tend to have a lot of them lying around, I used 1K ohm resistors. The brightness is not substantially lower on my display. Check your datasheet to be sure you use the right resistor for your matrix.

Troubleshooting

It's really important to check your connections, and I almost can't emphasize this enough. If one of the rows or columns doesn't light up or if you appear to be getting funny lines on the matrix, you have probably got one of the wires connected incorrectly. Go back and double-check all your connections. Even a seasoned tinkerer can get flummoxed by a crossed wire and spend a long time sorting it out. If you simply can't track down the problem, it's not out of the question to just pull out all the wires and start over from scratch. I've done this on many occasions and finally hammered out pesky problems.

On the other hand, you might be seeing that a single LED doesn't light up or that one row is noticeably dimmer or brighter than all of the others. If you've checked all your connections and can't identify the problem, you might have a bad connection inside the unit or, more likely, a burned out LED. It doesn't happen very often, but on occasion you will get a faulty unit from the manufacturer. In this case, the only way to fix the problem is to get another display.

Getting creative

Now that your sign is working, you can try out a few ideas. Play around with the direction of the scrolling by altering the index variable or sequence in which the Arduino pins are used in the colPins[] array. If you have a bi-color display, try wiring it up turning on both LEDs to mix the red and green into a yellow color. You'll need more wires to connect the additional columns of LEDs.

You can also try your hand at using shift registers to light up your matrix display. A shift register is an integrated circuit that can be used to reduce the number of Arduino pins that are needed to drive LEDs. With a MAX7221, you can reduce it down to three pins!

Chapter 7

Building an Arduino Clock

*E*veryone seems to be running short on time. You can't make more time, but by building this project you can at least keep track of time and set an alarm with a pitch and duration of your choice.

The Arduino is at the heart of this project, but its right-hand man is a Real Time Clock (RTC) module. After you have an idea of how the RTC works, you can add timekeeping to other projects where it's important, such as putting a timestamp onto data that you collect. When you are finished with this project, you will have a working clock that keeps time reasonably accurately. You can set an alarm and program your own messages to display. You also find out how to use an RTC module, how to display text on a 16 x 2 LCD display, and how to accept user input with buttons and switches.

This project is built in stages. You add hardware, and then you add some code to test that it works, and then more hardware, and so on, until the clock is finished. This way, you can easily spot problems as you go, rather than connecting everything all at once and having to troubleshoot the entire clock, if something's not working.

 You can download schematics and full-color parts placement diagrams from the companion website (www.dummies.com/go/arduinoprojectsfor dummies).

It's About Time!

If you want to keep accurate time on an Arduino project, you need a real-time clock of some kind. The Arduino can keep track of time very accurately by using the millis() function, but only since the last time it was powered up.

If you lose power to the Arduino, the `millis()` function gets reset to zero — not very handy if you are trying to log real time precisely.

What you need is an additional way to keep time, while consuming only a little power. A real-time clock is just that. It's more or less a wristwatch. It has a tiny button battery for power, so it works even if there's a power outage and your Arduino shuts down. When the power comes back, your clock will still be ticking away. Because it's very efficient, the RTC battery lasts for several years.

Although the RTC is your timekeeper, you use the Arduino to handle the display of the time and responding to inputs and outputs as you change its settings. The main features for your clock are

✔ Keeping track of the time of day

✔ Displaying the time

✔ Setting an alarm and sounding it

This project uses a lot of wiring, so checking your progress along the way is important. You put it together in four stages:

1. Assemble the RTC module and set the current time.

2. Add the LCD display and make sure it works.

3. Add buttons and a switch for programming the alarm.

4. Add the alarm sounder module.

First, you need to get everything together.

Selecting and Preparing Your Parts

Figure 7-1 shows the parts you need for this project. In this project, you build it on a breadboard, but you may want to move it to a suitable housing after you've got it working. In that case, make sure your housing can accommodate your breadboard or consider moving the circuit to a stripboard when you've finished building it. Here are the parts you need:

✔ An Arduino

✔ A full-size breadboard or two half-size ones that are connected

✔ Adafruit Industries Real Time Clock DS1307 Breakout Board

✔ An HD44780 standard parallel 16 x 2 LCD Display (such as Adafruit ID: 181, Jameco 2118598, or the 16 x 2 display from oomlout.co.uk)

✔ A 10K ohm potentiometer to control contrast (included with the displays from Adafruit and Oomlout)

✔ Two momentary pushbutton switches (widely available, such as Jameco 2076148 or from oomlout.co.uk)

✔ A single-pole dual throw (SPDT) or double-pole double-throw (DPDT) slide switch with ON-NONE-ON positions (such as Jameco 1915801 or Farnell 1813681 or 1437711)

✔ A piezoelectric sounder (such as Jameco 1956776 or Maplin N16CL)

✔ Four 220-ohm resistors

✔ A suitable housing, if you want to package it up nicely

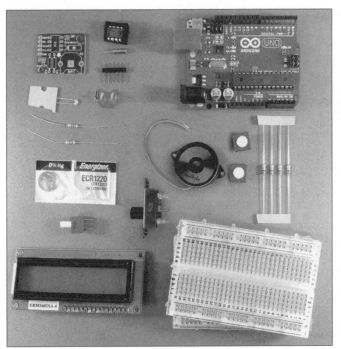

Figure 7-1:
The parts you need for this project.

Many RTC modules are on the market in a variety of physical packages. In terms of its ease of use, one of the best is the RTC DS1307 Breakout Board module from Adafruit Industries. Figure 7-2 shows an enlarged view of the parts in this kit. It is based on the Dallas Semiconductor DS1307 Integrated

Circuit (IC), which is an inexpensive and rugged real-time clock. It's on the low-end cost-wise, so it may lose or gain a small amount of time over extended periods. More precise products are available, but they are much more expensive. You could skip getting the kit, purchase the various parts necessary to use the DS1307 and build it yourself, but the breakout board kit contains all the parts and the printed circuit board makes it very simple to connect the components correctly.

A breakout board is any printed circuit board that makes it easy to physically access all the pins on an integrated circuit or other device for prototyping, building, and testing. In a sense, the Arduino is a breakout board for the ATmega328 Microcontroller IC.

The Adafruit Industries RTC Breakout Board module comes as a kit with a small number of parts, so you need to do a little soldering to reap its benefits. But a little soldering is always rewarding! This kit is inexpensive and readily available, and has excellent online assembly instructions and documentation. As a bonus, the battery *is* included! The best part about using an RTC with a battery backup is that you never have to see the flashing 12:00 if the power goes out!

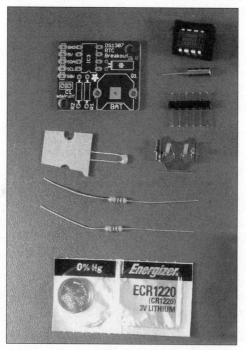

Figure 7-2:
Inside the Adafruit Industries RTC DS1307 Breakout Board kit.

With the RTC breakout board at the heart of your clock, you need to be able to display the time, as well. Although there are dozens of ways to do this, one of the simplest is using a 16 x 2 LCD display. These are inexpensive and easy to control. There are Arduino code *libraries* for LCD displays, which make it easy to update text on the screen. Another benefit of using a 16 x 2 LCD display is that you can add some text on the screen to make your clock a little more verbose and interesting than the standard, 7-segment display you find on most clocks out there.

The term "16 x 2" refers to the number of characters on a 16 x 2 display. These LCD displays can display two lines of text, composed of 16 characters each.

You need the following two switches:

- ✓ The momentary pushbutton switches are for incrementing the hours and minutes of the alarm time. The parts listed are suitable for easily inserting into a breadboard, but you may want to use different switches if you are going to place this clock into a separate housing.

- ✓ The slide switch is used to control three states: time display mode, alarm set mode, and alarm armed mode. This means the switch must have three positions, so make sure to get one that is: ON-NONE-ON and not simply a two-position, ON-ON switch.

For the alarm, you need a piezoelectric sounder. These come with or without a plastic housing. You should get one that is enclosed already, because the enclosures are designed to amplify the sound of the piezo element. If yours is not enclosed you can mount it on a hard surface (such as the inside of your enclosure), but it's better to get one that is designed to be clearly audible in the first place.

Assembling your RTC module

Assembling the RTC module is fairly simple, if you have some experience soldering. If not, it's a good opportunity to practice your skills. After the kit is assembled, you add the battery and connect it to your Arduino. Then, you set the time on the clock IC with an Arduino sketch just for this purpose.

Nine parts are in the kit:

- ✓ Real–time clock PCB
- ✓ Dallas Semiconductor Real Time Clock Chip (DS1307)
- ✓ Crystal (32.768 KHz)
- ✓ Two resistors (2.2K ohm)

✔ Capacitor (100 nF)

✔ Header (male 5 pin)

✔ Battery (CR1220)

✔ Battery holder

The RTC module has excellent assembly documentation and photographs online, and you can solder it fairly quickly. The printed circuit board (PCB) of the kit is labeled with the locations where all the components should be placed. Refer to Figure 7-2 and solder them in the following order:

1. **Solder a little bead of solder onto the battery solder pad, so that there is be good contact between the button cell and the pad on the PCB.**

2. **Solder the resistors (R1 and R2) in place.**

   The orientation of the leads does not matter.

3. **Add the capacitor (C1) and the crystal (Q1).**

   Again, the orientation of the leads does not matter.

4. **Add the DS1307 Integrated Circuit (IC).**

   Make sure that the little notch in the IC is pointing downward, and matches the printed outline on the PCB. If you solder it on the wrong way, it won't work at all, and it is a big pain to remove it!

5. **Solder the chrome battery holder in position.**

6. **Insert the male pin headers into a breadboard and place the RTC module on top of them to make it easier to solder them in place.**

   The pin headers should be on the underside of the board, so that the short ends of the pins are just sticking up through the printed side of the PCB.

Now that you have completed soldering, you can insert the battery, with the positive side facing up. Make sure you have a battery in the RTC or it won't work correctly and you won't be able to program it.

With the battery inserted, it's time to wire up the RTC to your Arduino so that you can program it with the correct time. Refer to Figure 7-3 to make the following connections:

1. **Create a ground rail and a power rail on your breadboard by connecting your Arduino's +5V and GND pins to the long columns of pins on the sides of the breadboard.**

2. **Connect the ground pin (GND) to your ground rail.**

3. **Connect the 5v pin on your RTC to +5V power rail.**

4. **Connect the pin labeled SDA to Analog Pin 4.**

5. **Connect the pin labeled SCL to Analog Pin 5.**

The last pin is labeled SQW and can be used to get a square wave from the RTC chip. It's not used on the clock, so you can ignore it.

After the module is connected, it's time to program it with the correct time. This is done with an Arduino *library* called RTClib, provided by Adafruit Industries, for the kit. You can download the library from the Downloads tab on this book's companion website (www.wiley.com/go/arduinoprojects fordummies) or from Adafruit Industries' website.

Arduino libraries are bundles of code that contain related procedures. See Chapter 3 for details on how to install and use libraries.

After you have installed the RTC library, notice that there is a new item called RTClib in your Examples menu. Load the one called Examples⇨RTClib⇨ ds1307. This sketch conveniently sets the time on your RTC module.

The important part of this code is in `setup()`:

```
RTC.adjust(DateTime(__DATE__, __TIME__));
```

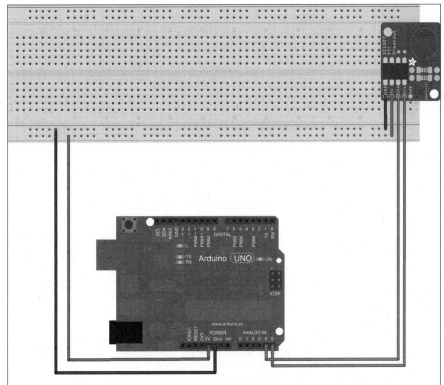

Figure 7-3:
Wiring up the RTC module.

In this line, the `RTC.adjust()` function requests the system time from your computer at the time the program is compiled, just before it is sent to your Arduino. This is what sets the time on your RTC module. If you ever want to change the time of your RTC module (say for example, after Daylight Saving Time, or if the module drifts a bit too much), you need to remove the battery for three seconds, replace it, and then rerun this sketch.

If you haven't already done so, upload this code to your Arduino and click the Serial Monitor button in your Arduino IDE. You should see something like the output in Figure 7-4. Make sure your serial monitor is set to 57600 baud in the lower-right corner. Otherwise, you'll just see gibberish!

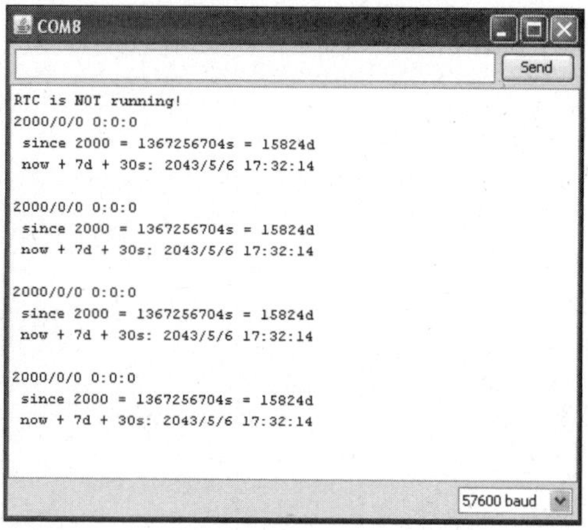

Figure 7-4:
Program-
ming the
RTC time
and check-
ing it with
the Serial
Monitor.

```
COM8                                      [-][□][X]

[                                        ] [ Send ]
RTC is NOT running!
2000/0/0 0:0:0
  since 2000 = 1367256704s = 15824d
  now + 7d + 30s: 2043/5/6 17:32:14

2000/0/0 0:0:0
  since 2000 = 1367256704s = 15824d
  now + 7d + 30s: 2043/5/6 17:32:14

2000/0/0 0:0:0
  since 2000 = 1367256704s = 15824d
  now + 7d + 30s: 2043/5/6 17:32:14

2000/0/0 0:0:0
  since 2000 = 1367256704s = 15824d
  now + 7d + 30s: 2043/5/6 17:32:14

                               [ 57600 baud ][▼]
```

You can also arbitrarily set the time of the RTC module. This is a little trickier, because the time is set to UNIX system time, which is simply the number of seconds since midnight on January 1, 1970. For example, the following code sets the time to February 27, 2012, at 8:50 p.m.:

```
RTC.adjust(DateTime(1330375800));
```

There's a convenient website for looking up UNIX time, should you need it: www.onlineconversion.com/unix_time.htm.

After you've set the RTC with your system time, you are ready to get the display wired up and fired up.

Adding and testing your LCD display

Now that you've programmed and tested the beating heart of your Arduino clock, you need a way to display the time without using the serial monitor. This is where the LCD display comes in.

This one is fairly inexpensive and it uses the very common Hitachi HD44780 driver. These LCD modules are easily recognized because they have 16 pins in a single row and use what's known as a *parallel interface.* Because of this, the Arduino uses several digital pins to make the display work. This process is somewhat complicated, but luckily, there is an Arduino library for it already that makes it very easy to send text to the screen without worrying about the low-level commands that would otherwise be needed.

You use 4-bit mode to display text, which needs only seven Arduino digital pins to control the display. You also need power for the LCD itself, and for the backlight. Finally, you control the contrast of the display by using the potentiometer.

Connect the following:

1. **Add your LCD display and potentiometer to your breadboard roughly in the positions shown in Figure 7-5.**

2. **Connect the power and ground pins on your LCD, which are Pins 15 and 16, respectively.**

3. **Connect the ground and power for your LCD's backlight, which are Pins 1 and 2, respectively.**

4. **Connect the control pins for your LCD to the digital pins on your Arduino, as shown in the following table.**

16 x 2 LCD Display Pin	*Arduino Digital Pin*
1 (to GND rail on breadboard)	
2 (to +5V rail on breadboard)	
3	2
4	3
5	4
6	5
7 (no connection)	
8 (no connection)	
9 (no connection)	
10 (no connection)	
11	11
12 (to GND rail on breadboard)	
13	12
14 (to potentiometer middle pin)	
15 (to +5V rail on breadboard)	
16 (to GND rail on breadboard)	

5. **Now connect the potentiometer, which controls the display's contrast.**

   The center pin of the potentiometer should go to Pin 14 of the LCD display and the other two pins of the potentiometer are connected to power and ground, in any order.

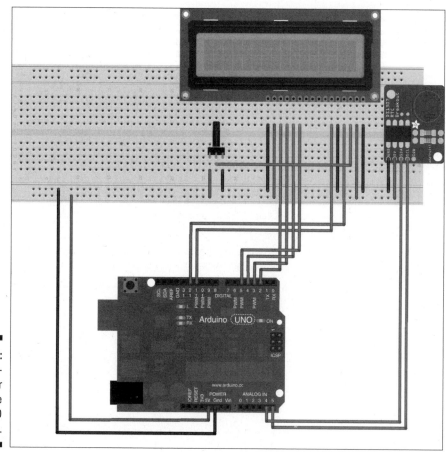

Figure 7-5:
Parts place-
ment for
adding the
16 x 2 LCD
display.

Now that you have connected your LCD, it's time to make it do something interesting! First you need to upload some code to make sure that the LCD is working properly. This code is the first part of your alarm clock sketch. You build upon it to add all the other functions for your clock.

You can copy the code for the clock all at once from the companion website (www.dummies.com/go/arduinoprojectsfordummies), but I'd recommend adding it in sections, as described here. That makes it easy to troubleshoot problems and test the clock in stages, as you build it.

Enter the following code into the IDE, or download it from the companion website and upload it to your Arduino:

```
// Chapter 7: Arduino Alarm Clock
// An alarm clock that uses the Adafruit Industries DS1307 RTC Breakout board
// and a 16 x 2 Parallel LCD Display

#include <Wire.h>      // I2C Wire Library for communicating with the DS1307 RTC
#include "RTClib.h"    // Date and time functions for the DS1307 RTC connected
#include <LiquidCrystal.h> // Display functions for the LCD Display

RTC_DS1307 rtc;                         // Create a realtime clock called rtc
LiquidCrystal lcd(12, 11, 5, 4, 3, 2);  // Create an LCD called lcd

void setup () {
  Wire.begin();       // Enables the communication for the LCD
  rtc.begin();        // Enables the RTC
  lcd.begin(16, 2);   // Enables the LCD
  lcd.print("  It's Alive!");    // Print a message, centered, to the LCD to
            confirm it's working
  delay(500);                    // Wait a moment so we can read it
  lcd.clear();        // Clear the LCD

}

void loop(){
}
```

When this code is uploaded, you should see the message "It's Alive!" displayed for a half-second on the LCD. If you don't see anything, or if the display has garbled characters, you've connected something incorrectly. Go back to the wiring table (shown earlier, in Step 4) and Figure 7-5.

The first three lines of this code include the libraries that are be used for your clock. The first includes the I2C library that enables communication with the RTC module. I2C, pronounced "eye-squared cee" or "eye-two-cee," is a communication link (also called a *bus*) for talking between integrated circuits — in this case your Arduino and the Dallas DS1307 chip. It's also useful for communicating with lots of other accessories, such as GPS modules. The useful thing about I2C is that it only requires two pins, plus power and ground. This library makes communication pretty easy with most I2C devices.

The next library is the RTCLib. It's a version of a library written by JeeLab and modified by Adafruit Industries for communicating with the RTC module. It's used for getting the time from the RTC module and uses the I2C library to negotiate that communication.

The last library is the LCD display library, which handles the parallel communication with your display. Unlike the RTC library that you added manually, it's included as a standard library in the Arduino software distribution.

After including the libraries, the code creates two objects: a clock object called `rtc` and a LiquidCrystal object called `lcd`. This object has parameters that determine which digital pins the Arduino uses to communicate with the LCD.

After creating those objects, the `setup()` function gets things going. The I2C, RTCLib, and the `lcd` all have to be enabled, which is done by the `begin()` function for each one. The `lcd.begin()` function takes two parameters, the number of columns and the number of rows, which on your display are 16 and 2. After this has been set, you can write messages to the screen simply by using the `lcd.print()` function:

```
lcd.print("  It's Alive!");
```

The two spaces at the beginning of this text center the 11-character message within the 16-character space on the top line. You normally control the position of text with the `setCursor()` function, but it's not needed here — one less instruction to put into `setup()`. After a brief delay so that you can see that it has been printed to the screen, the `lcd.clear()` function wipes all the text, ready to go for the main `loop()`.

If you haven't been able to get the test message to print, check your connections. Make sure you have all the pins in the right locations and that you've provided power and ground connections for both the LCD and its backlight. They are separately powered.

Displaying the time

Now that you've got something on the display, it's time to read the time from the RTC module and display it. Later, you add buttons to program the alarm, and a switch to change between Time Display, Alarm Set, and Alarm Armed modes.

There are really only two things you can display with this clock: either the current time or the time you want the alarm to go off. Rather than including the code for both in the main `loop()`, it makes sense to put the display procedure in its own function so that it is modular and easy to modify.

Add the following code to the variable declarations section at the top of your code (new code is in boldface):

```
RTC_DS1307 rtc;                       // Create a realtime clock called rtc
LiquidCrystal lcd(12, 11, 5, 4, 3, 2); // Create an LCD called lcd

DateTime now;
```

This creates a DateTime object called `now`. The DateTime object is part of the RTC library and is the only way to get the time out of the RTC module, though it has a lot of options and can provide hours, minutes, seconds, and the year, month, and day.

Next, add the code in your main loop that reads the current time from the RTC module, and add a function to update the display with the current time:

```
void loop(){

now = rtc.now(); // Get the current time

// Refresh the display
  updateDisplay();
}
```

The now DateTime object stores the current time taken from the rtc.now() function to display the time and to check whether it's time to trigger the alarm.

To keep the code modular, updating the display is done in its own function, outside the main loop. After closing the main loop, add the updateDisplay() function by entering the following code:

```
void updateDisplay(){

    int h = now.hour();   // Get the hours right now and store them in an
            integer called h
    int m = now.minute(); // Get the minutes right now and store them in an
            integer called m
    int s = now.second(); // Get the seconds right now and store them in an
            integer called s

    lcd.setCursor(0, 0);  // Set the cursor at the column zero, upper row...
    lcd.print("  The time is: ");  // ...with spaces to clear characters from
            setting alarm.
    lcd.setCursor(4, 1);  // Move the cursor to column four, lower row
    if (h<10){            // Add a zero, if necessary, as above
      lcd.print(0);
    }
    lcd.print(h);         // Display the current hour
    lcd.setCursor(6, 1);  // Move to the next column
    lcd.print(":");       // And print the colon
    lcd.setCursor(7, 1);  // Move to the next column
    if (m<10){            // Add a zero, if necessary, as above
      lcd.print(0);
    }
    lcd.print(m);         // Display the current minute
    lcd.setCursor(9, 1);  // Move to the next column
    lcd.print(":");       // And print the colon
    lcd.setCursor(10, 1); // Move to the next column
    if (s<10){            // Add a zero, if necessary, as above
      lcd.print(0);
    }
    lcd.print(s);         // Display the current second
  }
```

Send this code to your Arduino and see what happens. If all is well and your code compiles correctly, you should be in business! The display should show a time that matches the one on your computer (having been set with the DS1307 sketch that you sent earlier). Congratulations! You've just built a basic clock!

In the code, the current time is requested from the `now` object and placed into three integer variables used only in the `updateDisplay` function. These variables have a *local scope,* meaning they only can be used within `updateDisplay()`, and the rest of the program doesn't know anything about them — which explains why they are not declared at the beginning of your code. You request time minutes, hours, and seconds separately with `now.hours()`, `now.minutes()`, and `now.seconds()`. Assigning each of these separately to its own integer variable (h, m, and s) is much easier than requesting the current time all at once using `rtc.now();` and then separating out (called *parsing*) the hours, minutes, and seconds.

Having parsed the time into three variables, the main thing going on in `updateDisplay()` is positioning the cursor on the LCD and printing the relevant text. Positioning the cursor is done with `lcd.setCursor()`, which takes two parameters: column number and line number. Setting the cursor only puts it in the correct position. You then have to tell the display what to print. The numbering starts at zero, so the upper-leftmost character is in column 0 and row 0. The cursor is positioned at the top left of the screen and the first line of text is printed with `lcd.print("The time is:")`.

There are two space characters before and after the text. These write over any text that's already on the screen — which is not an issue now, but it would become a problem later, when you display the Alarm Set mode. The characters printed from that mode need to be erased. Writing spaces overwrites any other text that might be already on the screen from Alarm Set mode.

You could use instead the `lcd.clear()` function, which clears all the text on the whole screen. However, your clock is constantly refreshing the display, so clearing the LCD every time the `updateDisplay()` function executes can introduce just a bit of noticeable flicker. A simpler approach (which uses one less instruction) is just to write the space characters over what might have been already on the display.

Next, the cursor is moved four spaces to the right and on the second row, so that the time is centered on the screen:

```
lcd.setCursor(4,1);
```

One tricky bit about using integers to get the hours, minutes, and seconds, is that they do not have a leading zero for values below 10. You need to add those in manually, both to make the clock look right (for example, 01:05) and to keep the hours minutes and seconds in the same place on the screen. Otherwise, they'd jump around and would be hard to read. It would be confusing. For example, without leading zeros, 5 minutes after 1 a.m. would be displayed: 1:5.

Some would argue that you could also use the *char* data type since the `rtc.now()` method returns chars, but this makes it more complicated to logically compare the current time to the alarm time. It's much simpler to use *ints*.

Adding the leading zeros is accomplished in the same way for hours, minutes, and seconds (I'm just discussing hours, for the sake of brevity):

```
if (h<10){        // Add a zero, if necessary, as above
   lcd.print(0);
   }
   lcd.print(h);   // Display the current hour
```

The conditional `if` statement tests whether the current time is less than 10, and if so, the `print()` statement prints a zero. After this, the LCD automatically advances to the next column position, so when you print the current hour (1 through 9), stored in the integer variable h, it will have a leading zero. The same goes for minutes and seconds. You must also advance the cursor to the correct position for the leading zero for minutes and seconds. You insert a colon between them with the `lcd.print(":")`; statement.

You've now got the basic information you need to display the time and move the cursor around a bit. You can also easily change the text. Perhaps it should be in French or Klingon? With the time displayed, you can now get down to building the input and output hardware to handle the alarm.

Adding your input buttons and a switch

First, add one of the pushbutton switches and one of the resistors, which you use as an input to increment the alarm hours. Refer to Figure 7-6 to make sure you have made the right connections. The pushbutton works by allowing +5V to be applied to Pin 7 when it's pressed. When current flows through the switch, it encounters the resistor, and instead takes the easier pathway to ground through Pin 7 (there are connections to ground internally, within the ATmega328 microcontroller IC). Reading Pin 7 with the `digitalRead()` function returns a value of HIGH (+5V).

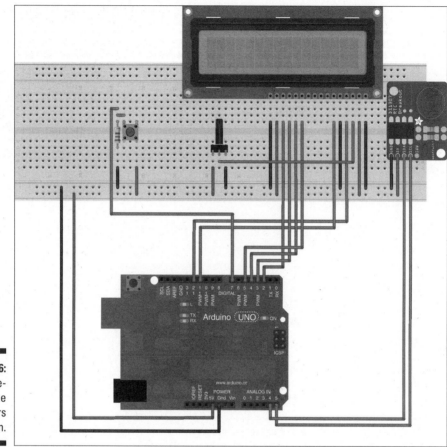

Figure 7-6:
Parts place-
ment for the
alarm hours
pushbutton.

When it's not pressed, Pin 7 is connected through the resistor to GND, via the ground rail. Reading Pin 7 with the `digitalRead()` function returns a value of LOW (0V).

Now add the second pushbutton switch and resistor, which increments the minutes. It should be connected to digital Pin 8.

Finally, add the slide switch, which has three positions, and two resistors. You can see from Figure 7-7 that the electrical connections for the slide switch are very similar to the two pushbutton switches. But because it's a slider, it stays in the position that you put it in. In the left position, it keeps +5V on digital Pin 10. In the right position, it keeps +5V on digital Pin 10. In the center, it makes no connection, and both of the digital pins are connected only to the ground rail.

Reading these pins, you can determine whether the clock is Alarm Set Mode (Pin 6 is HIGH), Alarm Armed Mode (Pin 10 is HIGH), or simply in Display Time mode (no connection; Pin 6 and Pin 10 are LOW).

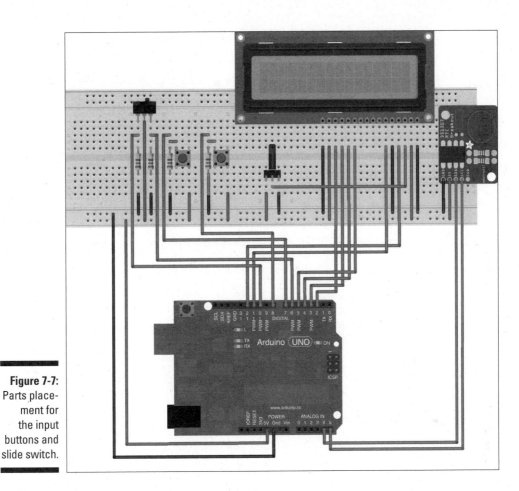

Figure 7-7:
Parts place-
ment for
the input
buttons and
slide switch.

Now add the code necessary to read and respond to the hardware. You need a few variables to store the system state and keep track of when to trigger the alarm. In the variable declaration section, add the following code:

```
...
DateTime now;

boolean displayAlarmSet = false;  // Whether we are in the show time mode or
                show alarm set mode
boolean alarm = false;  // Whether the alarm is currently happening
boolean armed = false;  // Whether the alarm is armed or not

int alarmHrs = 12;    // You can set the alarm time in code, here
int alarmMins = 00;
```

The variable displayAlarmSet allows you to switch between showing the clock time or showing the alarm time, that you use in the updateDisplay()

function, a bit later. You can use the slide switch to change the value of this variable.

The "alarm" variable keeps track of whether or not the alarm is currently happening, so that you can sound the piezoelectric sounder, if necessary.

You also need to keep track of when to trigger the alarm. This is done with two integers, `alarmHrs` and `alarmMins`. If you want to set the alarm time from within the software and not from the buttons, you can set that by changing the starting value of these variables. I've set it to 12 hours and 00 minutes to start.

Counting the two pushbuttons, and the two states that can be set by the slide switch (Time Display mode or Alarm Display mode), you have four inputs. So, you need four digital pins to read them. You use them for input, so they need to be enabled in the `setup()` part of your code. You'll also use the piezo sounder for output, later, but it can be added now, so add the following code:

```
// User input to set alarm time
const int alarmSetPin=6;           // Used to change to alarm set mode
const int incrementAlarmHrsPin=7;  // Used to increment the alarm hours in alarm
                set mode
const int incrementAlarmMinsPin=8; // Used to increment the alarm minutes in
                alarm set mode
const int piezoPin = 9;            // Used for the piezoelectric sounder
const int alarmArmedPin=10;        // Use to enable the alarm to go off
...
setup(){
...
  lcd.clear();

  // Set several pins for input and output
  pinMode(alarmSetPin, INPUT);
  pinMode(incrementAlarmHrsPin, INPUT);
  pinMode(incrementAlarmMinsPin, INPUT);
  pinMode(alarmArmedPin, INPUT);
  pinMode(piezoPin, OUTPUT);
```

Note, the ellipses (...) indicate the code you added earlier — no need to repeat that here. There are five new integers, which handle the input pins. These don't change throughout the program so they are integer *constants*. You connected the slide switch to Pin 6 and Pin 10 to handle either setting the alarm or arming it to go off. You connected the pushbutton switches to Pin 7 and Pin 8. Each one separately controls incrementing the hours and minutes. You can only increment upward. Otherwise, you either need additional buttons to decrement hours and minutes or a way to switch between incrementing and decrementing, which would be unnecessarily complicated. Finally, these pins are all used for input, so they have to be explicitly set to be used for INPUT with the `pinMode()` function. Later in this chapter, you connect the piezoelectric sounder to Pin 9, so it is also included here, and set to OUTPUT.

Checking, setting, and displaying the alarm

Next, you can add the main `loop()` code that is running on the clock. It checks the time, whether to sound the alarm, and refreshes the display (the new code is shown in boldface):

```
void loop(){

now = rtc.now(); // Get the current time
int alarmArmed=digitalRead(alarmArmedPin);

if (alarmArmed==HIGH){
   armed=true;
 } else {
   armed=false;
 }

  // Determine whether to sound the alarm or not
if(armed){        // If the alarm is armed and...
  if (!alarm){    // If we are not currently sounding the alarm
    checkAlarm();  // Check to see if it is the time it should be triggered
  }
  else {
    soundAlarm();  // Otherwise, we should be sounding the alarm, so do it.
  }
}

// Check whether we are in Alarm Set mode
  int setMode = digitalRead(alarmSetPin); // Read the pin that the switch is on
  if (setMode==HIGH){      // If the pin is high
    displayAlarmSet=true; // Set displayAlarmSet true. It's used by
              updateDisplay to switch between showing alarm or current time
    setAlarm();           // Go read the switches to set the alarm
  }
  else {                  // If we aren't in set mode
    displayAlarmSet=false; // We are not in set mode, so make sure the flag is
              correct
  }

  // Refresh the display
  updateDisplay();
}
```

There's a lot going on here!

After the `rtc.now()` function (which you added previously) gets the current time, you use the local variable `alarmArmed` to hold the value of the `alarmArmedPin`, and then use the conditional `if` statement: `if (alarmArmed==HIGH)` to evaluate whether it's HIGH. If so, that's because the slide switch is in the activated position, and is allowing +5V to be present on Pin 10 of the Arduino. In that case, the boolean variable armed is TRUE; otherwise, it's FALSE. This variable determines whether to sound the alarm when the alarm time is reached. You probably don't want to do that once a day, *every* day!

Next, there's a nested loop, which determines whether to sound the alarm. The conditional if statement checks this condition by evaluating whether the clock is in armed mode:

```
if(armed){
```

This is a bit of coding shorthand. It could also be written:

```
if(armed==TRUE){
```

and it would work the same way.

If the alarm is armed and the alarm is *not* currently already being played, then it's time to check whether it should be played, using the checkAlarm() function. This is tested by the !alarm condition. The ! indicates a logical "not." On the other hand, if you are currently in the alarm state, then it's time to sound it, using the soundAlarm function, which you add to the code later, when the piezoelectric sounder hardware is added. The checkAlarm() function just compares the current time to the alarm time. At the bottom of your code, add the following function:

```
void checkAlarm(){
  if(alarmHrs==now.hour() && alarmMins==now.minute() && now.second()==0){  // If
              the alarm time is now, and it's zero seconds
    alarm=true;  // set the alarm flag to be true. The next time the main loop
              executes, the alarm will be activated
  }
}
```

This function uses the global integer variables you created at the beginning of your code to hold the alarm time: alarmHrs and alarmMins. You obtain the current hour and minute using now.hour() and now.minute(), and test whether they are both the same value as alarmHrs and alarmMinutes, using the logical AND operator: &&. You only want to check this the second that the alarm time is reached, so you use the && operation to test this, too. Without checking this, the boolean variable alarm would be set to true for an entire minute, even if you were to cancel the alarm, with the result that you wouldn't be able to turn off the alarm for a whole minute! That's all you need for the checkAlarm() function. You'll add the soundAlarm() function later.

Next, you test to see whether the user is setting the alarm. You use the local variable setMode to read and store the alarmSetPin(Pin 6). You are keeping track of this with the boolean variable displayAlarmSet. It is true when the slide switch position allows +5V to be present on Arduino Pin 6. If the slide switch is in Alarm Set Mode, then you read the buttons using the setAlarm() function. Therefore, the buttons are only read if the slide switch is in the proper position, which prevents accidentally changing the alarm time. You also update the display accordingly with the updateDisplay() function, not showing the current time, but rather showing the alarm time. I go over how you do this in a moment, but first you need to add the setAlarm() function, so that you can read and respond to the button presses and store the alarm time, accordingly.

At the bottom of your code, add the following:

```
void setAlarm(){
  int hrs=digitalRead(incrementAlarmHrsPin);
  int mins=digitalRead(incrementAlarmMinsPin);

  if (hrs==HIGH){      // If the hours switch is pressed
    alarmHrs+=1;       // Increment the hours upward
    delay(200);        // Wait a moment between incrementing the numbers
    if(alarmHrs>23){ // if the hour is over 23, set it back to 0
      alarmHrs=0;
    }
  }
  if (mins==HIGH){     // If the minutes switch is pressed
    alarmMins+=1;      // Increment the minutes upward
    delay(200);        // Wait a moment between incrementing the numbers
    if(alarmMins>59){ // if the minute is over 59, set it back to 0
      alarmMins=0;
    }
  }
}
```

In this function, you use two local integer variables, hrs and mins, to read and store the value on the digital pins that are connected to the pushbutton switches. If the hours button is being pressed, then hrs has the value HIGH. You update the alarmHrs variable by adding 1 hour: alarmHrs+=1. You need to pause for a moment so that the user won't increment upward too fast. The delay(200) statement waits for 200 milliseconds — just enough time for the user to increment quickly and stop accurately. There are only 24 hours in a day, so the last if statement resets the alarmHrs to zero if it exceeds 23 hours. Next, you follow the same process for detecting and incrementing the alarm minutes.

Now you need to be able to see what you're doing. To update the display with the Alarm Set time, add the following code (in boldface) to the very beginning of the updateDisplay() function you created earlier:

```
void updateDisplay(){

   if(displayAlarmSet){     // If we are in alarm set mode, DISPLAY ALARM SET TEXT
      lcd.setCursor(0, 0);  // Set the cursor at the column zero, upper row
      lcd.print("Set alarm time: ");
      lcd.setCursor(4, 1);  // Move the cursor to column four, lower row
      lcd.print(" ");       // Write over digits of the time previously displayed
      lcd.setCursor(5, 1);  // Move to the next column so the time will be
                centered
      if (alarmHrs<10){     // Integers of 0-9 are only one digit. If so...
        lcd.print(0);       // ... add a zero in front of it
      }
      lcd.print(alarmHrs);  // Print the current alarm hour
      lcd.setCursor(7, 1);  // Move to the next column
      lcd.print(":");       // And print the colon
      lcd.setCursor(8, 1);  // Move to the next column
      if (alarmMins<10){    // Integers of 0-9 are only one digit. If so...
        lcd.print(0);       // ... add a zero in front of it
      }
      lcd.print(alarmMins); // Print the current alarm minutes
      lcd.setCursor(10, 1); // Move to the next column
      lcd.print("  ");      // Write spaces over the digits of time that was
                previously displayed
   }
   else {

      int h = now.hour();   // Get the hours right now and store them in an
                integer called h
      int m = now.minute(); // Get the minutes right now and store them in an
                integer called m
      int s = now.second(); // Get the seconds right now and store them in an
                integer called s

      lcd.setCursor(0, 0);  // Set the cursor at the column zero, upper row...
      if(armed){
        lcd.print("* The time is: ");
      }
      lcd.print("  The time is: ");  // ...with spaces to clear characters from
                setting alarm
      lcd.setCursor(4, 1);  // Move the cursor to column four, lower row

      if (h<10){            // Add a zero, if necessary, as above
        lcd.print(0);
      }
      lcd.print(h);         // Display the current hour
      lcd.setCursor(6, 1);  // Move to the next column
      lcd.print(":");       // And print the colon
      lcd.setCursor(7, 1);  // Move to the next column
      if (m<10){            // Add a zero, if necessary, as above
        lcd.print(0);
```

```
    }
  lcd.print(m);          // Display the current minute
  lcd.setCursor(9, 1);   // Move to the next column
  lcd.print(":");        // And print the colon
  lcd.setCursor(10, 1);  // Move to the next column
  if (s<10){             // Add a zero, if necessary, as above
    lcd.print(0);
  }
  lcd.print(s);          // Display the current second
 }


}
```

Here, you are simply updating the display with the current hours and minutes of the alarm set time. The first conditional `if` statement evaluates whether you are in Set Alarm mode. If so, you will show the alarm time. If not, the Arduino will jump to the `else` statement. You've already created the code that happens after the `else {` statement — it's what's normally displaying the current time.

Showing the alarm time is essentially the same process as showing the time, simply positioning the cursor and printing text to the display. The difference is what the text says: "Set alarm time: " (with a trailing space) and the alarm hours and minutes, separated by a colon. Note that you are also handling whether a leading zero needs to be added, as you did earlier.

One final modification needs to be made to `updateDisplay()`. You need to indicate somehow that the alarm is armed, if the armed variable is TRUE. A simple solution is to just add an asterisk when the current time is displayed. Right where you left off, modify the remaining `updateDisplay()` code:

```
  lcd.setCursor(0, 0);
if(armed){
    lcd.print("* The time is: ");
  }

else lcd.print("  The time is: ");
```

Now there's only one thing left to do: Play it!

Adding your alarm

This is the easiest hardware modification. You only need to attach the piezo-electric sounder, as shown in Figure 7-8. With that added, you simply create a function to play the alarm. Add the following code to the bottom of your Arduino sketch:

```
void soundAlarm() {
  float alarmFrequency=1400;   // The value for the alarm tone in Hz
  float period = (1.0 / alarmFrequency) * 1000000;
  long beepDuration=250000;    // the time in microseconds (0.25 seconds)
  long elapsedTime = 0;

  while (elapsedTime < beepDuration) {
    digitalWrite(piezoPin,HIGH);
    delayMicroseconds(period / 2);
    digitalWrite(piezoPin, LOW);
    delayMicroseconds(period / 2);
    elapsedTime += (period);
  }
  digitalWrite(piezoPin, LOW);
  delayMicroseconds(beepDuration);

  // Listen for either button to be pressed and if so, turn off the alarm
  int hrs=digitalRead(incrementAlarmHrsPin);
  int mins=digitalRead(incrementAlarmMinsPin);

  if (hrs==HIGH || mins==HIGH){
    alarm=false;
  }
}
```

This code uses the standard formula to obtain the period of a frequency; the period is the duration of a single cycle in a repeating event and is the reciprocal of the frequency. You specify the frequency of your alarm tone in *Hertz* (Hz) and assign it to the `float` variable `alarmFrequency`.

Your alarm will alternate between playing a tone at this frequency (I've chosen 1440 Hz).

Two long integers, `beepDuration` and `elapsedTime`, store the elapsed time the tone has been playing and the duration that you want it to play. The `while` loop uses these to limit the time the note is played to 0.25 seconds (beep duration).

With the period calculated, you use this value to rapidly write HIGH and LOW values to the `piezoPin`. One cycle includes both on and off times, so the amount of time to write the pin HIGH and LOW is half the total period. This is written to the digital pins using:

```
digitalWrite(piezoPin,HIGH);
delayMicroseconds(period / 2);

digitalWrite(piezoPin,LOW);
delayMicroseconds(period / 2);
```

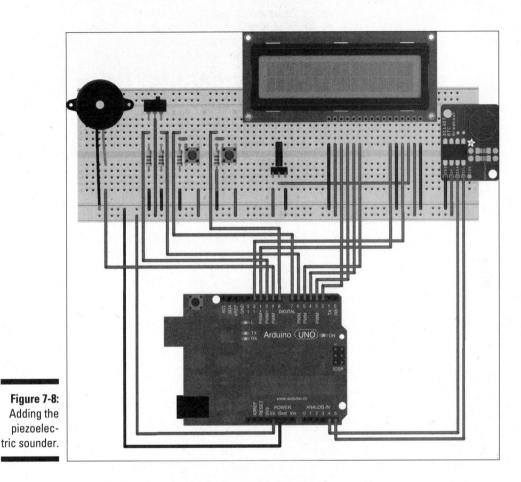

Figure 7-8:
Adding the
piezoelec-
tric sounder.

The `delayMicroseconds()` function is the shortest amount of time you can delay the Arduino, and is needed for generating a tone. After the tone has been played, the following two lines create silence for the same duration, 0.25 seconds, by holding the `piezoPin` LOW:

```
digitalWrite(piezoPin, LOW);
delayMicroseconds(beepDuration);
```

The very last thing to do is provide a way to silence the alarm, if you press either of the buttons. The local integers, `hrs` and `mins`, store the value of the buttons used to program the alarm. If the hours button or the minutes button goes HIGH because the button was pressed, the alarm condition is set to false. The vertical bars | | indicate a logical OR evaluation:

```
int hrs=digitalRead(incrementAlarmHrsPin);
  int mins=digitalRead(incrementAlarmMinsPin);

  if (hrs==HIGH || mins==HIGH){
    alarm=false;
  }
}
```

Whew. That was a lot of code; but now the clock is ready to have its trial run. In the code, set the alarm time to be something in the next minute or so; then send the code to the Arduino. Make sure the slide switch is in the armed position and that your asterisk is displayed. Pretty soon, you should have your rewarding alarm.

If you have any trouble, check your connections. I've also included a schematic diagram to help you track down any problems, as shown in Figure 7-9. Then check your code to make sure it's correct. If all else fails, check the trouble-shooting tips in Chapter 17.

Beep! Beep!! Beep!!! It's time to pat yourself on the back for building a fully functional alarm clock from scratch!

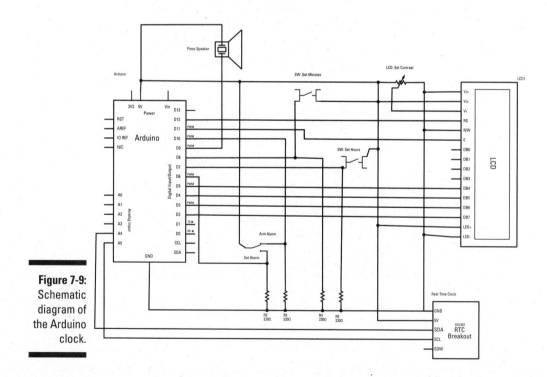

Figure 7-9:
Schematic diagram of the Arduino clock.

Part III
The Interactive Home and Garden

Find out how to add the RFID reader to your keypad entry system from Chapter 8 at
www.dummies.com/extras/arduinoprojects.

In this part . . .

- ✔ Find out about using sensors and home automation
- ✔ Build an automatic plant watering system
- ✔ Program your Arduino to take temperature and light readings
- ✔ Build a homemade Arduino shield
- ✔ Discover how to post data from your Arduino to the Internet
- ✔ Program your Arduino to send tweets

Chapter 8

Building a Keypad Entry System

*N*o self-respecting mastermind would leave his fortress unsecured against intruders. The project steps in this chapter guide you through building a keypad entry system that unlocks a door when you enter the correct code into a standard 10-digit keypad. The system also displays the code on a seven-segment LED display while you are entering it, and when you've keyed in the correct code a welcome message is displayed.

The project uses a four-digit ("quad"), seven-segment display — the kind you've seen in every spy movie since the 1960s and a widely available standard keypad with a telephone-style layout. The door is secured with an electric locking mechanism that is activated once you type in the correct code.

You can buy systems like this from specialty lock and security suppliers, but it's more fun to build it yourself and pick up a few Arduino skills along the way. You can also modify the system to accept input from the RFID card reader (see Chapter 9).

Selecting and Preparing Your Parts

Figure 8-1 shows the parts you need for this project.

You create a prototype on a breadboard to make sure that everything works properly and then put it into a suitable enclosure after you've got it working. When you transfer it to your enclosure, you might want to rebuild the circuit on a piece of stripboard, in which case you need a small piece of that, too. There are a lot of wires in this project, so you might also want to pick up some ribbon cable to make all those connections. Here's what you need:

- An Arduino
- A numeric keypad (SparkFun COM-08653 or Rapid 78-0305)
- A quad, common cathode, seven-segment LCD display (Lite-ON LTC-4727JR from Digi-Key 160-1551-5ND, or HDSP-B09G from Farnell 1003341)
- A Max 7219 or 7221 8-digit LED display driver
- Two capacitors: a 10µF (microfarad) electrolytic capacitor and a .01 µF ceramic disc capacitor
- Two resistors: 2.2kΩ and 33kΩ. These may be different depending on your LED module and type of relay.
- A 5V DC miniature relay (such as Hamlin HE721A0510, from Jameco #1860109, or Farnell #9561757)
- A 2N2222 or similar NPN transistor
- A 1N4001 or similar diode
- A strip of pin headers
- An electric door locking mechanism, 12V DC. There are several types (see below) to choose from, such as an electric door strike (item #5192 from `SmartHome.com` or GAE Series Electric Strike from `online securityproducts.co.uk`)
- A two-conductor, low-voltage wire (18-22 AWG) to run power from your transformer to your project box and door locking mechanism
- A suitable enclosure to package it up nicely (such as Serpac A27BK, Jameco #373456, or Farnell #775538). Minimum dimensions of approximately 15 x 8 x 4 cm (6 x 3 x 1.5 inches).
- A small piece of stripboard (optional)
- Some short lengths of ribbon cable (optional)
- Wire mounting clips
- A hot glue gun and some glue sticks
- A measuring tape
- Small hand tools to make holes in the enclosure and to install the door locking mechanism into your doorjamb

You can download schematics and full-color parts placement diagrams from the companion website (`www.dummies.com/go/arduinoprojectsfor dummies`).

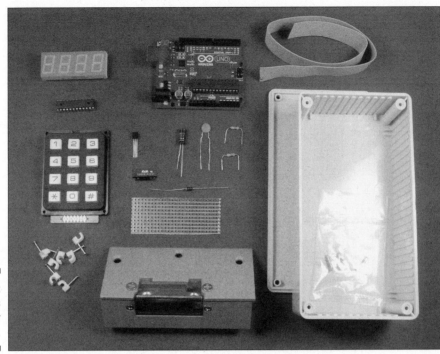

As with the other projects, this one is built with an Arduino Uno. But there's nothing unusual about the code, so you should be able to run it on any Arduino.

The keypad contains conductive traces on the printed circuit board inside. Pressing a button closes a switch that connects two of these traces — one for the row and one for the column underneath that button. Each row and column is connected to an output pin on the keypad, and you connect those output pins to your Arduino's digital pins. When you press a button, the connection between a row and a column is made. You detect this connection by reading the state of your Arduino's digital pins.

Manufacturers assign different keypad output pins to the rows and columns. Two of the commonly available keypads are listed previously and are used in the sample code. You can see how they are laid out in Figure 8-2. If your keypad is different, you'll need to test it or read the keypad's datasheet to determine how to connect your keypad's output pins to your Arduino's digital pins. I show you how to test your keypad later in the chapter.

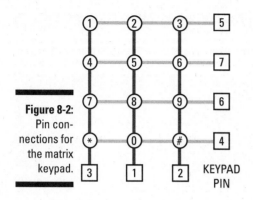

Figure 8-2:
Pin con-
nections for
the matrix
keypad.

The power supply should be rated at 12V DC. Most electronic lock mechanisms are available in 12V DC models and this is an acceptable input for your Arduino. Also, make sure your transformer will supply enough current to handle the needs of both your Arduino and your electronic lock. Your Arduino can operate at a bare minimum of 250mA, but it is safer to estimate it at 500mA. The spec sheet of your lock mechanism should say how much current is required to operate it. If not, you can use your multimeter to measure the current flowing through the coil of your lock, while it is activated. The GAE electronic door strike in the parts list operates at 12V DC at 400mA. Combined with the Arduino, that's a current requirement of 950mA. You should exceed this by a small margin, so that means your power supply must provide a minimum output of 1.0A. You can use one with a higher rating, but not a lower rating.

The display is a four-digit, seven-segment display of the type that you've seen just about everywhere. Using a quad display is a bit simpler than using four individual seven-segment displays because they are all packaged up into a single housing. It has shared *cathodes* to reduce the number of pins needed to drive it. The cathodes and anodes for the digits and the colon/decimal points (on the Lite-On display) are connected to just a few pins on the back of the unit. Again, different manufacturers use different *pinouts*. The datasheet shows which pins are connected to each segment. You can use a different module than the ones listed here, but make sure you are using a common cathode (CC) display, which the code in this chapter is designed for. A common anode (CA) display won't work.

There are also seven-segment displays that you can address directly over the serial interface on your Arduino. This makes connecting it up and writing to the display a lot simpler (SparkFun COM-11442, for example), but they do cost a bit more. The code in this chapter won't work with one of these modules, but once you understand the code, it is pretty easy for you to modify it to do so.

The display is driven by the Maxim 7219 or 7221 display driver (72xx, for short). This integrated circuit (or IC) makes it very easy to control up to eight digits. It handles addressing each segment, storing the state of each digit, and even controlling the brightness through pulse-width modulation (PWM). Conveniently, you send commands using the Serial Peripheral Interface (SPI) Arduino library. The chip requires only one resistor to set the LED current and two capacitors, which keep power fluctuations from harming it. Best of all, it only uses three Arduino digital pins.

The lock mechanism is controlled by a relay. Turning on the relay allows power to flow from the power supply to the electric door lock. The switching transistor, resistor, and diode control the relay. The transistor is a 2n2222 general purpose NPN switching transistor. The 2.2KΩ resistor used with it prevents too much current flowing to the base of the transistor.

The diode prevents *blowback,* or *back voltage,* a phenomenon that occurs when power to the relay coil is switched off and its magnetic field breaks down. You don't want stray current flowing back through to your microcontroller.

Selecting an electric lock mechanism

Carefully consider the door you plan to use for the project. You need to modify your door or the doorjamb to accept an electric lock mechanism, which may require some light carpentry skills and tools, if you have to cut the door or jamb to fit your lock mechanism. There are several different types of doorjambs you can use, and you need to choose the one that is right for your door and door frame. The most common types of electric door locking mechanisms are electric door strikes, magnetic locks, and drop bolt locks. You can choose any of these for the project. You should choose one that will be easiest for you to install. Electric door strikes are generally easiest to work with and use an internal relay to actuate a pin that allows the strike plate to swing open. The inside of one is shown in Figure 8-3. Also keep in mind that you need to run a power supply to your door, so you may need some extra wire for this.

Electrically activated door locking mechanisms come in two modes:

- ✔ **Fail safe:** Fail safe systems will not leave the door locked if the power goes out. That way if there's a fire or other safety situation, you can still get out the door. It fails safely, so the occupants can escape.

- ✔ **Fail secure:** Fail secure systems work the opposite way. If there's a power outage, they remain locked. That means they require no power to stay locked either. The benefit of using a fail secure system is that you do not have to have any power to keep the door in a locked state. But if you choose a fail secure locking mechanism, you need to make sure that there is a way to open the door in case of an emergency, such as a manually activated latch bolt.

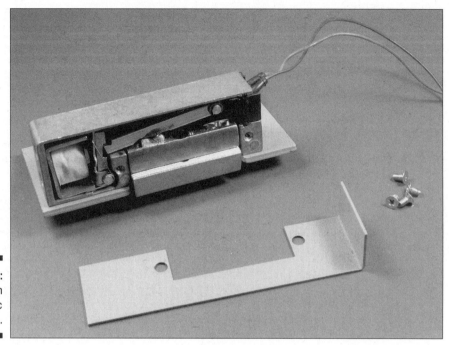

Figure 8-3:
Inside an
electronic
door strike.

I used an electric door strike for this project because it was easiest to install. The door strike is the metal plate fitted into the doorjamb, which has a ramped surface to receive the door latch. The electric strike has a relay mechanism inside. When power is applied to the relay, the strike plate releases and allows the door latch to pass freely. My door has a spring bolt latch. You can turn the bolt on the inside of the door to move the latch, but the latch slides back into place automatically. This means that it fails securely, but can be opened in case of an emergency or power outage.

Electric lock mechanisms come in both DC and AC voltage ratings. Choose a 12 volt DC (or selectable 12/24V DC) device. That way, you can use the same power supply for your Arduino.

You also need some wire to run from the enclosure for your keypad to the electric door mechanism and optionally some ribbon cable, if you plan to transfer your circuit from the breadboard to stripboard. Standard low power 18-24 gauge wire should be sufficient because this is a low power system. You can even use solid core telephone wire or an old Ethernet cable if you have them lying around. The connection to the door strike should only require a few inches of wire, enough to pass through the wall and up to your door strike. You shouldn't need much, because the keypad assembly will be mounted not too far from your door frame.

The nearest wall socket will determine the length of your power supply lead. Measure the distance from your door to the nearest power outlet to estimate the length of wire you need.

Make sure to add plenty of extra wire so that you can mount it near the door frame and baseboards with wire mounting clips.

You'll definitely need to put this project into a housing so that all the components are protected. You should choose an enclosure that will be large enough to fit your keypad, display, the Arduino, and either a small breadboard or a section of stripboard for the MAX72xx IC. Specifying exactly the enclosure you'll need for your system can be difficult. You need to consider what kind of finish you want (wood, metal, or plastic?) and whether you have the tools to cut the square openings for the LED display, keypad, and through holes for the wires. A power drill and a small saw, such as a jeweler's saw or coping saw, should be sufficient for you to make the necessary openings. The minimum practical internal dimensions to fit the display, keypad, Arduino, and relay circuit are approximately 15 x 8 x 4 cm (6 x 3 x 1.5 inches).

You also may need a hot glue gun and glue sticks, and probably a small hammer and chisel to install your locking mechanism into the door frame.

Prototyping your keypad and display

This project has a lot of connections, so it's a good idea to prototype it first using a breadboard. After you've built and tested your prototype, you can then install the breadboard into an enclosure or transfer the circuit to a more permanent substrate, such as a stripboard.

Figure 8-4 shows the electrical schematic for your system's components.

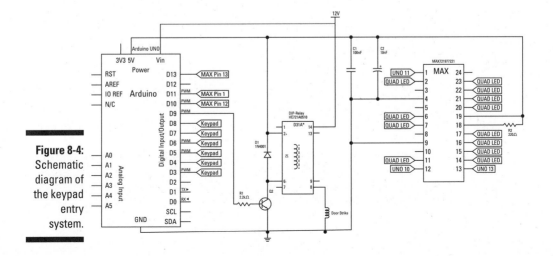

Figure 8-4: Schematic diagram of the keypad entry system.

You need to solder pin headers onto your keypad so that you can insert it into your breadboard for testing, as shown in Figure 8-5. Later, this will make it easier to connect a ribbon cable either by soldering it to the pins or with a header socket that is soldered to the ribbon cable. After the pins are soldered on, you can start assembling your breadboard.

The parts layout on your breadboard diagram is shown in Figure 8-6, which shows the connections for the Rapid Keypad and Avago LED display. If you are using different parts, your connections will probably be slightly different. Add components to your breadboard as follows:

1. **Add your keypad.**

2. **Insert your quad LED display on the left side of the breadboard.**

3. **Add the 7219 display driver to your breadboard.**

4. **Connect your keypad to the digital pins of your Arduino, making sure the keypad pins for rows and columns correspond to the correct digital pins on your Arduino.**

5. **Double-check your connections.**

   It's easy to make a mistake.

Figure 8-5: Soldering pins to your keypad.

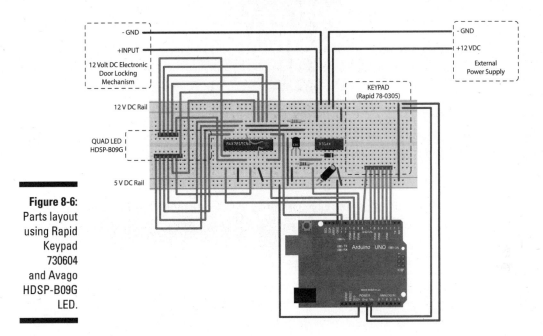

Figure 8-6: Parts layout using Rapid Keypad 730604 and Avago HDSP-B09G LED.

It's always worthwhile to check your datasheet to be sure of your connections. Sometimes there may be extra pins on the unit that are not connected to anything. It depends on the manufacturer. Table 8-1 shows how to connect your Arduino to two of the more commonly available keypad units. If you are using a different unit, you can test its connectors to determine how to connect it to your Arduino. Instructions for doing this are detailed in the "Identifying pins on your keypad" sidebar, a little later in this chapter.

At the time of writing, the datasheet for the Rapid Keypad part #78-0305 shows the wrong pinouts.

Table 8-1	Connecting Your Keypad to the Arduino	
Arduino Digital Pin	*SparkFun/Rapid Keypad Pin*	*Keypad Row/Column*
2	7	Row 1
3	6	Row 2

(continued)

Table 8-1 *(continued)*

Arduino Digital Pin	SparkFun/Rapid Keypad Pin	Keypad Row/Column
4	5	Column 2
5	4	Row 3
6	3	Column 0
7	2	Row 0
8	1	Column 1

Now connect the Max 72xx Driver IC to your Arduino by connecting jumper wires, as shown in Table 8-2. Pretty simple, because you are using the SPI library to communicate with the IC, and it only needs three connections!

Table 8-2   Connecting Your Max 72xx to the Arduino

Arduino Digital Pin	Max 72xx Pin
10	1
11	12
13	13

Add your capacitors to the breadboard. As shown in Figure 8-6, the .01 µF capacitor straddles the IC. To be most effective at preventing electrical noise from disturbing the IC, it needs to be as close as possible to output Pins 9 and 19. Straddling the IC is an easy way to do this. The 10 microfarad electrolytic capacitor simply needs to be placed across the ground and power rails, as shown in Figure 8-6.

The 10 µF is "polarized," meaning it operates correctly in only one direction. Make sure that the negative leg is connected to the negative power rail on your breadboard. You identify the negative side by a "–" printed down the side of the capacitor. The leg on that side is the negative leg.

You may be tempted to omit the two capacitors, especially if you don't have them lying around your workbench. Don't! This can lead to erratic behavior and even permanent damage. They prevent noise on the power input and should be placed as close as possible to the V+ and Ground pins of the IC.

Identifying pins on your keypad

If you have a keypad from a different manufacturer, you can easily test which pins are assigned to its rows and columns using your multimeter. If you find it difficult to juggle the test probes and your keypad and pen, attach some alligator clips to your probes and use them to clamp onto the pins. Do the following steps:

1. Make a keypad diagram like the one in Figure 8-2, but with no numbers.

2. Set your multimeter to test for continuity.

3. Starting at the left and proceeding to the right side of the keypad, connect your probes to Pins 1 and 2 of your keypad. These are the leftmost two pins and may or may not be labeled with numbers.

4. Press every button on the pad until you detect continuity.

5. Make a note of the row and column of the key that you just detected. For example,

if you are connected to Pins 1 and 3 and your meter reacts when you press number 7, write a 1, for Pin 1 under `COL0` and a 3 next to `ROW2`.

6. If you didn't detect anything, that's fine; it just means that the two pins are either both columns or both rows (and so will never be connected). Move your probe from Pin 2 to Pin 3 and repeat Steps 4 and 5.

7. Continue this way until you have reached the end with the second meter probe.

8. Now start moving the first meter probe toward the end to meet the second probe and keep testing.

9. Eventually you will have documented all the connections and you can set the correct pins for the `rowPins` and `colPins` variables.

Next, add your resistor between Pins 18 and 19 of the Max 72XX Driver IC. This is used to limit current through each LED segment. The maximum current rating for your display determines the value of the resistor value, which limits how much current flows through the LED. The 72xx datasheet has a table that specifies the resistor values that should be used for your LED display. The HDSP-B09G has a maximum of 25mA per segment at a *forward voltage* of 2.2V. Checking the table, this would indicate a resistor value of somewhere between 17KΩ and 28KΩ, but it's good to have a bit of a safety margin, so I've specified a 33KΩ resistor. This works for both the Lite-On and Avago displays, but you might need a different value if you are using a different display. Using a lower value could reduce the life of your LED or your driver IC.

Now connect your Max 72xx to your quad LED display. The way you connect your LED display to your Max 72xx will depend on the layout of its pins. The schematic diagram in Figure 8-4 doesn't show both displays. The pinouts for the quad LED vary by manufacturer, so in the diagram they aren't labeled by pin number. Table 8-3 lists the connections for the two seven-segment quad displays in the parts list. Refer to Figure 8-6 to see the breadboard placement for the Avago display.

Table 8-3	Pin Connections to the MAX72xx for Popular LCD Displays	
MAX 7219/7221	**Lite-On LTC-4727JR**	**Avago HDSP-B09G**
1		
2	1	12
3		
4		
5		
6	6	8
7	8	6
8		
9		
10		
11	2	9
12		
13		
14	14	11
15	11	10
16	16	7
17	15	5
18		
19		
20	13	4
21	5	1
22	7	2
23	3	3
24		

Coding and testing your keypad

At this point, you have everything but your relay and door strike assembled. Now that you've got the keypad and display components in place on your breadboard, it's time to load up the code to your Arduino. In your IDE, open the code for this chapter from the Downloads tab of the companion website (www.dummies.com/go/arduinoprojectsfordummies). Take a moment to look at the code to understand how it works, and then upload it to your board.

Declaring your variables

In the first section, before setup, you declare variables for the keypad and display.

```
const int numberOfDigits = 4; // The number of digits in the 7-segment display
const int numRows = 4;        // Number of rows in the keypad
const int numCols = 3;        // Number of columns in the keypad
const int debounceTime = 20;  // Number of milliseconds for switch to become
           stable
const int doorOpenTime = 5000; // How long you want the door strike to remain
           open

const int strikePin = 9;      // The pin that actuates the relay for the door
           strike
const int slaveSelect = 10;   // Pin used to enable the slave pin on the MAX72xx

char code[4]= {'1','2','3','4'}; // Set your code here
char codeBuffer[4]; // Stores the code that currently is being entered

boolean DEBUG=true;  // Set to true to print status messages to the serial port
int keypressCount=0; // Counts how many times a key has been pressed

// The keyMap defines the character returned when its key is pressed
const char keyMap[numRows][numCols] = {
  { '1', '2', '3' },
  { '4', '5', '6' },
  { '7', '8', '9' },
  { '*', '0', '#' }
};

const int rowPins[numRows] = { 7, 4, 2, 5  }; // Keypad Rows 0 through 3
const int colPins[numCols] = { 6, 8 ,3 };     // Keypad Columns 0 through 2
```

The `numberOfDigits` variable sets your LED driver IC with the proper number of digits. `numRows` and `NumCols` store the number of rows and columns on your keypad, 4 and 3, respectively. You use these to look up which key is being pressed. The `debounceTime` (20 milliseconds) ensures that the key being pressed is accurately detected. You set the amount of time the door will be held open with the `doorOpenTime` variable. Play around with this until you get it set to your liking.

The `strikePin` variable defines which digital pin will be activated when the correct code is entered. This applies power to the relay, which closes to actuate your door lock mechanism. I use an electronic door strike in the project, so I call this "strikePin." You might want to use a different name if you are using a different kind of mechanism, such as a magnetic door lock or a drop bolt lock.

slaveSelect defines a digital pin that you use to indicate you are sending data. The slave select (or "chip select") pin (SS) is a command pin on your IC that connects the external pins to the internal circuitry.

In applications with several LED drivers that are all connected to your input wires, you want to be able to select whether or not a specific driver IC is enabled. The IC only responds to commands when its slave select mode pin is activated, which allows you to differentiate between this driver and other ones you might be using.

You are only using a single IC in this project, but you still need to let the chip know when you are going to send it data, and that's what the SS pin does.

Two char variables are used for handling access code. The first one, code[], stores the access code digits. You can set this to be whatever you like. The second char, codeBuffer[], stores (or "buffers") the keys that have been pressed. When these two match, presto! The Arduino activates strikePin. There's no way to set the code from the keypad — you have to do it programmatically. But after you understand how the code works, you could easily create a secret key sequence that would allow you to store a new access code directly from the keypad.

This program has a handy little debug feature built in. That's what the next variable is for: a boolean called DEBUG. Recall that boolean variables can only be true or false. By setting this to true, you can use a conditional if statement to execute certain lines of code that won't be executed if you set it to false. For example, in this code, you print a lot of variables on the serial port to test that your keypad is working properly. But after your system is installed on your door, you don't need to print anything. Rather than deleting all those Serial.println() statements, you can simply go back to the DEBUG variable and set it to false. When the statement evaluates to false in your code, nothing within the condition's curly brackets will be executed.

The keypressCount stores how many digits have been pressed so far. When the fourth is pressed, the real action happens.

The char variable keyMap[][] is a two-dimensional array. A two-dimensional array is simply an array of arrays. Imagine a menu for an Italian restaurant. You might have a dozen menu items to choose from: breadsticks, soup, pizza, lasagna, salad, red wine, and so on. You could store these as simply a single array, but you could also organize them by type: starters {breadsticks, soup}, main courses {pizza, lasagna, pasta}, drinks {water, red wine, white wine}. This way you can refer to items either individually or as collections. A single dimension array, as with your code[] array, stores *elements* (individual data items) like this:

```
Int anArray[] = { 0,1,2,3 };
```

A two-dimensional array stores elements like this:

```
Int anArray[][] = { {0,1,2,3}, {3,2,3,0}, {4,3,8,1},
        {2,3,4,5} };
```

When you read from a two-dimensional array, the first value in the square brackets specifies which element you wish to read; the second value in brackets specifies the element within the element you specified. In working with arrays, the numbering system starts from zero. So, for example, in the two-dimensional array above, `anArray[2][0]` is holding the value 4.

The `keyMap` is simply used to store which digits are on the keypad. It's literally a map of the keys.

Consider this. The Arduino doesn't know what number is in each position of the keypad. It can't read the number 1 that's printed on the key in the upper left, which could just as easily be labeled "platypus" — the Arduino doesn't have a clue until you specify it.

When a key is pressed, you use the `keyMap` to identify which number is at that location, so you can compare it to your predetermined code.

The final two variables are arrays that store which of your Arduino's digital pins the rows and columns of your keypad are connected to. This is the code that implements what is shown in Table 8-2.

Defining the setup

In the `setup()` section of your code, you prepare the Arduino to run this sketch.

Now you set up the Max Display Driver chip. The `sendCommand()` function toward the bottom of your code is used to make it a bit easier to send instructions to the chip using the SPI interface. Every time you send an instruction, you have to set the `SlaveSelect` pin to `LOW`, send the byte corresponding to the command you want to issue to the chip, send the byte with the value for the command, and then set `SlaveSelect` back to `HIGH`. You don't want to have to do these steps every time you talk to the Max chip, so the `sendCommand()` function packages these up nicely:

```
void sendCommand(int command, unsigned char value)
{
  digitalWrite(slaveSelect,LOW);
  SPI.transfer(command)
  SPI.transfer(value);
  digitalWrite(slaveSelect,HIGH);
}
```

You merely send the command code you want and its value. For example, command 10 is for brightness. The following sets it to 8 (out of 15):

```
sendCommand(10, 8);
```

You set the chip to normal mode (ready to display something), turn off its test feature, set the brightness at medium, and tell it how many digits there are on your display (4). Then you set the chip to decode mode. This means it will automatically decode the byte sent to it and light up the corresponding segments of the LEDs: 0-9, the characters H, E, L, P, a dash, and a blank space. (If you wanted only to light up individual segments, you'd set it to no-decode mode.)

You now set up the pin controlling your relay that powers the door mechanism. It's set to output.

You also need to set up the pins that are used for reading the keypad. You use a special technique, which I explain in the next code section, that takes advantage of "pull-up resistors" that are on your Arduino. These resistors are on the ATmega328 chip itself and can be set to hold a pin HIGH. Later, if it goes LOW for some reason (a keypress), your Arduino can respond appropriately. You are setting all the rows to be used for input and writing these pins HIGH, which activates the pull-up resistors. You'll use all the columns for output. You set these pins HIGH for now, but will change this later on.

The last thing is to clear the display. Sometimes when powering up the system (and especially when uploading code), stray characters appear on the display. The `clearDisplay()` function at the bottom of your code sets all the digits to be blank:

```
void clearDisplay(){
   sendCommand(1, '_');
   sendCommand(2, '_');
   sendCommand(3, '_');
   sendCommand(4, '_');
}
```

Running the main loop

There are only a few things the code does to operate your entry system. The main loop operates as follows:

1. **Listen for a key.**

2. **If a key has been pressed, send it to the LED display.**

3. **Increment the number of key presses by one.**

4. **Enter it into the code buffer in the next available position.**

5. **Determine whether four digits have been entered.**

   If so, check whether the code is valid.

6. **If the code is valid, open the door and reset everything for the next time around.**

The main thing you need to do is check whether a key has been pressed. The first statement creates a local `char` variable called `key` to store the character that is sent back from a function named `getKey()`, which I discuss in a moment. Remember the `keyMap`? That's where this number ultimately comes from.

The char value from `key` is also assigned to the `codeBuffer[]` array, which you use to test whether the code is valid. It is added to the position stored by `keypressCount`, which is incremented upward every time a new character is detected. Remember, array numbering starts from zero, so the "zero-th" character is the first keypress detected. So `codeBuffer[0]` contains the first key pressed on the keypad, `codeBuffer[1]` contains the second key pressed, and so on.

The next conditional `if` statement executes only when a key has been pressed, at which point Steps 2 through 6 from the preceding list are processed. If a key hasn't been pressed, the program just waits for that to happen. When it does, the `sendCommand` function executes:

```
sendCommand(keypressCount+1, key);
```

The `sendCommand` takes two parameters: which seven-segment module number to change, and what to change it to. You use `keypressCount` not only to keep track of the number of times keys have been pressed so far, but also to tell which seven-segment digit to light up. However, `keypressCount` starts at zero because the `code[]` and the `buffer[]` char arrays start their numbering at zero, and you want to store those values in the right place. But the Max chip starts numbering digits from 1. Therefore, to use `keypressCount` to light up the correct seven-segment digit, you have to add one (+1) to its value.

The next statement implements that handy debugging feature I mention earlier. If you have set the `DEBUG` boolean to `true`, the code will print out all your variables to the serial port.

Next, you increment the `keypressCount` by one and then test to see if four digits have been pressed. If so, it's showtime. The `delay(500)` statement gives you a half-second to see the last access code digit entered because the display will change depending on whether the right access code was entered. This test is done with a little bit of native C language code:

```
if (memcmp(codeBuffer, code,4)==0) {
    if(DEBUG){Serial.println("MATCH!");}
    unlock();
}
```

The function `memcmp()` compares two items in memory and takes as its parameters the two items and their expected lengths. In this case, you are comparing the `codeBuffer` array and the code stored at the beginning of the program. Both have a length of four bytes. If they are exactly the same, the `memcmp()` function returns a zero and that is exactly what you are looking for in the conditional statement. If they are the same (and `DEBUG` is true), `MATCH!` is printed to the serial port and the `unlock()` function is executed. If the memory comparison fails, then the function does not return a "0," meaning the wrong code was entered.

In either case, you want to clear the display, ready for the next time around. So you call the `clearDisplay()` function. Another native C language instruction does a little memory housekeeping:

```
memset(codeBuffer, 0, 4);
```

This clears out the `codeBuffer` explicitly by setting it to 0. Its length is 4, which is the second parameter. Some might argue that this instruction is not necessary, but it's good practice to explicitly manage memory rather than leave things to chance.

Lastly, because this was the fourth keypress and there are only four digits to evaluate, the `keypressCount` needs to be reset to zero so you are ready for the next iteration.

Specifying your user-defined functions

The final part of the code contains four functions that handle identifying the key pressed, sending commands to the Max chip, clearing the display, and activating the door mechanism.

The truly clever part of this code is how the keypress is determined. It uses code by Michael Margolis in his indispensable reference book *Arduino Cookbook* (published by O'Reilly Media). Recall that the digital pins for the rows were pulled up HIGH during `setup()`. This means that reading those pins will always evaluate to HIGH, unless something else is pulling them low — like a keypress connecting them to a LOW column pin. The `getKey` function goes through each of the digital pins connected to the column pins of your keypad and sets the pin for LOW. It then checks to see if any row pins are now also LOW. The pull-up resistors you used in `setup()` keep the row pins HIGH — unless a key has been pressed, connecting it to a LOW column pin! There's a short delay of 20ms to make sure that the key was actually pressed (debouncing).

The `while` statement only operates while a condition exists, in this case when one of the row pins has become LOW due to a keypress. At this moment, the `keyMap` is consulted to find the corresponding number for that row and column, and this is stored in the variable `key`. Next, you do a little housekeeping, setting all the column pins back to HIGH, for the next time around. Finally, the value for `key` is returned to the part of the program that requested it. Whew!

The only thing remaining is to unlock the door to your fortress/castle/ laboratory. If you haven't already done so, add the last part of your code at the end. In the `unlock()` function, the four `sendCommand()` instructions print the message "HI" to the display. It's nice to receive a warm welcome — if only a brief one. Then the action happens. The `strikePin` is written HIGH, which will provide power to the transistor controlling the relay (which you add in the next section). When it activates, power is allowed to pass to your unlocking mechanism for the duration specified by `doorOpenTime`. Then you set `strikePin` to LOW to keep out any nefarious intruders, spies, and miscreants.

If you haven't already done so, upload the code and cross your fingers. When you press a key, you should see its number displayed in your LED module. Open the serial monitor in the Arduino IDE and observe what happens when you press a key. If everything is connected correctly, you should see the keys identified and the `codeBuffer[]` gradually being filled with the values you have entered. If you don't see the digits lighting up on your LED module, check your connections again. If you don't see the correct values on your serial monitor, make certain that there is not an error in your code and that the values for `rowPins` and `colPins` are correct. After you've confirmed this is all working, you can move on, to add the relay and door opening module. If it's not working, you won't be able to test the relay and door mechanism.

To prepare your Arduino for its working life as a security guard, set `DEBUG` to `false` and upload the code one last time. Remove the USB connection from your Arduino because you won't need it anymore. Power will be supplied from your power transformer.

Adding and testing your relay

You now need to add the relay that controls the door mechanism and the power supply. You use the same power supply to operate your Arduino, because it won't be getting power from the USB connection anymore. Follow the breadboard layout in Figure 8-6 to make the connections. Don't plug your power transformer into the wall until you are ready to power up and test the system.

Connecting your power supply

You set up the breadboard with two *power rails:* a 12V DC rail on top for your Arduino and door lock, and a 5V DC rail on the bottom, which supplies the Max 72xx. First, connect the output lead of the 12V DC power transformer to the top two columns of your breadboard. You probably need to cut and strip the output wire from your transformer to do this. You solder the wires to pin headers to make it easy to connect them into your breadboard.

Use your multimeter to test the transformer's output wires, identifying the positive and negative connections. Don't rely on the diagram on the transformer or markings on the wires. If you get the *polarity* of the connections wrong, you could fry your Arduino.

You can now supply the power for your Arduino, using the Vin and GND headers at the bottom of the board, instead of the USB port or the black "barrel connector" on the left side. Use a jumper wire to connect the 12V power rail to the Vin pin and connect the ground rail to GND.

The last step is to create a *common ground* between the two power rails. Use a jumper wire to connect the negative column of the 12V DC rail to the negative column of the 5V DC rail.

Connecting your transistor and relay

You also need to supply power to operate the 5V relay. Use a jumper wire to connect from the 5V header on your Arduino to the bottom power rail. As shown in Figure 8-6, the relay simply controls whether the door mechanism receives power and when it does, the lock is released. The door locking mechanism needs about 400mA to operate, which is ten times the amount of current your Arduino's digital pins can provide. Switching power is one of the basic and common tasks that electronic circuits do, so there are many ways to control power. This project uses an Arduino digital pin to apply power to a *transistor* (itself a solid-state switch) that actuates your relay.

Figure 8-7 shows a transistor like the one in your parts list. The transistor has three pins — an emitter, a base, and a collector, labeled E, B, and C. Current will flow between the collector and emitter when current from a digital pin is applied at the base of the transistor.

The current from the collector is what actuates your relay, closing its contacts together and allowing power from your power supply to activate the door locking mechanism. In effect, you have a digital switch (the Arduino pin) that controls a digital switch (the transistor), which in turn controls an electro-mechanical switch that activates the door mechanism!

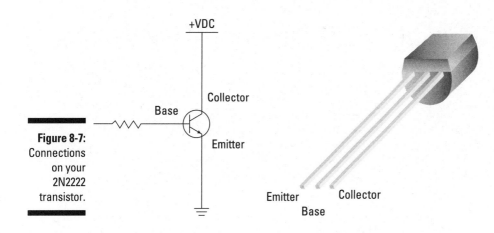

+VDC

Collector

Base

Emitter

Emitter   Collector

Base

Figure 8-7:
Connections
on your
2N2222
transistor.

It is also possible to use a power switching transistor to control the door lock directly (doing away with the relay entirely), but the 2N2222 transistor is cheaper and easy to find. Plus, there are a lot of applications where relay control is handy, especially if you want to electrically isolate the circuit being controlled from your Arduino (to control household electricity, for example). You could easily adapt this part of the project to other applications.

Add your relay, diode, and transistor to the breadboard, as shown in Figure 8-6. Make sure the transistor is in the right orientation. The emitter should be connected to ground. Add the 2.2kΩ resistor as shown. It prevents too much current from flowing to the transistor's base. Connect the collector to your relay and connect Pin 9 of your Arduino to your transistor's base.

Now take a moment to double-check all your connections, paying close attention to the positive and negative polarity of the wires. It's a pain, but you don't want to power things up incorrectly because you might end up damaging your hardware. After checking your connections, plug in your power supply.

After your Arduino boots up, you're ready to roll. Enter your code into the keypad to test the relay. You'll probably hear a faint click as the relay coil is energized. Add jumper wires to the relay's output pins and connect your multimeter's probes to them. When you enter the right code, the meter should show a connection.

The final step is to connect the two leads of your door mechanism to the ground rail and the output of your relay. Do that and enter your access code again. If everything's working properly, you should be rewarded by a satisfying "click" as your Arduino does its magic and opens the lock.

Assembling and Installing Your System

The parts placement diagram in this chapter (see Figure 8-1) shows a full-size breadboard, which makes prototyping easy. But when you put it onto the enclosure, you might want to transfer the circuit to a half-size breadboard that takes up less space and accommodates the Max72xx driver, transistor, and relay circuit, as shown in Figure 8-8. The LED display and the keypad are mounted to the front faceplate of your enclosure, so you won't need extra room for them on the breadboard. Alternatively, you can transfer the circuit to a piece of stripboard and solder the components together for a more rugged finished project.

Whether you will keep the project on a breadboard or transfer it to a stripboard or perfboard, ribbon cable makes it easy to attach all the connections to the IC, and your enclosure won't end up as a rat's nest of wires. If you are using a breadboard, attach pin headers to the ribbon cable to ensure a stable connection, as shown in Figure 8-9. If you are using stripboard, you can solder your ribbon cable directly to the board. A dab of hot glue applied at the point the ribbon cable meets the stripboard will relieve some of the strain on the soldered connections so that you don't damage them during installation.

Figure 8-8: Installing the control assembly into an enclosure.

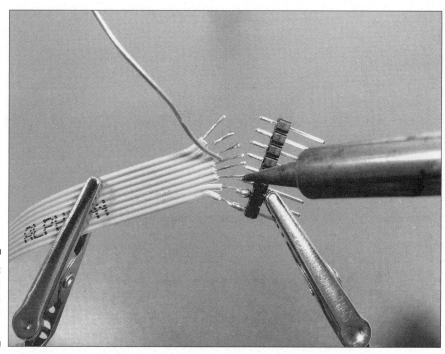

Figure 8-9:
Using ribbon
cables to
make wiring
neater.

You can also use the glue to hold your display, Arduino keypad, and circuit board. For a really professional finish, use an enclosure that has internal *bosses* (the small plastic pillars into which you can fix a screw) onto which you can bolt your Arduino, stripboard, and keypad. However, choosing the right one for your components can be tricky, and these enclosures can be expensive. I find a bit of hot glue goes a long way.

If you use a stripboard to mount your LED Driver IC, the copper strips on the underside will electrically connect all the pins of your LED Driver IC together, which you do not want to do. To avoid this, use an X-ACTO knife or a stripboard trace cutting tool (Rapid #34-0600) to cut the traces, as shown in Figure 8-10. A 3mm drill bit will also do the job.

You run power leads from the wall to your enclosure and from your enclosure to the door strike or other lock actuating mechanism, as shown in Figure 8-11. You need to drill a small hole through the interior wall to the exterior wall. How you do this will depend greatly upon the circumstances of the door you are securing. Is it an interior door or an exterior door? Do you need to drill through brick or masonry? Your particular circumstances will determine how you mount the enclosure and run the wire.

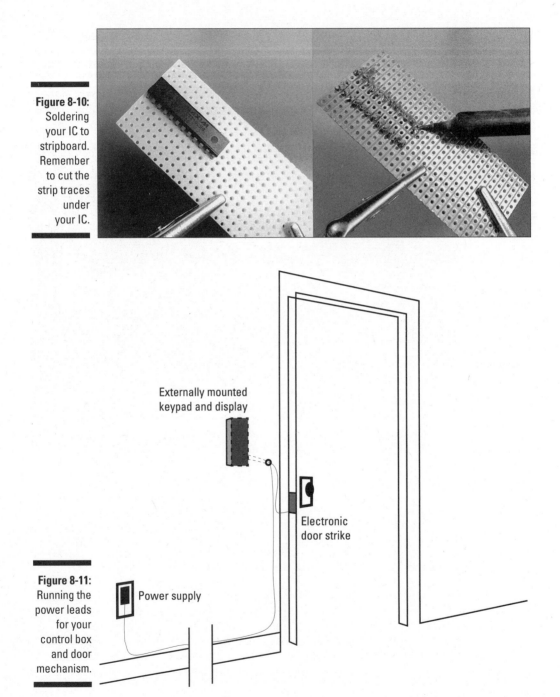

Figure 8-10: Soldering your IC to stripboard. Remember to cut the strip traces under your IC.

Externally mounted keypad and display

Electronic door strike

Figure 8-11: Running the power leads for your control box and door mechanism.

Power supply

The power leads pass through holes in your enclosure, and you need to secure them to make sure they won't pull out or put stress onto your internal components. You can either use cable strain relief glands, or you can create a sort of strain relief by affixing a wire tie (zip tie) to the cables on the inside of the enclosure, as shown in Figure 8-12. That way they won't be easily pulled out. A dab of hot glue on the interior will keep the cable from moving around.

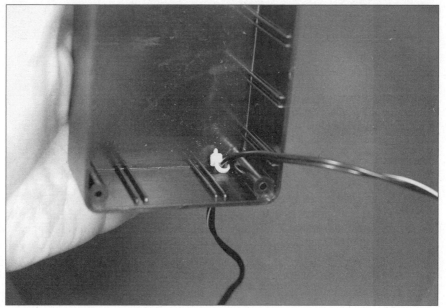

Figure 8-12:
Securing
the cables
with a strain
relief.

The only remaining task is to install the door locking mechanism itself, which in my project is an electronic door strike. You will likely need to use some light woodworking tools to shave off additional wood from your doorjamb to accommodate the electronic strike. Remove the existing strike plate to reveal the bare jamb underneath. Mark the profile of the strike plate onto the wood and use a small chisel and hammer to carefully tap out the excess wood to accommodate your strike plate, as shown in Figure 8-13. You need to ensure that you have enough room in the door frame to secure it.

Figure 8-13:
Installing
the door
strike.

The final task is to screw the strike plate into the jamb and test the fit. Make sure the door latch travels freely into the strike plate. On most models, you can adjust the depth of the strike plate assembly to match your door latch.

Now, shut the door for the final test, and for good measure, lock yourself on the outside!

Chapter 9

Building an RFID Tag Reader

*1*f you're reading this book, you've probably heard of radio frequency ID (RFID) tags and know that they are used for tracking things like packages and small inanimate objects. They can also identify animate objects, such as pets, cattle, and even people! In addition to things like inventory control and security, RFID also serves as a quick and easy mechanism for handling small secure payments and other simple transactions.

You can easily get your Arduino to read RFID tags and act upon the unique ID that is encoded on them. In this chapter, you find out about a few of the different kinds of RFID systems and how they work. You use an Arduino to control an RFID reader module and respond to the information it spits out when a tag is brought near the reader. With this knowledge, you can add RFID to just about anything, including other projects in this book, such as the keypad entry system in Chapter 8.

You can find many different kinds of RFID readers. The one you need to use is based on your project's requirements and how much you want to spend. I've selected one of the most common and relatively inexpensive ones, which can read things like RFID key fobs. It operates at the 125 KHz frequency. With the easy-to-build relay circuit, you can control just about anything else, from the door opener in Chapter 8, to a toaster, and beyond!

You can download schematics and full-color parts placement diagrams from the companion website (www.dummies.com/go/arduinoprojectsfor dummies).

Understanding RFID

RFID is a radio frequency system, as its name indicates. In that sense, it's similar to other kinds of radio frequency systems, such as FM radio, but operates within a different frequency range. Unlike broadcast systems, with RFID, radio signals are exchanged between two objects, a reader module and a tag. It's a bidirectional communication, and is typically within a relatively short range compared to broadcast systems. The acronym "RFID" can refer to either the reader or the tag, or both. The range of an RFID system depends on the particular RFID frequency standard that's used. This depends on the size of the antenna and the strength of the signal.

The reader sends the radio signal. Each RFID tag holds a unique ID code that is returned back to the reader when they exchange the right sequence of commands. Other kinds of information can also be stored on RFID tags, and some systems support both reading from and writing to tags, which means you can do simple transactions like handling fares for busses and subways.

The tag is an electronic circuit that is usually embedded within some kind of practical physical package, depending on the particular application. Figure 9-1 shows some examples. For security access, the circuit is embedded into plastic cards the same size as credit cards, which are easy to carry around in wallets and purses. Other examples include key fobs and self-adhesive labels. The variety is almost endless. Thinner and cheaper systems are used for inventory control. More expensive and bulkier systems are used for things such as shipping container tracking and electronic toll road systems, including SpeedPass or E-ZPass.

There are several different RFID frequencies, which are used by the two categories of systems, *passive RFID* and *active RFID*. The system described in this chapter is passive, as is the one in the bonus chapter online.

About passive RFID

Passive RFID tags operate at relatively short distances only, anywhere from a few inches to a few feet. They are called *passive* because they do not provide their own power and can only send their information when they enter the electromagnetic field of a reader. Entering the field energizes the tiny radio transceiver circuit through a tiny antenna within the passive tag, so that it can receive signals from the reader and respond to them. Because the field is relatively weak, and the power induced into the tag is very low, the operating range of these tags is short. Usually they must be within a few inches of the reader or at most, a few feet. Passive systems are generally relatively cheaper than active systems. The passive tags themselves are usually made to be as inexpensive as possible so that they can be produced and sold in mass quantities and are, more or less, *losable* because they are cheap. However, long range readers that can detect tags up to three or four feet away can cost thousands. The systems in this chapter are short range (only a few inches at most) and cost under $50.

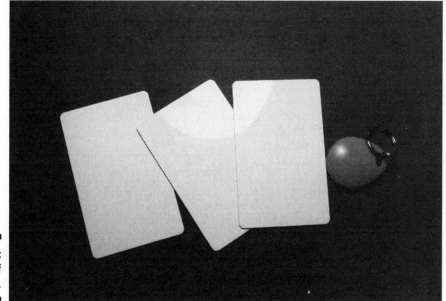

Figure 9-1:
Examples of
RFID tags.

Passive RFID systems shouldn't be confused with electromagnetic article surveillance (EAS) systems that are used to make sure expensive items in shops aren't stolen. These are acousto-magnetic, microwave, or in some cases, radio frequency systems and don't contain any kind of identification mechanism.

About active RFID

Active RFID systems have a powered reader and a powered tag. When the tag gets a message from the reader, it responds with its encoded information. These systems cost more and are more accurate and faster. They also can read tags much farther away than passive systems. You need all these features if you are deducting money from someone's account as she flies by at 30 miles per hour. However, the higher cost means it's impractical to use such systems for simpler applications, such as entry systems.

RFID frequencies and protocols

Passive systems operate at both low and high frequencies. Two common ones that I describe in this chapter are the low frequency 125 kilohertz (kHz) band and the high frequency 13.56 megahertz (MHz) band. The high frequency system is faster to read and write to. It also has a greater range, but does cost slightly more.

In addition to having different frequencies, there are several different communication *protocols* — the conversation rules that are used between the reader and the tag — that govern how they *speak* to each other. These standards are set by the International Standards Organization (ISO) and different manufacturers implement different ISO standards in their products.

The reader I use in this chapter is the 125KHz ID-Innovations reader chip and tag system that uses the EM4001 protocol. This reader is easy to use and inexpensive. Its antenna is self-contained within the chip.

The high frequency system is the 13.56MHz Philips MiFare/MiFare UltraLight system using the ISO 14443 standard, which costs a bit more. This system is used by many transit systems, so you should be able to read a transit pass with this one. SparkFun sells a really handy Arduino prototyping shield for this one, based on the SonMicro SM130 reader. It has an external antenna that is included on the shield. You just solder your reader into it and start scanning. It even has a little prototyping area, so you can add additional components, such as the relay.

Not all readers and tags operate at the same frequency or protocol. When shopping for an RFID system, make sure to match the RFID reader and tag type; otherwise, your system won't work at all.

Building an ID-Innovations RFID Reader

This project uses the ID-Innovations ID-20 chip, which is super easy to work with because it has its own internal antenna. You can build this on a breadboard and then transfer it to a homemade perfboard Arduino shield if you want to put it into a more permanent enclosure.

Selecting your parts

The parts you need to build the reader are shown in Figure 9-2. This list only includes the parts for the reader, but you also need a tag or tags to read. You can choose from literally hundreds of RFID tags. The key fob 125kHz RFID tag shown in Figure 9-1 would work just fine.

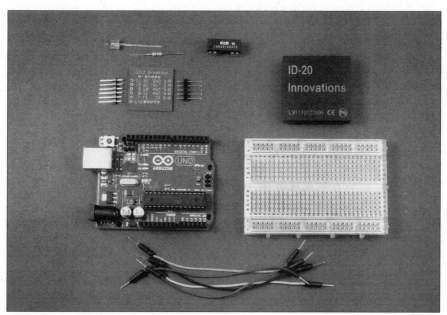

Figure 9-2:
The parts you need for your RFID reader.

You use the relay so that you can switch on and off some other device. It's optional, but pretty cool to be able to control things with an RFID tag, so I'm showing you how to do that with this project. You need

- An Arduino

- A full size or mini breadboard

- An ID Innovations 12, or ID Innovations 20 RFID Module (SparkFun SEN-08628/ Cool Components #000155)

- A SparkFun SEN-08243 breakout board (SparkFun SEN-08423 / Cool Components #000108)

- Eleven long pin headers

- An LED

- A 220Ω resistor

- An assortment of several jumper wires

- A miniature Dual In-Line (DIL) reed relay (such as Jameco #138431 or Rapid #60-2400)

- A 125kHz RFID tag, such as the key fob tag shown in Figure 9-1 (Cool Components #000648). SparkFun sells a plain white credit card style tag, too (SparkFun #COM-08310).

ID Innovations makes a range of several 125kHz RFID readers, of which the ID-12 and ID-20 models contain their own built-in antenna and are advertised to read tags 12cm and 16cm away, respectively. However, to get this kind of range you have to build a tuning capacitor circuit.

Fine-tuning to get optimum range is best done with an oscilloscope, which is not a piece of gear most people have. But I've found that you can get away without a tuning circuit and still read tags within several centimeters, so the tuning circuit is not described in this book. If you want to go for the gold, the tuning circuit is described in the ID Innovations datasheets for the series.

The LED is used as an indicator, so that you can see when a tag has been read. The 220Ω resistor is used to limit the current going to the LED.

The SparkFun breakout board allows you to work with your reader on a breadboard, and it fits any of the ID Innovations readers (even though it's labeled ID-12). Their pins have a 2mm pitch, so they do not fit into a regular breadboard, which has holes spaced at 0.1" (2.54mm), so you have to use the breakout board for any prototyping. In fact, even if you aren't planning to use a breadboard, the breakout board is handy because the 2mm pins are really pretty inconveniently close together to work with. The breakout board also is registered to fit into the RFID reader in only the correct orientation. One of the pins on the reader is missing, and the breakout board aligns with this missing pin, as shown in Figure 9-3.

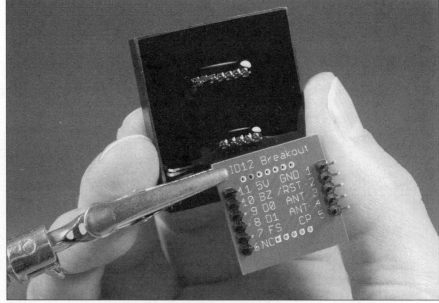

Figure 9-3: The SparkFun breakout board is keyed to fit the ID Innovations readers.

To go along with the SparkFun breakout board, you also need some pin headers, in either regular or long variety. I'd strongly suggest long headers, since on a breadboard the reader overlaps the jumper wires, making it difficult to see the connections and (more importantly, depending on the type of jumper wires you use) putting strain on the wires themselves, which can make for bad connections and cause the sensor not to work.

It doesn't come with them. You connect the pins to your breakout board so that you can insert it into your breadboard. You could also simply solder wires directly to the breakout board if you are going to put your reader some distance away from your Arduino.

The relay is an extremely convenient little guy called a reed relay, and it's in a dual in-line (DIL) *package,* so it fits perfectly onto your breadboard. The relay has an internal coil resistance, which means you can connect it directly to an Arduino digital pin and operate it. You could control any of the other projects in this book with it, too.

This reed relay can only switch up to 100V DC and 1A or less. Don't connect it to an AC electricity circuit, such as a household appliance would use. If you want to do that, you need to connect a bigger relay to this one or use a power transistor instead.

Assembling your RFID reader

After you have all the parts, you are ready to assemble the reader. You first build the breakout board and then connect it to your RFID reader. Then you add the reader assembly to your breadboard and complete it with the additional components.

Adapting your reader to your breadboard

Do the following steps to build your breakout board:

1. **Snap off a group of five pin headers and a group of six pin headers, which will go into the holes on your SparkFun breakout board.**

2. **Insert the pins into your breadboard so that they can accommodate the breakout board, as shown in Figure 9-3.**

   This is so that you can hold the pins steady while you solder them to the breakout board. It's a really convenient technique to use for soldering pins, when you can do it! See Figure 9-4.

Figure 9-4:
Holding your
pins with a
breadboard.

3. **Add your board to the top of the pins, with the SparkFun logo facing up. You need to make sure the pins are pointing the right way or you won't be able to add your RFID reader!**

   Make sure that you solder the pins to the breakout board with the SparkFun logo facing up!

4. **Carefully solder the two rows of pins in place, as shown in Figure 9-5.**

5. **Remove your breakout board from the breadboard.**

   Gently slip your finished breakout board-with-pins assembly onto the RFID reader, as shown in Figure 9-6. It will only fit on the reader in the correct orientation.

   Pay special attention to make sure that your breakout board is snug and parallel with the reader, or it won't sit flat on your breadboard and will look funny.

Figure 9-5:
Soldering
your pins on
the break-
out board
with the
SparkFun
logo
facing up!

Figure 9-6:
Fitting your
breakout
board to the
reader.

6. **Carefully solder the breakout board to your reader.**

You should work carefully, but quickly when soldering any integrated circuit (IC). The pins are rated to withstand a certain amount of heat during soldering, but lingering too long on one could damage your reader. If you're working slowly, it's a good idea to take a break for a few moments between pins so the heat doesn't build up during the process. Don't rush. Carefully solder the breakout board to your reader, as shown in Figure 9-7. The RFID reader IC isn't going anywhere!

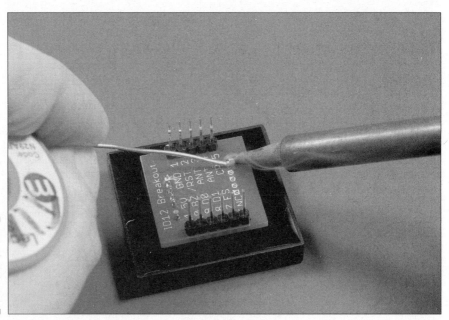

Figure 9-7:
Soldering
your pins
on the RFID
reader.

Building your circuit

Now that your reader assembly is ready, you can complete the rest of the circuit. The schematic diagram in Figure 9-8 shows how the reader is connected. It's a fairly simple connection, requiring only four wires to the Arduino! The rest of the connections go to the LED and relay.

The parts layout diagram in Figure 9-9 shows how to connect everything on your breadboard. Note that two wires trail off to the top. Here is where you could connect something to the relay so that you can switch it on and off. The relay circuit is optional, of course. To start out, you may only want an indicator LED. You can always add the relay later.

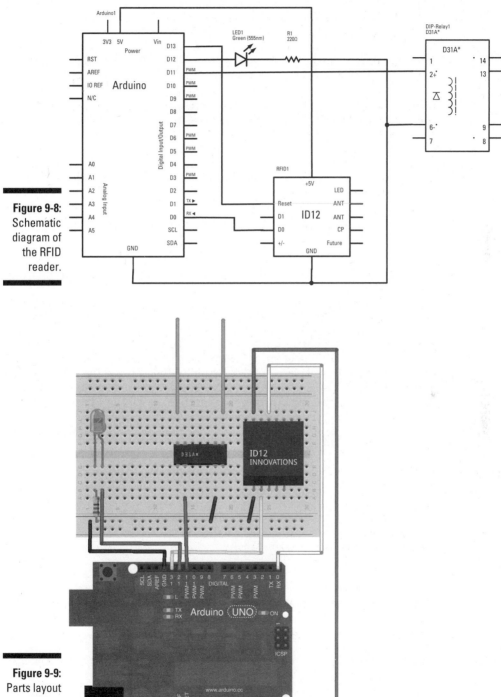

Figure 9-8:
Schematic
diagram of
the RFID
reader.

Figure 9-9:
Parts layout
on your
breadboard.

Programming your RFID reader

After you've built the circuit on your breadboard, you can send your code (download it from the companion website at www.dummies.com/go/arduinoprojectsfordummies). But to get it to work right, take a look at it before uploading. You need to set it up with the correct RFID tag ID before it will work with your LED and relay. Most RFID tags do not come with any indication of what their unique ID is. Fortunately, you can use the serial monitor to figure out what ID is encoded on your tag.

Take a look at the code to see how you do this before you upload your code to your Arduino and test your reader.

Variable declarations

You start with four variables:

```
const int relayPin = 11;
const int ledPin = 12;
const int RFIDResetPin = 13;
const int relayOntime = 5000;
```

These four *integer constants* hold the values that don't change in your program (and are hence "constant"). You're using three digital pins on the Arduino for this project. Two control output to the LED and the relay, respectively. The third is a reset pin. The reader doesn't automatically reset itself to be able to read the next tag, so you have to tell it specifically that you are ready to do that by sending a reset signal on this pin. You simply toggle it HIGH and LOW. The last constant sets how long you want to operate the relay, once a tag is detected.

Next, you add several *char arrays* that store the ID numbers:

```
char tag1[13] = "3B00DDBF9FB6";  // Your scanned tag ID goes here
char tag2[13] = "010203AABBCC";  // these are example Iag IDs only
char tag3[13] = "020304BBCCDD";  // these are example Iag IDs only
// etc. for more tags
....
```

I've shown three tags here, as an example, but you can add many more, limited only by the memory on your Arduino. The tags consist of 13 bytes of data consisting of 12 values, plus an end-of-line character (which *char arrays* usually have as the last character).

The IDs are stored as *hexadecimal numbers,* not the regular *decimal* numbers from 0–9. Hex numbers include the values for 10–15 as the letters A through

F. So, each single digit in the ID represents a number from 0–15 (in decimal terms).

Note that these IDs are just examples. You need to replace them with your own, which you probably don't know yet. That's why the code includes a way to show your tag IDs. However, you can't leave them out altogether. You need to have at least one char array because the main code expects there to be one to which to compare any new tag. So leave these in place, even if you don't know your ID yet. You can substitute the correct value(s) for your tag later.

Setup

Now you are ready to set up your Arduino running environment for reading tags. Take a look at the next part of the code. It should seem pretty familiar if you've done any of the other projects in this book already:

```
void setup(){
  Serial.begin(9600);
  pinMode(RFIDResetPin, OUTPUT);
  pinMode(ledPin, OUTPUT);
  pinMode(relayPin, OUTPUT);
  digitalWrite(RFIDResetPin, HIGH);

  Serial.println("Ready.");
}
```

The first line sets up a serial port for communication with your computer at 9600 bps (over the USB port). Both your computer and the RFID reader communicate with your Arduino using the serial communication protocol. Your Arduino's serial port is connected to your USB connection, and the same port is shared with digital Pins 0 and 1. Pin 1 is used to transmit information, and Pin 0 is used to receive information. This is why they are labeled TX and RX. You connected your reader to Pin 0 so that your Arduino can also receive information from the reader on the RX pin. Because you are sharing the serial connection with both your computer and the RFID reader, you need to use the same speed for both your Arduino and the tag reader, which expects to be using 9600.

The three pinMode instructions set your toggle pin (to reset the reader), the LED pin, and the relay pin for output. The `Ready` statement provides confirmation everything went okay.

The main loop

Now you're ready to get on with things. Check out this code for the main loop:

```
void loop(){

  Serial.println("Looking for a tag...");
  char tagString[13];
  int index = 0;
  boolean reading = false;

  while(Serial.available()){
    int readByte = Serial.read();
    if(readByte == 2) reading = true;
     if(readByte == 3) reading = false;
      if(reading && readByte != 2 && readByte != 10 && readByte != 13){
      tagString[index] = readByte;
      index ++;
     }
  }
  checkTag(tagString);
  clearTag(tagString);
  resetReader();
}
```

You want to know that everything is proceeding according to plan, and the "Looking for a tag..." message provides confirmation of this, for every cycle of the loop. You then create a char array called `tagString[]` that holds the 13 bytes of anything that the reader detects and reports to the serial port. You will write each individual byte to this array, one position at a time. To keep track of which byte you are writing in the array, you create the `int` variable called `index`. Every time you write another byte, you will increase it by one. The boolean `reading` keeps track of whether you've been advised there is a new tag to process.

Next is a `while` statement. As long as the condition in parentheses is met, that there is a valid connection from the serial port, and it is receiving data, everything inside its curly brackets is executed. First, you create a local variable to store the next byte that is being read from the serial port with the `Serial.read()` command. The tag reader sends a value of 2 first, if it has a tag ID to report. Otherwise, you'll read a 3. Depending on which it is, you set the boolean value reading to true (if the value is 2) or false (if it's 3).

This is where the real action is:

```
if(reading && readByte != 2 && readByte != 10 && readByte != 13){
  tagString[index] = readByte;
  index ++;
 }
```

The two ampersands && are a *logical* AND, and the != is a *logical* NOT EQUAL TO comparison. This line says that if there is a reading (because the boolean variable reading has been set to true), AND the byte read is not 2, AND also is not 10, AND also is not 13, then do what's in the curly brackets. The values 2, 10, and 13 mean beginning, end, and linefeed, respectively. If the byte is not one of those, then it must be the tag data you're seeking. So, in the next line, you store the value of readByte in the array tagstring[] at the position index. You are keeping track of this index position for each character you read in. The last step is to bump up the index by 1 so that the next stored value will be at the next place in the array.

Remember that array numbering starts from 0, so the first byte is index 0, the second is index 1, and so on through 11 bytes. After you go through all 12 bytes of the ID, each of the bytes you read has its own numbered position in the tagString[] array and you can compare it to your list of valid ID tags.

There are three final steps in the main loop that are done with three *user-defined functions*. The main loop is then closed with its ending curly bracket.

User-defined functions

There are six user-defined functions, some of which are called within other functions. It may seem a bit complicated to branch from one function to the next this way, but it keeps each of your code's operations modular and self-contained, and is good coding practice. You should try to keep your functions as modular as possible, so that if you need to change how a particular function works, you only have to change it in one place, and every time that function is needed it will behave the same way.

The checkTag() function checks whatever is in the tagString[] array (whether or not it's a valid tag), against the list of valid tags. This function accepts a char array as its input. This is specified within the parentheses, where you are *defining* what the function should expect to receive so that it can evaluate it. In this case, that's a char array. In the main loop when you checkTag(tagString), you are *passing* the char array called tagString to this function, so that it can evaluate whatever is in tagString:

```
void checkTag(char tag[]){

  if(strlen(tag) == 0) return;

  if(compareTag(tag, tag1)){
    lightLED();
    triggerRelay();
  }
  else if(compareTag(tag, tag2)){
    lightLED();
```

```
    }
    else if(compareTag(tag, tag3)){
      lightLED();
    } else {
      Serial.println("New tag found: ");
      Serial.println(tag);
      delay(5000);
    }
  }
```

If the length of the string is zero, there's nothing in it. This is not likely to happen, but it's good to be on the safe side. You test this condition with the `strlen()` function. The value of (tag) is whatever char array was just passed to this function. There are two `==` signs because this test is a *logical* IS EQUAL TO evaluation. The `return` means to drop out of this function altogether if there is nothing in the array.

The next `if` statement tests whether the data passed to this function matches one of your stored tags. It uses another user-defined function called `compareTag()`, which takes two char arrays as inputs. It works by comparing two arrays: the one you just read in, and the one stored at the top of your program called `tag1`. I get to the details of how it does this later in this chapter.

If the comparison is valid, you've got a known tag. So you execute the `light LED()` and `triggerRelay()` functions listed in the next code segment.

You then repeat this test for each tag in your variable declarations at the top of the program, `tag2`, `tag3`, and so on. You can add any number of tags that you want to check for in the `else if` test for each one.

If none of those tags checks out, then this must be a new and unrecognized tag. In that case, it's handy to know what its ID number is, so you print this to the serial monitor with the `Serial.prinln` statements. The delay provides five seconds, so you can write it down.

So, let's take a look at how `compareTag()` works. It is a boolean function, so it just returns a value of TRUE or FALSE, no matter what comparison you ask it to do:

```
boolean compareTag(char one[], char two[]){

  if(strlen(one) == 0) return false;
  for(int i = 0; i < 12; i++){
    if(one[i] != two[i]) return false;
  }
  Serial.println("Valid tag found!");
  return true;
}
```

This function takes two char arrays as input (the one you just read and any of the ones in your list of valid tags), and if there is a match it returns the value TRUE to the part of the program that called it (the `checkTag()` function). If the length of the string is zero, there's nothing in it, in which case the function returns a value of FALSE. Again, just to be on the safe side.

Otherwise, the `for` loop goes through each character of the two arrays and compares them. If any one of these characters is not equal to the other one, then the tags do not match, and the comparison is returned as FALSE. However, if you go through all the characters successfully, then the two arrays match and the function returns a value of TRUE. The good news is reported to the serial monitor. And that, friends, is how you compare the two ID numbers.

The `lightLED()` function turns on the digital pin for the led (ledPin), waits for a quarter of a second (250 milliseconds), and then turns it off. That way you will know a valid tag was read, even when your Arduino is no longer connected to a computer:

```
void lightLED(){
  digitalWrite(ledPin, HIGH);
  delay(250);
  digitalWrite(ledPin, LOW);
}
```

The `triggerRelay()` function works the same way but using the `relayPin`, and it holds the relay open for the duration specified by `relayOnTime` in your variable declarations:

```
void triggerRelay(){
  digitalWrite(relayPin, HIGH);  // Turn on the ledPin
  delay(relayOntime);                  // Wait a moment
  digitalWrite(relayPin, LOW);   // Turn off the ledPin
}
```

Then, you clear the `tagString[]` array so that the next reading can be taken, using the `clearTag()` function. It uses a `for` loop to go through each index position of the array that was passed to (which is always `tagString`), and sets the value of each position to zero:

```
void clearTag(char one[]){
  // Clear the tag reading char array by filling it with ASCII 0
  // If not null, it could indicate another tag read
  for(int i = 0; i < strlen(one); i++){
    one[i] = 0;
  }
}
```

With this function, you've effectively erased the tag you just read from memory.

Finally, your `resetReader()` function tells it to get ready for another reading by toggling the reset pin LOW and then HIGH. The delay ensures this was properly achieved, but is probably not really necessary:

```
void resetReader(){
   // Toggle the reset pin so the RFID reader will read again
   digitalWrite(RFIDResetPin, LOW);
   digitalWrite(RFIDResetPin, HIGH);
   delay(150);
}
```

Testing and Setting Your RFID Reader

Now that you've built your reader and you understand the code, the first thing you need to do is test your code and read the code from your RFID tag(s). Remember that the wire connected to digital Pin 0 is also connected to your USB serial port. If you try to send code to your Arduino with this wire attached, it will cause errors, because both your tag reader and your USB connection will be writing to the same serial port. You don't want your reader to be sending stray data on that connection while you are uploading your sketch to your Arduino.

To avoid problems uploading your code, *always* disconnect the wire on Pin 0 before uploading your code and then reconnect it after you've confirmed the transfer.

If you forget this, it won't damage anything, but you probably will get orange error messages and have to restart your Arduino or your Arduino IDE, or both!

So, disconnect that wire and then upload your program. Then reconnect the wire and click on the serial monitor in your Arduino IDE. Scan your tag over the ID Innovations reader, as shown in Figure 9-10. I'm holding my hand about three to five centimeters above the reader.

Because you probably won't have this tag listed in your code yet, something like Figure 9-11 should appear. The new tag ID is printed to the screen in hexadecimal numbers. Write down this number so you can add it as a valid tag in your variable declarations later. Also, you should get any other tags you want to track and do the same.

Figure 9-10:
Scanning
an unknown
tag.

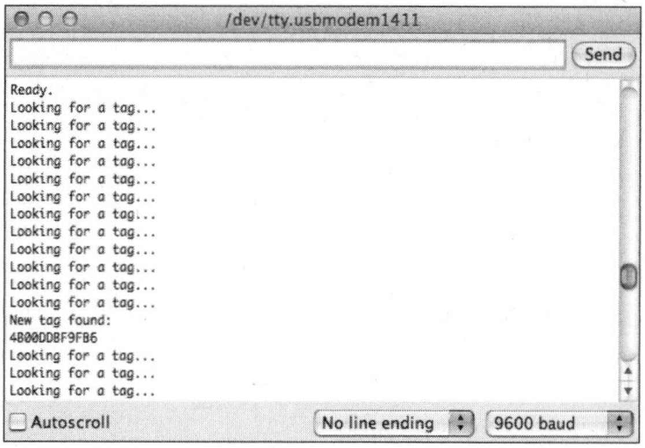

Figure 9-11:
Getting the
value of an
unknown
tag in
the serial
monitor.

After you've completed scanning all the tags you want to track, edit the
tag[] arrays:

```
char tag1[13] = "0123456789AB";
```

Change the numbers in the quotation marks to be the hexadecimal value of your tag. There should only be 12 digits. Occasionally, you may see a stray number at the very end, but ignore that if it occurs. Keep going until you've added new arrays for every tag ID you want to track.

Make sure to also update the `checkTag()` function at the end of your code, so that it checks the same number of tags you've stored at the beginning of your program.

Now, disconnect your tag reader from Pin 0, upload your new code, and check whether it works. You should see something similar to Figure 9-12. Your LED should also turn on for a moment, and your relay will activate. To be sure, you can connect your multimeter to its wires to see whether they've been connected.

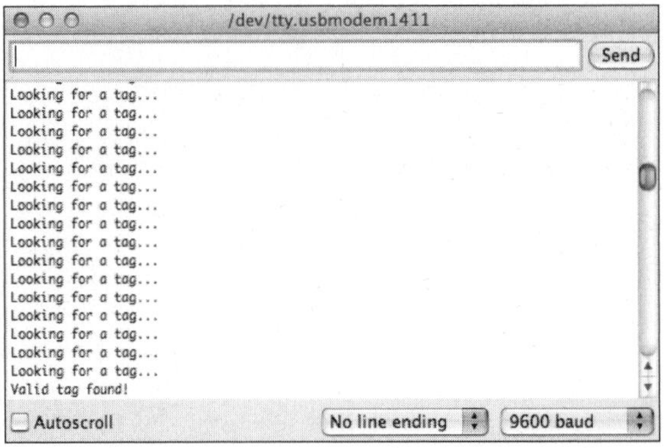

Figure 9-12:
Reading a
valid tag
successfully.

```
/dev/tty.usbmodem1411

Looking for a tag...
Looking for a tag...
Looking for a tag...
Looking for a tag...
Looking for a tag...
Looking for a tag...
Looking for a tag...
Looking for a tag...
Looking for a tag...
Looking for a tag...
Looking for a tag...
Looking for a tag...
Looking for a tag...
Looking for a tag...
Looking for a tag...
Valid tag found!

Autoscroll          No line ending    9600 baud
```

Now you're ready to start tagging, scanning, opening, closing, and activating. If you're like me, you won't hesitate to start tagging . . . and bragging!

Chapter 10

Building an Automated Garden

*H*ow many plants do you have to kill before you decide you need a help-ing hand? I went through three or four before guilt took over. When my wife's new miniature olive tree bit the dust, my creative tinkering hat went on. An Arduino is perfect for patiently — really patiently — waiting for some-thing to happen and then responding quickly and reliably.

I whipped up this system to prevent more plants from going to the great com-post heap in the sky. Even though my wife and I see the tree every day, we sometimes forget to water it. But my trusty Arduino is keeping the new olive tree happy.

Having your Arduino stand in for you as a plant minder can also be handy if you are going on an extended trip and won't be around to make sure your plants don't get too parched.

You can download schematics and full-color parts placement diagrams from the companion website (www.dummies.com/go/arduinoprojectsfor dummies).

Creating a Watering System

In this project, you build a system to automatically water a houseplant when the soil in its pot becomes dry. To monitor your plant's hydration, you use inexpensive and readily available materials to whip up a simple homemade sensor that measures soil moisture (also known as soil moisture *tension*). This sensor is inserted into the soil of the thirsty plant. You calibrate this sensor to tell your Arduino when to water it.

The water comes from a homemade reservoir made from a 2-liter soft drink bottle that you mount above your plant. You run a water supply tube from the bottle to your plant. You program your Arduino so that when your sensor detects that the soil is too dry, it opens an electronic *solenoid valve* that is inline with the supply tube.

The 2-liter supply should be enough to keep your plant going for a long time, and you can refill the reservoir every week or so, depending on how thirsty your plant is. You can extend this system easily to monitor multiple plants and water them independently.

Selecting Your Parts

Figure 10-1 shows the parts you need for this project. Aside from the electronic components, most of these are readily available at hardware stores and home centers.

Your Arduino can control up to six plant irrigators independently. The parts listed here are enough to build one sensor and one mechanism. If you want to water more plants (up to six), you should get all the extra accessory parts for the sensors and the watering reservoir.

Your exact requirements depend on how many plants you are monitoring and whether you want to use a single 2-liter reservoir. Here's what you should get:

- An Arduino
- A thirsty plant
- A 9–12V DC, 1 amp power transformer for your Arduino
- A length of 2-conductor, low voltage wire (22–24 AWG) to run power from your transformer to your project box and solenoid valve (not shown)
- A very small plant pot filled with rice
- A small enclosure for your Arduino

For each sensor, you need:

- A 10kΩ resistor
- A length of two-conductor, low voltage wire (not shown)
- A very short length of 15mm (⅝ in.) outside diameter (OD) clear vinyl tube (not shown)

✔ Two 50mm (2-in.) galvanized finishing nails

✔ About 50g (⅛ cup) measure of plaster of Paris (calcium sulfate hemihydrate) such as DAP Brand plaster of Paris or Herculite 2 (Formula brand) (not shown)

✔ Adhesive tape

For each irrigator and reservoir:

✔ A TIP120/TIP121 power transistor

✔ A 1N4001 or similar diode

✔ Two pin headers

✔ A 12V DC 2-port water/air solenoid valve, such as SMC part number VDW21-6G-2-M5-Q (such as RS#701-3233). See Figure 10-2.

✔ Two male parallel threaded elbow connectors, M5x6mm. See Figure 10-2.

✔ About a meter (3 ft.) of 6mm (¼-in.) outside diameter (OD) flexible nylon tube (such as Newark # 95M4630 or RS #386-6190)

✔ A 2-liter beverage bottle and a small to medium plant pot to use as a stand for it (not shown)

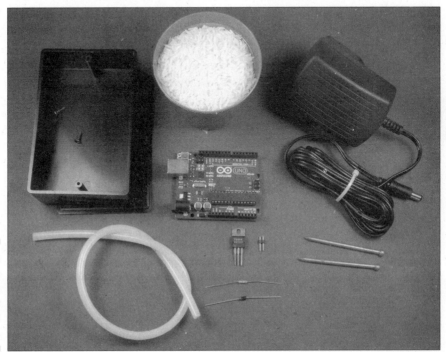

Figure 10-1:
Some of the key parts you may need for this project.

It doesn't matter which Arduino you use for this project. I used an Arduino Uno. Any thirsty plant will do, but ideally one that has a fearsome thirst to satisfy.

The power supply should be rated at 9–12V DC. It needs to supply the needs of both your Arduino and your solenoid valve(s). Your Arduino needs 500mA to operate, and each solenoid will need about 300mA. Combined with the Arduino, that's a current requirement of 800mA. You will only ever actuate one valve at a time, so that means your power supply needs to provide a minimum output of 800mA. It's okay to use one with a higher rating, but if you use a lower rating, there won't be enough power to operate everything and your Arduino may reset when the valve activates.

The two-conductor wires can be used for both your sensors and powering your valves. The kind with a "figure 8" profile is easy to cut and work with. You should estimate running one wire pair from each sensor to the Arduino and a second wire pair to power your solenoid(s). Adding all these distances determines the length of wire you need for your whole system.

You need to buy the correct quantity of parts for the number of sensors and irrigators that you want to build. For the sensor(s), the only electronic component you need is a 10kΩ resistor (and the wire). You need the larger vinyl hose, the galvanized nails, plaster of Paris, and adhesive tape to build the sensor itself. Make sure to get galvanized nails because the protective zinc coating prevents them from rusting. They'll be embedded in moist soil, so this is sure to happen if you use ordinary nails. You use the rice and the small plant pot to help you build the sensors. Afterward, you can eat the rice as a tasty snack.

The solenoid valve (see Figure 10-2) does the work of controlling the flow of water from the reservoir to your plant. It has an electromagnetic coil inside that opens a tiny valve mechanism when powered up. They are used for a huge number of industrial applications for controlling fluids or compressed air. A familiar example is the fountain beverage dispenser, which controls the flow of syrup and carbonated water into your soft drink cup when you (or a bartender) press the button. They are fast, quiet, and relatively inexpensive and come in a huge number of types, styles, and options. Make sure that there are two ports (for water in and water out) and that they are the right size for your supply tube. The valve in this project has M5 size threads, and you use threaded elbow adaptors to attach your water supply line to the valve. One side of the adaptor has threads that match the valve and the other has a push-fitting (6mm) into which you simply insert your water line. The other consideration for the valve is its electrical rating. The valve in the parts list from RS components is rated for 24V DC but will operate at 12V DC. If you have difficulty obtaining this exact valve, any one will do, as long as its power requirement matches your power supply and its ports match your supply lines.

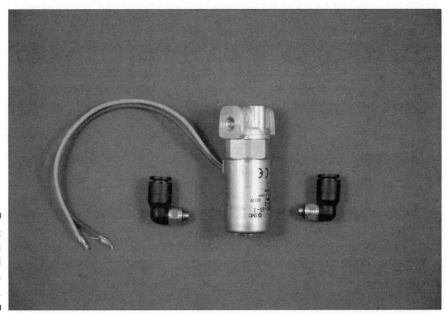

Figure 10-2:
A solenoid valve and supply line adaptors.

Each solenoid valve and water reservoir requires its own set of electronic parts. The *discrete components,* such as the transistor, diode, and resistors, control the power for each solenoid valve. Each connection requires a pair of pin headers so that you can connect the power wire to your Arduino. The number of valves is up to you, but you need at least one for each water reservoir. You could also build a single, larger reservoir with multiple solenoid valves attached to it and likewise, you could attach multiple plants to a single sensing/irrigation system. It's up to you and your plants to determine what's best. You also need flexible nylon/plastic tubing that runs from your reservoir(s) to your plant(s). You can buy this from the suppliers listed earlier, but you may be able to get both this and the larger tubing for the sensors from a well-stocked pet supply store. These parts are often used for fish tanks.

In addition to the usual, small hand tools that are part of your workbench setup (listed in Chapter 2), you will also need a small hand drill and 6mm (¼-in.) general purpose drill bit, or some other way of drilling a neat hole into the cap of the 2-liter bottle.

Building Your System

To build the system, you need to construct your sensors, fabricate and assemble the reservoir and valve assembly, and run the supply line(s). When you've got the system working and tested, you can set up the code and calibrate it.

Building your moisture sensor

The moisture sensor is simply a block of gypsum with two galvanized nails in it. When the soil is dry, the block is dry and there is infinite resistance between the two nails (or *probes,* if you want to sound technical). When the soil is wet, some of the moisture penetrates into the block and between the two nails, allowing electrons to pass between the probes. You measure this electron flow by using an analog pin on your Arduino. The more water, the lower the resistance. When the soil is completely wet, there will be little or zero resistance. You use the range of values measured on your analog pin to determine whether or not it's time to water the plant.

You wouldn't want to use this system to measure a precise value for soil moisture because after the plaster gets moist, its resistance drops very low. This is not good for measuring gradual changes in soil moisture (say for plotting a graph), but it's fine for simply determining when to water your plant.

To build the probes, you attach wires to your nails and insert them into a mold made from the vinyl tube. If you are going to build several probes, it's a good idea to do them all at once. That way, you only have to mix the plaster once. Make at least a couple of them, so that you have a spare. Plug in your soldering iron and fire up your hot glue gun. If you have a low power soldering iron (under 35 watts) you might not be able to heat the nails hot enough for solder to stick to them. In that case, skip the soldering (Steps 1 and 2) and wrap your wires around the nail heads after your plaster has set.

Do the following steps:

1. **Strip and twist the ends of a piece of your two-conductor wires long enough to reach from your plant to where the Arduino will be sitting.**

2. **Coat the wire ends with a small amount of solder.**

   This is called *tinning* the wire.

3. **One at a time, clamp each nail in your helping hands and apply a lot of heat to the head of the nail with your soldering iron, gradually adding a little bit of solder until it sticks.**

   This step may take 20 to 30 seconds and the nail will get pretty hot. Refer to Figure 10-3.

4. **When the solder is molten on the tip of your nail, add your wire, melting everything together, and hold it there a couple of moments, until the solder hardens.**

5. **When the nails cool, hold them about 5mm (¼-in.) apart and apply some hot glue to the space between them.**

   Doing this prevents them from touching each other when you add them to the plaster mold.

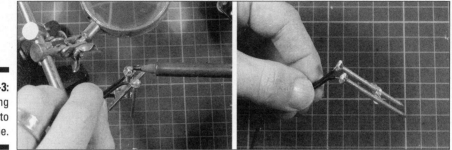

Figure 10-3: Soldering wires to your probe.

To prepare your mold, follow these:

1. **Cut a small section of the large vinyl tube, about 2cm (a half-in.) longer than your nails, as shown in Figure 10-4.**

2. **Make a vertical slice in your tube so that it will be easy to remove from the hardened plaster.**

3. **Place a piece of tape on the bottom of the tube to prevent plaster escaping from the bottom of the tube.**

   The tape also holds its sides together.

4. **Gently press the tube into the pot of rice, which holds it upright while the plaster sets, as shown in Figure 10-5.**

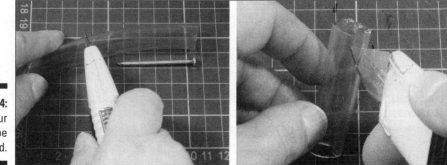

Figure 10-4: Cutting your vinyl tube mold.

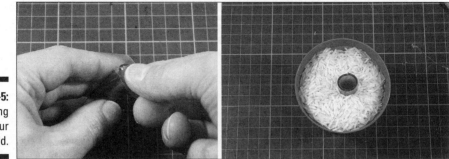

Figure 10-5:
Applying
tape to your
mold.

5. **Use a disposable stick and a paper cup to mix your plaster at a ratio of two parts of plaster to one part of water.**

   Fifty grams (⅛ cup) of plaster will make enough for two probes. Mix it until it's nice and smooth. Wait for a minute or two so the plaster starts to set a bit. It should be the consistency of thin pudding.

6. **Carefully fill the vinyl tube(s) with the plaster, leaving about 5mm (¼-in.) at the top, since some plaster will be forced up the tube when you put in the nails, as shown in Figure 10-6.**

7. **Insert the nails into the plaster and hold them there for a minute or two while it thickens.**

   Make sure they are vertically centered in the tube and they don't touch the sides. You can use a small block of wood to hold the wire in place while the plaster sets, or rest the wire on the side of the plant pot.

8. **After an hour, remove the probe and peel off the vinyl tube, as shown in Figure 10-7. It can be discarded or saved to make more probes.**

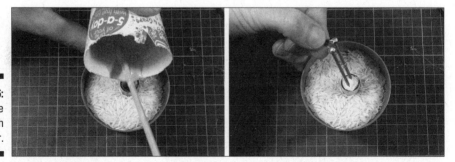

Figure 10-6:
Filling the
mold with
plaster.

9. **If you are using the twist-on method to attach your wires, strip about an inch of insulation off the wires and gently wrap each wire around one nail head, as shown in Figure 10-8.**

10. **Apply a neat coating of hot glue to the top of your probe. Refer to Figure 10-9.**

   This protects it from getting wet on top and provides strain relief for the wire.

Figure 10-7:
Removing
your probe
from the
mold.

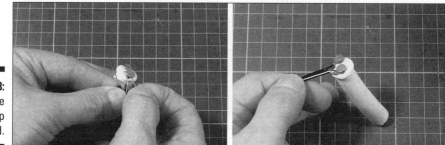

Figure 10-8:
Using the
wire wrap
method.

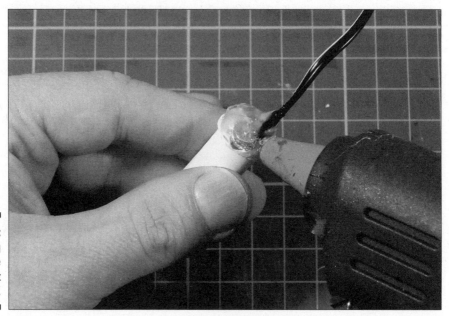

Figure 10-9:
Finishing
your probe
with hot
glue.

The plaster needs time to set fully so it will be completely hard and dry. You need to ensure that it's dry before you calibrate the probe to your Arduino. Set aside the probe(s) to dry for a good 24 hours. This is a good time to get on with building the reservoir and writing the code.

Building your reservoir

The water reservoir is cheap and simple to make. The only tricky part is drilling into the cap. You need to use a small hand drill or a power drill to do this. I use a 6mm wood drill bit, which goes through the plastic pretty easily. You could more easily bore a hole into the side of the bottle, but the bottle walls are very thin, so your hose won't be very secure. To build the reservoir, complete the following steps:

1. **Drill a hole into the bottle cap, as shown in Figure 10-10.**

   Drill slowly so that the downward pressure from your drill will prevent the cap from spinning or flying across the room.

2. **Insert one end of the plastic tubing into the cap so that a short amount protrudes on the interior side of the cap, as shown in Figure 10-11.**

   This should form a snug fit.

3. **On the underside of the cap, apply a small mountain of hot glue heaped up on the sides of the tube.**

   Be careful not to get any glue into the threads of the cap, or the very bottom flange where the cap makes a seal. Otherwise, it will leak!

4. **Apply a similar amount of glue on the outside and hold the tube firmly until the glue cools.**

5. **Poke a small hole into the bottom of the bottle, which will allow air to get inside when it is inverted.**

   Otherwise, the gravity feed won't work very well because a vacuum will build up in the top half of the bottle.

6. **Cut a hole in the bottom of your medium plastic plant pot, which acts as a support for your two-liter bottle. See Figure 10-12.**

7. **If needed, cut a hole out of the side of your pot so that the tube can pass through.**

When you've finished fabrication, install your reservoir onto your base to check the fit, as shown in Figure 10-12. For the ultimate test, fill the bottle with water, covering the small hole in the bottom. Screw on your supply line assembly and invert it to check for leaks.

Figure 10-10:
Drilling a hole for your supply line.

Figure 10-11:
Inserting the
supply line.

Figure 10-12:
Fitting the
reservoir
onto the
base.

Running the water supply

Determine exactly where you want to place the irrigation system. For the gravity feed system to work, your water supply reservoir needs to be elevated above the plant that you want to water. You may need to place it on a small box or shelf to achieve the correct height.

You need to determine a suitable location for your solenoid valve. It doesn't matter too much where you put it, so long as you can mount it to a stable surface. You also need to make sure that your control wires are long enough to reach your Arduino. I mounted mine to the Arduino enclosure itself, so I used the existing wires on the valve.

You can now measure the correct distance for your supply lines. Cut the tubing to the desired length to reach the place where your valve is located and from there to the bottom of your plant pot. Make sure to run the output line to the bottom of your plant pot — that's where the roots are located!

Building the breadboard circuit

This project has a very simple schematic, shown in Figure 10-13. It consists of a voltage divider circuit that is connected to your Arduino's analog pin and an actuator circuit connected to a digital pin, which switches the power to your solenoid valve on and off.

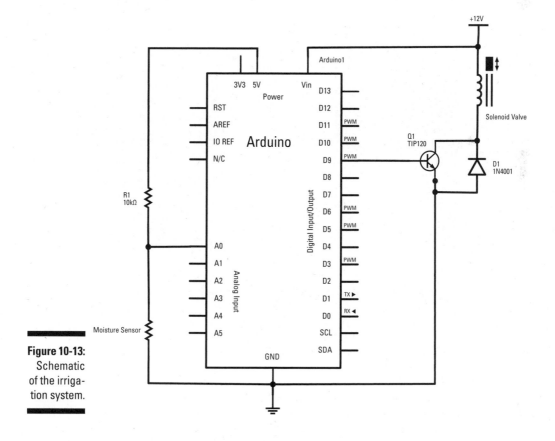

Figure 10-13: Schematic of the irrigation system.

The parts placement diagram in Figure 10-14 shows the setup for 1 sensor and 1 solenoid valve, but you can extend it to accommodate up to 6 sensors on an Arduino Uno — and if you are feeling really ambitious, up to 15 on an Arduino Mega!

When you've completed the wiring and testing, you can build this project on a half-size breadboard and fit everything into your enclosure, as shown in Figure 10-15. I've made an "Arduino sandwich" by stacking the breadboard underneath the Arduino inside the enclosure. You need to drill a couple of small holes for your power supply line and your sensor leads, so make sure to get an enclosure you can cut into easily with the tools at your disposal. A small 7.5 x 10 x 5cm (3" x 4" x 2") ABS plastic or wood enclosure should be sufficient to fit both the breadboard and your Arduino.

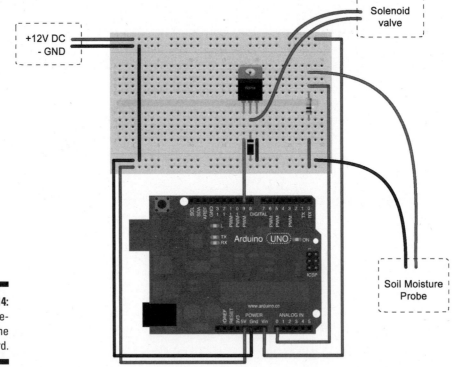

Figure 10-14:
Parts place-
ment on the
breadboard.

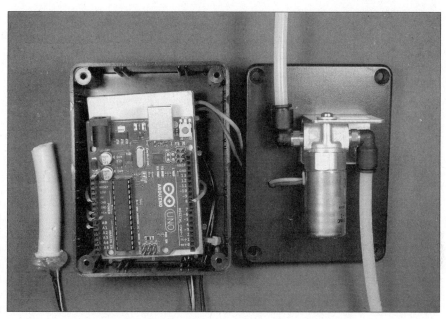

Figure 10-15:
Putting
everything
into an
enclosure.

Coding, Calibrating, and Testing

The code for this project is pretty short and sweet. Now that you've got the components in place on your breadboard, check out this code, so you know how it works. Then, set your values as explained below and upload them to your Arduino.

In the first section, you declare your variables:

```
int sensorPin = A0;
int valvePin = 9;

const int dryThreshold = 900;
const long sampleInterval = 6000000;
const int irrigationTime = 5000;

boolean DEBUG=true;
```

The sensor is connected to analog Pin 0, and appropriately named. The valve is connected to digital Pin 9. If you have more than one valve or more than one sensor, you can simply add additional variables to handle them.

The integer value `dryThreshold` specifies the point of dryness at which you want your Arduino to take action. When the value from A0 is higher than this value, the irrigation is triggered.

The `sampleInterval` variable is used to delay the time between readings. There's no need to constantly check the analog port because timing isn't very critical. Evaporation is a slow process, so your probe dries out over hours or days.

You use `irrigationTime` to specify in milliseconds how long the water will be allowed to flow. You determine this value during testing and calibration.

I usually include a Boolean variable called `DEBUG` in my code. In most circumstances, the only way to see what's going on your Arduino (such as values of variables or readings) is to print statements to the serial port using the `Serial.println()` command. But you don't need to do this after you've perfected your code. No need to be clogging up the serial port (or even using it at all) once the bugs are worked out. If you place all of your debugging statements within a conditional `if` statement that is contingent on `DEBUG` being true, you can ensure they are executed only when you are debugging. You simply change the debug value to false when you are done testing. This is a matter of style really, but it can be very handy if you are building a project that uses the serial port for communication, in which you want to be able to debug the code as well.

Defining the setup

In the `setup()` section of your code, you prepare the Arduino to run the system.

```
void setup(){
  if(DEBUG){Serial.begin(9600);}

  pinMode(sensorPin, INPUT);
  pinMode(valvePin, OUTPUT);
  digitalWrite(valvePin, LOW);
}
```

The `if` statement checks whether you have set the `DEBUG` Boolean to be true and if so, activates the serial port.

You then use the `pinMode` function to tell the Arduino to use the `sensorPin` for input and the `valvePin` for output.

Make sure that the valve is closed when you fire up the sketch, so you do that with the last line in setup, using `digitalWrite()` to set `valvePin` to LOW explicitly.

Running the main loop

You only need your Arduino to check the sensor and, if the soil is too dry, release the floodgate(s). The main loop operates as follows:

1. **Take a reading from Analog Pin 0.**

2. **Compare this reading to the threshold value.**

3. **If the reading value is higher than the dryness threshold, activate the digital pin for the solenoid valve.**

4. **Wait for a few seconds.**

5. **Close the valve.**

6. **Wait until the next sample time and then start at the beginning.**

Here's the code:

```
void loop() {

  int sensorValue = analogRead(sensorPin);

  if(DEBUG){
    Serial.print("Sensor value: ");
    Serial.println(sensorValue);
  }

  if (sensorValue>dryThreshold){
    digitalWrite(valvePin, HIGH); // Open the water valve
    delay(irrigationTime);        // Keep it open for the irrigation time
    digitalWrite(valvePin, LOW);  // Close the valve
  }
  delay(sampleInterval);  // wait until the next time to take a reading
}
```

You use the local integer variable `sensorValue` to store a reading from the variable `sensorPin`, which you *initialized* as analog Pin 0.

The next statement checks whether you have set the `DEBUG` Boolean to be true and if so, prints out the reading taken to the serial port.

The conditional `if` statement then tests whether the reading taken from Analog Pin 0 is lower or higher than the dryness level specified by `dryThreshold`. If is higher, then the valve is opened by applying a voltage to the `valvePin`. This causes the transistor to switch the valve on, and water can flow. The duration of flow was set by `irrigationTime`. After this time has elapsed, the valve is closed by writing `valvePin` to a LOW condition.

The last statement tells the Arduino to wait for the `sampleInterval` duration, after which the next reading needs to be taken and the process starts all over.

Calibrating the sensor and flow rate

Now that your code is up and running, tweak it for your specific plant(s). You need to determine the range of values your sensor will obtain and the flow rate of your irrigation unit.

When you've added the preceding code, set the `sampleInterval` variable to something short, say 100 milliseconds, so that you can watch your sensor's output and upload it to the board.

When the code starts, open your serial monitor and take note of the readings. If your probe is bone dry, the sensor value should be at or near 1023, indicating infinite resistance. If it is something else, or something very low, you have a problem with your wiring or your probe. It should be very dry. Try another probe (remember the spare you made?) and see whether you have the same problem. If you do, check your connections and test again.

Now, grab a short glass of water and dunk your sensor in it. Make sure that there's no chance that the leads on the top of the sensor are exposed to the water, or you'll have a short circuit and nothing will be measured.

Now observe the readings reported from your probe, which should be gradually declining. Recall that the values measured on analog pins range from 0 to 1023. This range corresponds to the value of the voltage present on a pin, from 0 to 5 volts. If there is more resistance due to drier soil, there is less current flow and consequently, a low-measured voltage due to the relatively high resistance of dry soil. This value could be over 1000. If there is less resistance between your probes, more current will flow between them. Therefore, the measured voltage will be higher. A high-measured voltage means the soil is very wet and conducting electricity well. In this case, the value is not likely to go to zero, but will be in the low hundreds. In my tests, the sensors started at 1023 and declined over about two minutes to 110 or thereabouts.

Now that you've observed your sensor in action, remove it from the water and allow it to dry out. Depending on your ambient atmospheric conditions, your probe should dry out fully in a few hours and your readings should be back up to 1023.

Meanwhile, fill up your reservoir (making sure to cover the air vent in the bottom with your finger), screw in the cap, and hold your finger over the end of the tube. Now water your plant manually and count how many seconds it takes to give it a good soak. Make a note of that number and set the irrigationTime variable to be that number in milliseconds. My plant takes about 7 seconds to water, so that's 7000 milliseconds.

With a bit of testing, you can write the code differently, so that the flow shuts off after the sensorPin detects a wet condition, but it takes several seconds for the sensor to report this, so there is a danger you could overfill your plant pot while you are still waiting for your sensor to report that it's wet. To be on the safe side, I simply set a fixed value.

With everything tested and calibrated, you can set your Arduino free from the computer. Install the enclosure near your plant and plug in the power. Make sure to place the probe deep into the soil so that the moisture measurement will be taken from close to the roots (see Figure 10-16). But don't bury it entirely; otherwise you might get a short circuit from water touching the leads on the tops of the nails.

Figure 10-16:
The irrigation system in its jungle home — our kitchen window!

Adding more valves

If you are irrigating more than one plant, you can do it without adding additional power supplies. You can power all your solenoids from a single supply, so long as you do them sequentially. You probably don't need to water all the plants at once, so you can actuate the valves one at a time. This means that you don't have to use a bigger power supply. If you tried to power them all at once, your Arduino would have an undercurrent condition and nothing would happen.

Now sit back, relax, and enjoy the grow!

Chapter 11

Building a Tweeting Pet Door

In This Chapter

▶ Using Hall-effect sensors

▶ Attaching an Ethernet shield to your Arduino

▶ Using the Twitter library

▶ Sending a tweet

*W*ith everyone sending tweets these days, it only makes sense that your pet should be able to do the same! This project provides a (somewhat) credible excuse to create a Twitter account for your pet and has the practical benefit that you can see when your pet is in or out, even when you're not at home. I have an indoor/outdoor cat, who comes and goes as he pleases. Living in the city, we sort of want to be sure that he is safe and know what he is up to at any given time. What better way than to use the Internet to provide a data feed of his comings and goings?

In this project, you modify your pet door with sensors that detect when a magnet passes by them. A magnet mounted to the pet door flap triggers these sensors when your cat or dog (or badger) is entering or leaving. Your Arduino uses this signal to select a random message and sends this directly to Twitter as a tweet. You won't need to leave a computer connected to your Arduino — everything is self-contained onboard. Also, many examples on the Internet use an intermediary server to log in to Twitter and post your tweet. If the server goes down, you can't send tweets. The great thing about this project is that your Arduino communicates directly with Twitter, with no need to rely on an intermediary server.

After you finish this project, you'll be able to detect when your pet enters or leaves the house using Hall-effect sensors. You learn how to connect your Arduino to your home network and the Internet, which can be useful for other Internet-related projects of your own design.

Selecting Your Parts

The tweeting pet door detects your pet using a magnet and two magnetic sensors, called Hall-effect sensors. When the door swings inward or outward, the magnetic field alters the flow of electrons inside the sensors and varies an output voltage. You measure this voltage to detect when the door has been moved.

Figure 11-1 shows the parts you need for this project (except the pet door). I built it using a breadboard first, but then moved it to its own housing near the router, which is under the sofa.

Here's what you need to start the project:

✔ An Arduino Uno

✔ An Arduino Ethernet shield (many suppliers carry these, including sparkfun.com, shop.arduino.cc, coolcomponents.co.uk, and oomlout.co.uk)

✔ A pet door, available from your local pet supply center or online (not shown)

✔ A linear Hall-effect sensor, such as Allegro A1324 (Digikey 620-1432-ND, RS Online 680-7507), in a single in-line package (SIP)

✔ Several feet of 4-conductor wire, 22 AWG or similar (Radio Shack, Maplin)

✔ Four pin headers

✔ A small (3-5mm), strong magnet, such as a neodymium magnet (try eBay)

✔ A short Ethernet cable (not shown)

✔ A 7-12V DC power adaptor for your Arduino

✔ A suitable housing, if you want to keep the dust off of your Arduino and Ethernet shield (SparkFun PRT-09682, Farnell 1848692)

✔ Two small pieces of wood block or discarded plastic (2cm cubes), such as a LEGO block (not shown)

✔ Pet treats! (not shown)

Of course, you need some tools for the project — your wire stripper and side cutters, hot glue gun and glue, and your "helping hands" clamp. I'm assuming that you are working with an Arduino Uno, Ethernet shield, and the latest version of the IDE. The current versions of the hardware and IDE are the most reliable.

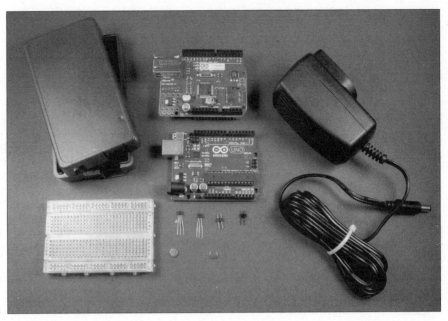

Figure 11-1:
The parts
you need for
this project.

If you don't already have a pet door, it's a bit easier to do this project because you can attach the sensors before you mount the door. But this project can be retrofitted onto any pet door you might already have.

The two Hall-effect sensors measure the strength of a magnetic field and give an output that depends upon the product you are using. You can find many types of Hall-effect sensors, and they can provide digital or analog output. You can find some that are *latching,* which means that they stay locked in the last magnetic polarity reading taken (north or south) until they are unlocked by a magnetic field in the opposite direction. You should not get a latching sensor, because of the way you'll be mounting the triggering magnets. I chose linear Hall-effect sensors because they can be used without any additional components like resistors or capacitors, making it very easy to build.

If you're like me, the pet door is far away from your router. You need several feet of wire to run between the sensors mounted to your door and the Arduino. You use two sensors, each with its own output signal, and you need to supply power and ground. That's a total of four conductors you need in the cable. Because it's a low power circuit, you could use spare telephone cable or Ethernet network cable that you might have handy. Otherwise, any inexpensive, small gauge (22 AWG or higher) 4-conductor cable will do nicely.

You need a small (3-5mm), strong magnet to trigger the Hall-effect sensors. I suggest you get a neodymium magnet, one of those nickel-plated, extremely strong magnets you may have seen before. They are widely available and inexpensive. I usually get mine on eBay. You mount the sensors and the magnet to the side of your pet door. Use hot glue to provide a firm grip. It has the side benefit of being waterproof, so you don't have to worry about moisture ruining your sensors. I always say "hot glue is man's best friend" (besides your pet, of course!).

Because there are no buttons to press or other interactions with the Arduino itself, you can hide it behind the sofa where nobody will see it. So the housing doesn't have to be snazzy. But you might want to put your Arduino and shield into a housing to keep the dust off. You could simply use a small cardboard box or mini Pringles canister.

The pet treats are to lure him or her through the door for testing and final launch!

The lines of magnetic flux must be perpendicular to the plate in the Hall-effect sensor. You will test your neodymium magnet to determine its correct orientation.

You can download schematics and full-color parts placement diagrams from the companion website (`www.dummies.com/go/arduinoprojectsfor dummies`).

Testing Your Circuit

Before you jump into mounting everything on the pet door and running sensor wires, start by wiring up your circuit on a breadboard to get the threshold values. Follow the parts placement diagram in Figure 11-2.

First, stack the Ethernet shield on top of your Arduino. The pins on the bottom of the shield fit into the matching pin headers on your Arduino. It should slide into the pin headers smoothly but securely. Be careful not to bend any of the shield's pins when you're seating it. The pin sockets on your Ethernet shield are now directly connected to your Arduino below it. Next add your two Hall-effect sensors to the Analog0 and Analog1 pins of your Arduino and connect the power, ground, and signal leads.

Make sure that you place your Hall-effect sensors in the correct orientation. The beveled side printed with text is the front of the sensor. Make sure to connect your +5 volt supply to the leftmost pin, as viewed from the front. Otherwise, the sensor will get very hot and will most likely be permanently damaged! If you are using one that's not in the parts list, make sure to check its datasheet for the correct pinouts.

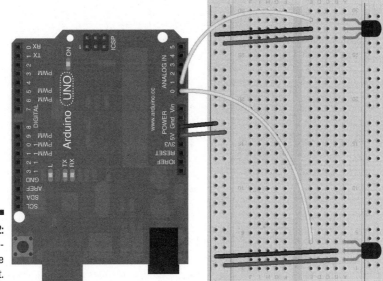

Figure 11-2:
Parts place-
ment for the
test circuit.

The A1324 sensors provide a linear output and require 5V, provided by your Arduino. When no magnetic field is detected, they provide an output voltage of one-half the input voltage, or about 2.5V. When the north pole of your magnet gets close to the sensor, the voltage increases to around 5V. When the south pole of the magnet gets close, the voltage drops to near zero. You use this property to detect when your cat or dog moves the pet flap.

The first step is to test your setup to get the threshold values that you are receiving from the Hall-effect sensors. By doing this, you can make sure that your sensors work correctly before you install them. Use the following code to test your sensors:

```
/*  Chapter 11
    Sketch to test Hall effect sensors for a tweeting pet door
 */

const int entryPin = A0;   // Define the input pin for entry sensor
const int exitPin = A1;    // Define the input pin for the exit sensor
int entryValue = 0;  // Define variable to store the entry value
int exitValue = 0;   // Define variable to store the exit value
```

```
void setup() {
  Serial.begin(9600);  // Open a serial connection to display the data
  pinMode(entryPin, INPUT);
  pinMode(exitPin, INPUT);
}

void loop() {
  entryValue = analogRead(entryPin); // Read the value from entry sensor
  exitValue = analogRead(exitPin);    // Read the value from exit sensor
  Serial.print("Sensor values: ");
  Serial.print(entryValue); // Print the entry sensor value
  Serial.print(", ");
  Serial.println(exitValue); // Print the exit
  delay(1000);  // Wait a moment, so we can read what's been printed
}
```

This code is pretty simple. First, you define two variables for the entry and exit pins. Their value is not going to change, so they are defined as integer constants. You then declare two integers to read the values from the Hall-effect sensors. The signal pin of each sensor outputs a voltage that is sent to the Analog0 and Analog1 pins.

The ATmega328 contains an onboard 6-channel analog-to-digital (A/D) converter, with 10-bit resolution (1024 values), which means the effective voltage resolution is about 0.004 volts.

The Arduino reads the voltage on the analog input pins and converts this to a numerical value from 0–1023. The input voltage to the Hall-effect sensors is at a constant 5V and they are designed so that when no magnetic field is detected, they output about 2.5V. When the south pole passes nearby, the input voltage drops low, and the Arduino assigns a numerical value closer to zero. When the north pole passes nearby, the value rises toward 1023. You use this change of value to determine when to send a tweet. Now test your setup to read the output values and make sure everything works correctly, as shown in Figure 11-3.

Click on the Serial Monitor button on in the Arduino IDE (the magnifying glass at the upper right), which will open up the output monitor so that you can see the printed values. Pass the magnet in front of each sensor and the values should change from the mid-500s to either near zero or near 1023, proportional to how close your magnet gets to the sensor. I had a stack of magnets that I stuck on the end of a drill bit to make them easier to hold. The effective range of the sensors is fairly small — about a centimeter for a really significant reading. Look for the side of the magnet that makes the output value drop toward zero, as shown in Figure 11-4, which shows what happens when you pass the magnet close to the exit sensor. It won't get to zero, since a small voltage still remains present on the analog pin. Mark that side of the magnet "S" with a Sharpie so that you won't forget which side is south. You'll mount the south facing pole on the pet flap so that it faces the sensor and passes close to it. You could also choose the north pole, but you'd have to change your code accordingly.

You don't have to get values that are at (or even close to) 0 or 1023. You just need to be able to detect a significant difference higher or lower when a magnet passes near the sensor.

Figure 11-3: Testing your sensors.

```
○ ○ ○                /dev/tty.usbmodem241111

                                              [ Send ]
Sensor values: 507, 508
Sensor values: 509, 507
Sensor values: 510, 508
Sensor values: 507, 507
Sensor values: 510, 508
Sensor values: 508, 22
Sensor values: 509, 22
Sensor values: 509, 22
Sensor values: 508, 22
Sensor values: 508, 22

☑ Autoscroll          [ Both NL & CR ◆ ]  [ 9600 baud ◆ ]
```

Figure 11-4: Checking readings on the serial monitor.

Preparing Your Twitter Account

After you've tested that your sensors are working, it's time to set up the pet door on your pet's Twitter account. You permit your Arduino program to use Twitter by using tools on the special Developer's area on the Twitter website. Lots of people are developing custom apps and features using Twitter all the time, so Twitter has set up special tools for them (for us!) to use, and ways for apps to use Twitter with an Application Programming Interface (API). You need to sign in to the Developer's area with your pet's Twitter account to access these features, as described here.

Your pet door has to have a way to authenticate to Twitter so that only it can send tweets. Twitter uses a secure authentication scheme called the Open Standard for Authentication (OAuth), which requires credentials so that you can allow your Arduino to use your pet's account. It can seem a bit complicated, but you don't have to be a security expert to use it. You are effectively delegating access to the Arduino to read or write tweets on your pet's behalf. The actual process is a bit complicated and uses encryption so that passwords aren't flying around the Internet unprotected. But put simply, it's like letting the Arduino borrow your pet's password whenever it needs to tweet.

The credentials you need are

 ✔ A consumer key

 ✔ A consumer secret

 ✔ An access token

 ✔ An access token secret

Fortunately, you can get all four in one click — after your account is ready. Do the following to prepare your account and request them (see Figures 11-5 and 11-6):

 1. **Of course, your pet probably already has a Twitter account — but if not, go to twitter.com and set one up, and while you are at it, why not upload a profile photo too?**

 2. **Navigate to** `http://dev.twitter.com` **and sign in with your pet's account.**

 3. **Hover over the profile picture in the upper right, and select My Applications from the options that appear on the menu.**

 4. **Click the Create New Application button.**

 5. **In the Name field, create a name for the app.**

    My cat Muon's is called MyPetDoor. Don't use any spaces in the name.

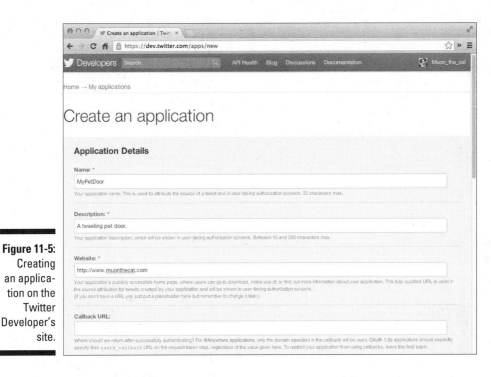

Figure 11-5:
Creating
an applica-
tion on the
Twitter
Developer's
site.

6. **Write a brief description in the next field.**

   "A tweeting pet door" will do.

7. **Put a link to your/your pet's website.**

   Most developers would specify the home page of their app here, so they can provide updates and support to users. But your pet doesn't need to provide user support, so what you put here is not critical. But you can't leave this blank and anything you put here must begin with "http://."

8. **Select the Yes I Agree check box and read the Rules of the Road if you have an extra hour or two.**

   Here's a summary: "Be nice."

9. **Enter the "Captcha" test phrases, which are there to ensure you are a real person and not a nefarious robot computer program (a "bot").**

10. **Click Create Your Twitter Application.**

If all goes well, you should see the new Details page for your application, as shown in Figure 11-6. Hooray!

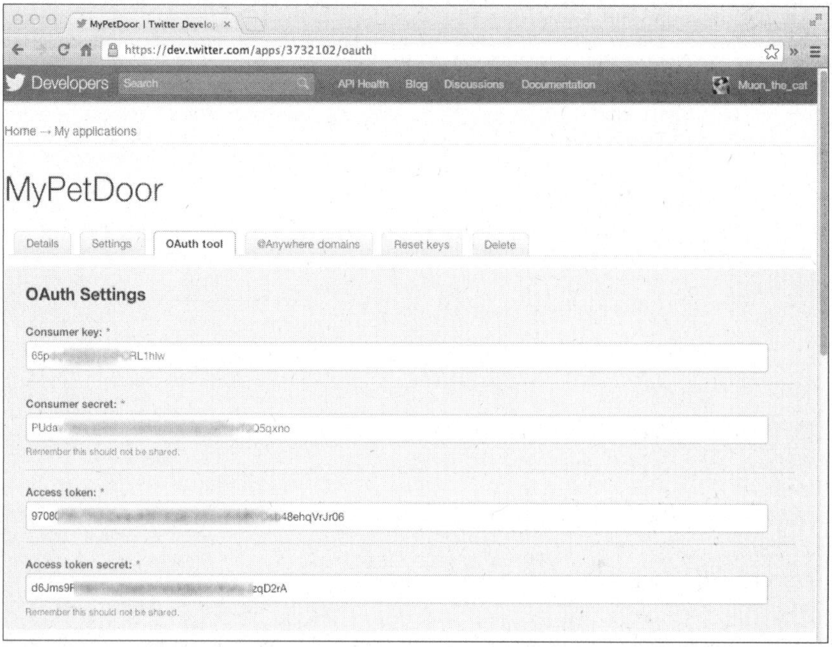

Figure 11-6:
Creating
an access
token
and key.

Now all you need to do is to request the Access Token and Access Secret key, so that your app can send tweets:

1. **At the bottom of the page, click on the Create My Access Token button.**

   A green notice at the top of the screen lets you know you've done this successfully.

2. **Click on the Settings tab and scroll down to the Application Type fields to begin the process of granting permission for the app to write tweets. There, you select the Read and Write radio button. At the bottom of this page, click the Update This Application's Twitter Settings button.**

   A green notice at the top of the screen lets you know you've done this successfully.

3. **To confirm the new settings, go back to the Details tab and make sure the Access level now reads Read and Write.**

4. **Go to the bottom of the details page labeled Your Access Token and click on Recreate My Access Token.**

   The access level in that bottom section should then update to reflect a Read and Write status. Now you've generated the needed authentication key, secrets, and token.

5. Click on the OAuth tool tab to view these.

Keep this window open or cut and paste them somewhere, because you need them for your code. Make sure to keep them where they'll be safe. You don't want stray cats hijacking your pet's Twitter account!

Crafting Your Code

Now you add to your sensor testing code to create your tweets, enable your network connection, and set up your Arduino to post to Twitter. You start by modifying your test code to select randomly from a list of clever tweets for your pet. You then test this with your sensor setup. Finally, you must add some Arduino libraries to test your tweeting capability before you mount everything in the pet door.

Specifying your tweets

Start by modifying your code to add some tweets for when your pet enters or leaves. Add the following code to the section where you declare variables, before setup() (shown in bold):

```
...
unsigned long timestamp;
boolean entering = false;
char* entryMessage = "I'm baaaack!";
char* exitMessage = "I'm outta here!";

const int entryPin = A0;      // the number of the pushbutton pin
const int exitPin = A1;       // the number of the pushbutton pin
int entryValue = 0;   // Define variable to store the entry value
int exitValue = 0;    // Define variable to store the exit value

void setup(){
...
```

The first unsigned long variable timestamp is used to get the time from Twitter in the main loop. You add this to the beginning of a tweet to create a unique message each time a tweet is posted.

The Twitter API requires that every tweet is unique so that zombies, bots, and malicious programs don't overload Twitter with useless junk. This means that you have to make each tweet a little bit different. The easiest way to do this is to add a unique count to each one with this counter.

The program sends different tweets, depending on whether your creature is coming or going. The tweets are stored in two variables of the data type *char**, called `entryMessage` and `exitMessage`. The fun part is in writing messages for your pet to tweet. Our cat is a bit cantankerous, so I've created messages to reflect his character. Here's where you can get really creative. Just make sure that your tweets are less than 140 characters!

Adding libraries for Ethernet and Twitter

Next, at the very beginning of the code, you add libraries to extend the capabilities of your Arduino to support your network connection using Twitter.

To enable Twitter, you need to add the Twitter library. This was developed by Markku Rossi, and you need to download it from the book's companion website, www.dummies.com/go/arduinoprojectsfordummies. Follow these steps to install the Twitter library:

1. **Download the Twitter library and save it somewhere convenient, like the desktop.**

2. **Quit the Arduino IDE if you are running it.**

3. **Extract the zipped files, which will leave you with a folder called /Chapter_11 containing three subfolders named Twitter, Time, and Sha.**

   The Twitter library uses Time to get the current time and Sha to perform encryption functions.

4. **Drag or copy these three folders into your Arduino libraries folder.**

   On Windows machines, this will likely be called "My Documents\Arduino\ libraries." On Macs, it will likely be called "Documents/Arduino/libraries." (On Linux, it will be the "libraries" folder in your sketchbook.) If the "libraries" folder does not exist, create it.

5. **Now restart the Arduino IDE. Make sure that the new libraries appear in the Sketch⇨Import Library menu item of the software.**

   If they do, you've installed the library correctly.

You add the Twitter features to your sketch by calling these libraries at the very beginning, and then you set up your Arduino's Ethernet shield by using the Ethernet library, which enables your network connection. If you are using the latest Arduino IDE, the Ethernet library is included, and all you need to do is add code to the beginning of your sketch. You also need the Serial Peripheral Interface (SPI) library to exchange data with the shield, which again, should be included already for you.

Now, add the following code to the beginning of your sketch (new code in bold):

```
#include <Ethernet.h>
#include <SPI.h>
#include <EEPROM.h>
#include <sha1.h>
#include <Time.h>
#include <Twitter.h>

byte mac[] = { 0x00, 0xAA, 0xBB, 0xCC, 0xDE, 0x01 };
EthernetClient client;

IPAddress twitter_ip(199, 59, 149, 232);
uint16_t twitter_port = 80;

char buffer[512];
const static char consumer_key[] PROGMEM = "*****YOUR CONSUMER KEY*****";
const static char consumer_secret[] PROGMEM = "*****YOUR CONSUMER SECRET*****";

Twitter twitter(buffer, sizeof(buffer));

unsigned long timestamp;
...
```

The libraries are included in your sketch by adding the #include command. You're no doubt familiar with IP addresses, but underneath that, at the hardware level, you also have what's called a Media Access Control address (MAC address). The variable mac[] is an unsigned integer array containing the 6 bytes of your MAC address.

All network devices are supposed to have a unique MAC address and your MAC address was burned on the shield at the factory. It is printed on the sticker on the underside of your shield. You can use the number on the sticker, but in fact, it doesn't matter and you can simply use the MAC address in the code listed here.

If you know that you are using a *static IP address* on your network, you can add that to the code after your MAC address. This is needed only if you are not able to use *dynamic host configuration prototcol (DHCP)* on your network. To use a static IP address, add the following, substituting the IP address you wish to use for the IP address in parentheses:

```
IPAddress ip(192,168,1,43); // the IP address may be different on your network
```

Next, you use the Ethernet Library's EthernetClient object to create an Ethernet client called "client." This allows you to send and receive messages with your Ethernet shield.

The IP address of Twitter is specified in the `IPAddress` variable. This is Twitter's current IP address and is not likely to change. You could also use Domain Name Service (DNS) to find (or "resolve") Twitter's IP address, but this would use up more memory on your Arduino, so I've opted to keep things short and simple. You also must specify a TCP port of 80, stored in the `twitter_port` variable.

Now, the important step is specifying the values you got from the Twitter Developer's site, shown in Figure 11-6. This is how your Arduino will authenticate with Twitter to send tweets on your pet's account. In the code above, do the following:

✔ Replace `*****YOUR CONSUMER KEY*****` with the long string of digits listed next to the Consumer Key field in the OAuth Tool tab of your account.

✔ Replace `******YOUR CONSUMER SECRET******` with the long string of digits listed next to the Consumer Secret field in the OAuth Tool tab of your account.

The last two variables are a character array called `buffer` that holds the message text and a Twitter object called `Twitter`, which provides connectivity and tweeting functions.

In `setup()`, you now need to enable the Ethernet connection for your shield. Unless you opted to use a static IP address, this sketch uses DHCP, which is a way for your router to hand out an IP address automatically. Most home routers are set up to do this because it makes it easier for you to add new network devices like printers, set-top boxes, tables, and mobile phones to your network. Add the bold code to `setup()`:

```
void setup(){
   Serial.begin(9600);
   Serial.println("Attempting to get an IP address using DHCP:");
   if (!Ethernet.begin(mac)) {
    Serial.println("Failed to get an IP address using DHCP, trying the static
             IP");
     Ethernet.begin(mac, ip);
 }
```

This code sends messages to the serial monitor so that you can make sure you are connecting to the Ethernet network. The last two lines are only needed if you can use a static IP address on your network and configured your code to do so.

Finally, add the code that specifies the last details that Twitter needs to authenticate your Arduino to use your pet's account at the end of the `setup()` section of your code:

```
void setup(){
  Serial.begin(9600);

  Serial.println("Attempting to get an IP address using DHCP:");
  if (!Ethernet.begin(mac)) {
   Serial.println("Failed to get an IP address using DHCP, trying the static
           IP");
    Ethernet.begin(mac, ip);


twitter.set_twitter_endpoint(PSTR("api.twitter.com"),
  PSTR("/1/statuses/update.json"),
  twitter_ip, twitter_port, false);
  twitter.set_client_id(consumer_key, consumer_secret);

#if 0
  // Read OAuth account identification from EEPROM.
  twitter.set_account_id(256, 384);
#else
  // Set OAuth account identification from program memory.
  twitter.set_account_id(PSTR("******YOUR ACCESS TOKEN******"),
  PSTR("******YOUR ACCESS TOKEN SECRET******"));
#endif
}
```

In the preceding code, the function `twitter.set_client_id` uses the values you defined at the beginning of the program, so you should leave those as is. You now have to add the access token and secret that were provided to you by Twitter:

✔ Replace *****YOUR ACCESS TOKEN***** with the long string of digits listed next to the Access Token field in the OAuth Tool tab of your account.

✔ Replace ******YOUR ACCESS TOKEN SECRET****** with the long string of digits listed next to the Access Token Secret field in the OAuth Tool tab of your account.

Adding your program logic

In the final part of crafting the code, you link the part of your code that detects the magnet to the part of the code that tweets. Replace the testing code in your main loop with the following:

```
void loop(){
  entryValue = analogRead(entryPin);

  Serial.println(entryValue); // Uncomment this line to monitor the readings

  if (entryValue < 50){
    entering=true;
    sendTweet();
  }

  exitValue = analogRead(exitPin);
  if (exitValue < 50){
    entering=false;
    sendTweet();
  }
  delay(10);
}

void sendTweet(){
  if (twitter.is_ready())  {
      char tweet[140];
      timestamp = twitter.get_time();


   if(entering){
      sprintf(tweet, "%02d:%02d:%02d: %s", hour(timestamp), minute(timestamp),
              second(timestamp), entryMessage);
   } else {
      sprintf(tweet, "%02d:%02d:%02d: %s", hour(timestamp), minute(timestamp),
              second(timestamp), exitMessage);
   }

      Serial.println(tweet);
      Serial.print("Posting to Twitter: ");
    if (twitter.post_status(tweet)){
      Serial.println("Status updated");
    }
    else{
      Serial.println("Update failed");
    }
  }
  delay(10000);  // wait 10 seconds to avoid double triggering

}
```

This is where the action happens. As with the code you wrote to test your Hall-effect sensors, the `main loop()` tests whether the magnet has been detected on either the entry pin or the exit pin, using the conditional `if` statement. I used the value of 50 or lower here, but your magnet might produce slightly different values, so you should adjust accordingly. Use a value that is significantly lower than the middle value shown when no magnet was present during your testing. If the magnet is detected by either sensor, the Boolean variable `entering` is set to either true or false, and the `sendTweet()` function is called.

The `sendTweet()` function selects which tweet to send and forwards it to Twitter. Before sending the tweet, it has to be put together. You use a temporary char array called `tweet` to store the contents of your message, which consists of a message number and the message text. Each tweet also has to be unique, or else Twitter will reject it as a duplicate message. You do this by getting the time from Twitter, using the `twitter.get_time()` function and assigning the results to the variable timestamp. This produces a value in UNIX time, which you convert to hours, minutes, and seconds when the tweet is assembled. This timestamp is placed at the beginning of each message, thereby ensuring that each tweet is unique.

The conditional `if` statement test selects whether to send entry or exit messages by checking the value of the variable `entering`. Both entry and exit tweets are assembled in the same way using the special C function `sprintf()`. Take a closer look at this function, in the case of the `entryMessage`:

```
sprintf(tweet, "%02d:%02d:%02d: %s", hour(timestamp), minute(timestamp),
                second(timestamp), entryMessage);
```

The `sprintf()` function concatenates the timestamp and the message text together into the `tweet` char array, which is the first item in parentheses. Next is the message itself, in quotation marks. The message is built up from the results of converting UNIX time from the timestamp variable into hours, minutes, and seconds, using the `hour(timestamp)`, `minute(timestamp)`, and `second(timestamp)` functions that follow the quotation marks. The results of these conversions are placed in sequential order within the quotation marks. The characters `%02d` specify that the hours, minutes, and seconds are decimal values and have two decimal places. The colons are simply printed out as normal text. Lastly, `%s` is where the `entryMessage` string is added. That's the text you are tweeting. The `exitMessage` is built up the same way.

The resulting tweet is printed to the serial monitor so you can easily debug it, along with the timestamp and status messages from Twitter.

The code initiates a Twitter communication using the `twitter.is_ready()` function. When this is true, Twitter is ready to receive your tweet.

The `twitter.post_status()` function actually sends the tweet you stored in the temporary variable `tweet`. The status response from Twitter is returned to the serial monitor, as shown in Figure 11-7, so that you can see whether or not the tweet worked and if it didn't, the reason that it didn't. The `delay()` instruction at the end of this function ensures that 10 seconds pass before the door can be checked again. This prevents false triggering if your pet is a bit uncertain about whether he's coming or going!

To prevent a flood of activity, Twitter limits you from communicating with the Twitter API to no more than 350 times an hour. If your pet is tweeting more than that, you've got problems. However, during testing you might want to be careful that you don't exceed this limit, which could be easy to do if you forget a line of code, such as the `delay()` instruction.

Now that you've entered all the code, you should test your setup before installing the sensors in your pet door. It's much easier to troubleshoot from your workbench than it is once the door is installed! Connect your Arduino to your router with the Ethernet cable. Leave the Arduino connected to your computer via the USB cable so that you can monitor the communication on the serial monitor and test that passing a magnet near the sensors sends a tweet. Use the neodymium magnet to send a tweet or two and confirm that everything is working properly.

After you are satisfied that it is working correctly, you can disconnect the USB cable and provide the power to the Arduino from the power adaptor.

Figure 11-7:
Sending a
tweet, and
the status
message
returned by
Twitter.

Modifying Your Pet Door

With the code written and tested, you can prepare the door and move your circuit off of the breadboard. First, tape the sensors temporarily into position on the pet door frame to help you estimate how long your signaling wire will need to be, as in Figure 11-8. The entry sensor should be placed on the inside of the frame and the exit sensor on the outside.

Deciding exactly where to put the sensors and the magnet requires a bit of finesse. You need to mount them in a position that guarantees that the magnet passes in front of the sensors so that it can reliably detect your pet's movement of the door. Make sure to place both sensors at the same height, so that the passing magnet can trigger either one. You shouldn't mount them too close to the top, or the door won't swing enough to trigger both sensors. You might need to do a trial run with your pet to see how far the door swings. This is where those treats come in handy!

Figure 11-8:
Taping your sensors in place to estimate the signaling wire length.

After you've estimated the location of your sensors, loosely run the cable from the location where your pet door is (or will be) mounted to your Arduino and router. Make sure to leave enough extra cable so that you can attach it to baseboards and door frames. Now cut the cable to the right length, but leave a little extra just in case. You can always just coil up any remaining wire later.

Your wire has four conductors. Power and ground are shared between the two Hall-effect sensors. The third and fourth conductors are for the signals from the sensors.

You need to solder the extension wire onto both of your sensors. At the Arduino end, use your wire strippers to remove some of the insulation and then solder pin headers to the four wires. Figure 11-9 shows how these will be connected to your Arduino and the pet door.

Make sure to keep track of the color of the insulation so that you will know which wires you used for power, ground, the entry sensor, and the exit sensor. While you've got the soldering iron fired up, solder the sensors to the other end of the signaling cable at the pet door. Use your helping hands to hold the sensors firmly so that you can make a good solder joint.

In the diagram, the lines that cross each other are only connected at two points, on the pet door frame near the sensors, and are indicated by the small, solid dots signifying the junction points. You should solder these wires together to create a reliable electrical connection.

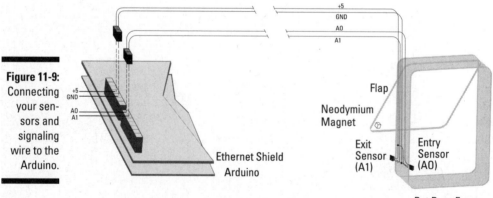

Figure 11-9: Connecting your sensors and signaling wire to the Arduino.

When you are soldering the wires to the sensors, be careful not to heat the parts for a long time. If it takes more than a couple of seconds, you could over-heat the sensor and it could be damaged.

With the sensors now soldered to the signaling wire, it is a good idea to test the setup once again, just to make sure the circuit is still working. You then mount your sensors to the door and if necessary, mount the pet door.

1. **Attach the sensors to the pet door with hot glue.**

   You may need a bit of plastic, wood or other material (like a LEGO block) to support the sensor, so that you can mount it to the surface of the door. I found a bit of discarded plastic and glued the sensor to it.

2. **Carefully coat the sensor with a layer of hot glue, which will protect it from moisture.**

3. **Glue the plastic block to the pet door frame, as in Figure 11-10.**

   The design of your door will determine exactly how you mount the sensor, but make sure that the path of travel is clear so it can swing freely.

Figure 11-10:
Mounting your sensors and magnets.

4. **The last step is to mount the magnet to the door itself.**

   Swing the door partway until it is in front of one of the sensors. Make sure that the south facing pole that you marked earlier points toward the sensors. Use a dab of glue to attach the magnet to the door. When you're done, it should look like Figure 11-10.

Now you can sit back, relax, and enjoy the tweets!

Chapter 12

Building a Home Sensing Station

*L*ots of people have been using their Arduinos to wire things up to the Internet, so much so that folks are starting to talk about an "Internet-of-Things." There are Internet-enabled lamps, weather stations, and even whole buildings that are wired up to post their data online. Your Arduino has a pretty powerful little microcontroller on board, and it can easily handle the tasks of collecting environmental data and sending it to the Internet.

In this chapter, you create a home sensing station that collects light and temperature data and posts it online. Your sensor station uses an Arduino Ethernet shield so that after your station is built, you don't have to leave a computer running. It just talks directly to the Internet over your home router. You also find out how to build temperature and light sensor probes and a homemade Arduino shield to connect them to your Arduino. I describe how to use Xively, an Internet-of-Things data service, to store your data and create cool charts. You can share your data with anyone, browse through other data feeds, and get a web page that automatically displays charts of your data.

 You can download schematics and full-color parts placement diagrams from the companion website (www.dummies.com/go/arduinoprojectsfor dummies).

Building Your Sensor Probes

Your sensor station uses two temperature probes (one for inside and one for outside) and a light sensor. After you get the hang of it, you can add more analog sensors. I'm even thinking of adding one to my refrigerator! You could also add other kinds of sensors, such as a relative humidity or a nitrogen dioxide sensor to gauge air quality.

Selecting your parts

To get started with the project, first wrangle all the parts you need, as shown in Figure 12-1.

- An Arduino Uno
- An Arduino Ethernet shield
- An Ethernet cable
- A 12V DC power transformer for your Arduino (not pictured)
- A length of multicore wire, with a minimum of three conductors (choose from a wide variety at Radio Shack or Maplin)
- An enclosure, such as Newark #13T9276 or Farnell #1848692 (as shown later in Figure 12-15)
- Two TMP36 temperature sensors (Jameco #278387 or Farnell #1438760)
- One light-dependent resistor (LDR)
- A 10kΩ resistor
- A drinking straw (McDonald's!)
- A small piece of stripboard (10 x 20 holes) (Radio Shack or Maplin)
- Six single row PCB pin headers (Jameco #103393 or Rapid #22-0520)
- A breadboard for prototyping (optional)

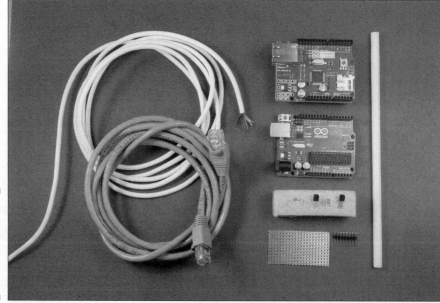

Figure 12-1:
The parts you need for your home sensing station.

I recommend using a relatively new Arduino Uno and Arduino Ethernet shield. The design of both products has changed slightly over the years, and I haven't tested this system with older hardware. I've found the newer Ethernet shields are also more reliable than the older ones. You need a 12V DC power supply for your Arduino because after you've programmed it, you no longer need to connect it to a computer.

If you have a hub or a router that has Power over Ethernet (POE), you can build this project without using an Arduino power supply. The whole shebang can draw its power directly from the Ethernet shield. POE is still not common yet, but more manufacturers are incorporating it into Ethernet hubs and routers, so it's a good idea to check yours to see if you can take advantage of POE.

You run your sensor cables to your Arduino, and your Arduino's Ethernet cable to your router. So the length of these cables is determined by exactly where you want to place your sensors and your Arduino. I recommend getting a shorter Ethernet cable (because it's cheaper) and placing your Arduino near the router, where there's also likely to be power.

Check to make sure your router has a spare Ethernet connection available and that a power socket is available for your Arduino's power transformer.

Get *multicore* cable (that's just cable that has several wires inside) for your sensor. It comes in both stranded and solid core varieties. Either will do, but stranded is more flexible and is easier to route along walls and corners. You need at least three wires (also referred to as *conductors*) inside the cable, but it doesn't have to be heavy gauge — 22 to 24 AWG is fine. You don't need to go overboard for this stuff. Inexpensive telephone extension cable works fine and is cheap. Just make sure that you get enough to run all your sensors from where they will be situated to your Arduino.

You can use any enclosure for this project. Any small box is suitable. If you're willing to spring for it, Newark and Farnell offer a custom-made Arduino enclosure that has room for an Ethernet shield, too (shown in Figure 12-16, later in this chapter). It's a perfect enclosure for this project.

You use TMP36 temperature sensors to detect the ambient temperature. These come in a tiny cylindrical black plastic package called TO-92 and have three legs. These sensors measure temperature by determining the voltage drop across an internal diode, which changes by a fixed amount, as temperature fluctuates. They are cheap, very reliable, and can be used to measure in either Celsius or Fahrenheit. Because they rely on your Arduino for power, TMP36 sensors can be subject to slight variations in accuracy depending on the amount of power your Arduino and Ethernet shield are using. But for the price, they are hard to beat.

You use a Light Dependent Resistor (LDR) and 10kΩ resistor to detect changes in ambient light level. The LDR has a chemical deposited on its surface that changes its resistance, depending on how much light falls on it. Like the TMP36 sensors, the LDR draws power from your Arduino, so the value it outputs is proportional to the ambient light but may be affected slightly by your Arduino's power consumption. The LDR doesn't provide light measurements in standard units, such as microcandelas or lumens. Sensors that do this are available, but much more expensive. So this project outputs values that range from 0 to 100 (dark to bright) instead. This is what you really want to know most of the time, anyway. But if you have access to one, you could use a light meter to calibrate these values to precisely measured lumens – or splurge for a more sophisticated sensor.

You use a drinking straw as a waterproof capsule for your sensors, hot gluing them inside. The straws from McDonald's are nice and fat, so there's plenty of room for your sensors to slide in. Go grab yourself a chocolate shake before you get started and save the straw for your sensors! A glue gun should be part of your workbench toolset, but if you don't have one, you'll need one for this project. They are pretty cheap and easy to buy at any hobby or craft store.

Your stripboard is the platform for your homemade Arduino sensor shield. They don't come in a 10 x 20-hole size, so you need to get a bigger one and cut it down to size. This is pretty easy to do with a utility knife and straightedge. You can score it a few times along the holes and then snap it apart. You solder the six pin headers to it so that you can slot it right into the Ethernet shield's header sockets and solder your sensor cables directly to the stripboard. You build your probes first and then your sensor shield. After that, you solder your sensors to the shield and plug it into to your Arduino for testing.

Building and testing your circuit

Before you build the shield, it's best to use a breadboard for testing the circuit and then move it to the stripboard after you know it works. The circuit diagram and breadboard layout are shown in Figures 12-2 and 12-3. Stack the Ethernet shield on top of the Arduino at this point. Later, after testing on the breadboard, you will connect to the headers on the shield, not on the Arduino directly. For the sake of clarity, the shield is not illustrated in the diagram or schematic.

Create a ground rail and a power rail on your breadboard by connecting the 5V and GND outputs to the column of pins on its side. Add your two temperature sensors and your light sensor, as shown in Figure 12-3.

Make sure you don't connect your sensors to analog Pins 0 and 1. These are used for the SD card slot on the Ethernet shield. Although you aren't using that for this project, it's best to keep the sensor signals connected only to your Arduino inputs and not to any other parts of the hardware.

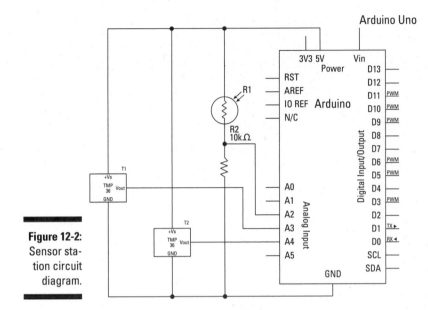

Figure 12-2:
Sensor sta-
tion circuit
diagram.

Make sure you use the resistor for your LDR. The LDR provides a resistance in relationship to the amount of light falling on it. This part of the circuit is a *voltage divider* because the ratio between the LDR and the fixed resistor provides a variable voltage that you measure on analog Pin 2. I tested this circuit in full sunlight as well as in total darkness and found that a 10kΩ resistor provides a good range of readings from about 10 to just over 1000. You can perform your own tests with the code below and determine whether 10kΩ is about right on your setup. The center legs of the TMP36 sensors provide the signals for analog Pins 3 and 4.

After you've built the circuit on your breadboard, enter the following sensor test code in the Arduino IDE:

```
const int lightSensorPin=2;
const int tempPin1=3;
const int tempPin2=4;

void setup() {
  Serial.begin(9600);
}

void loop() {
  float lightLevel = map(analogRead(lightSensorPin),0,1023,0,100);

  float temperature1 = ((getVoltage(tempPin1) -.5) * 100L);
  float temperature2 = ((getVoltage(tempPin2) -.5) * 100L);

  Serial.print("Temp 1 ('C): ");
```

```
    Serial.print(temperature1);
    Serial.print(", Temp 2 ('C): ");
    Serial.print(temperature2);
    Serial.print(", Light (V): ");
    Serial.println(lightLevel);
    delay(250);
}

float getVoltage(int pin){
return (analogRead(pin) * .004882814);
}
```

Before you upload this to your board, take a moment to understand how the code works. Your variable declarations for the three analog input pins that you use for your sensors come first. They are *integer constants* because their values won't change during the execution of the program.

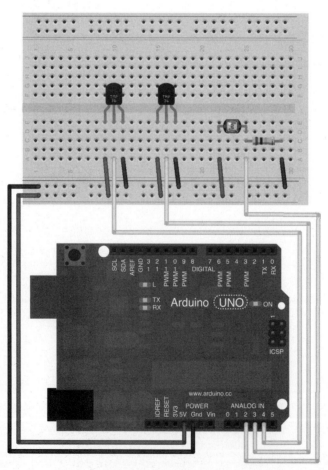

Figure 12-3:
Example
breadboard
layout.

`Setup()` only needs to prepare the serial port. Your analog pins are used for input by default, so you don't have to explicitly set them to INPUT. The main loop simply takes readings from the three analog pins, converts them to a useful numerical value, and prints them to the screen.

Doing your light-level conversion

As I mentioned earlier, the light level isn't calibrated to lumens or micro-candelas. It's just set to a value between 0 and 100 to give an idea of how bright or dark it is. I think a scale from 0 to 100 makes it easy to get a sense of brightness or darkness; over time, you'll be able to tell how bright something is just by checking out the scale. A voltage reading from analog Pin 2 is stored as a float, `lightLevel`:

```
float lightLevel = map(analogRead(lightSensorPin),0,1023,0,100);
```

The value provided by an analog pin ranges from 0 to 1023, in increments of about 5 millivolts. However, the `map()` function converts this to 0–100 for you. Its first parameter is the numerical value on the analog pin. The second two parameters specify the expected range of that value (0–1023), and the last two parameters specify that you convert any value taken in that range to a value from 0 to 100.

You can use the `map()` function in a lot of situations where you want to convert from one range of values to another, so it's a good idea to get familiar with how to use it.

Doing your temperature conversion

Your temperature sensors provide a value in millivolts (mV) proportional to the ambient temperature detected:

```
float temperature1 = ((getVoltage(tempPin1) -.5) * 100L);
```

This conversion first obtains the voltage on the analog pin using the `getVoltage()` function at the very end of the sketch. You specify in paren-theses which pin you want to get the voltage from. You convert the voltage to Celsius by subtracting a 500mV offset and then multiplying the result by 100. The "L" tells the Arduino to use a 32-bit integer to calculate the value. The result in degrees Celsius is stored in the *float* `temperature1`.

Although the Imperial units are quaint, and I have a gut feeling for them, I've been using the metric system for a long time now. If you want the satisfying shock of being able to take temperature readings that top 100 degrees, replace the temperature code with the conversion to Fahrenheit:

```
float temperature1 = (((getVoltage(tempPin1) -.5) * 100L) *9.0/5.0) + 32.0;
```

Next, you print the stored values for temperature and light to the serial moni-tor, so you can verify the sensors are working correctly.

The getVoltage() function takes an integer as input. The *integer* "pin" is a local variable that stores the number of the analog pin you want to read. When you call this function, you pass it that number (which is stored in the tempPin1 or tempPin2 variable). It then reads the pin specified and obtains a value from 0–1023, multiplying this by .004882814 to convert it to a voltage. The number .004882814 is used because the numbers 0 to 1023 actually represent voltage values between 0 and 5V, in increments of about 5mV. The result is then passed back to the part of the program where you called the function.

Now try out the code on your Arduino. Upload it and then open your serial monitor. The output should look like Figure 12-4.

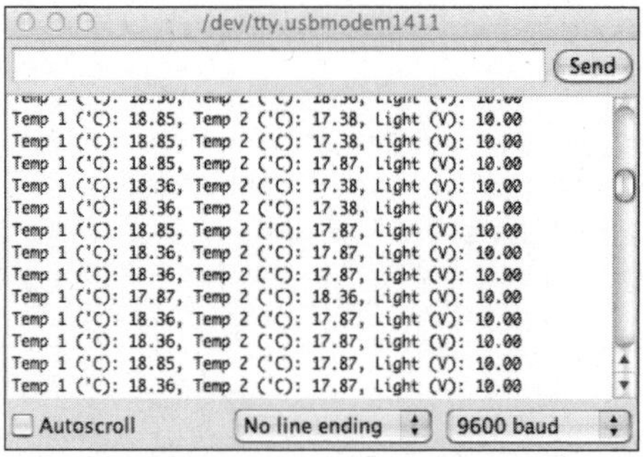

Figure 12-4:
The output from your sensor test.

Calibrating your light-level mapping

Examine the values you get for your light level by covering the LDR with your hand and taking it away. You should make a note of the values you get when the sensor is completely covered and when it is a bright day in the place where the sensor will be situated. Your values will range from near zero (dark) to anywhere up to (or nearly) 1023.

Replace the values in your code so that these numbers are the range of values for your light-level conversion. Suppose you got the values of 5 when the sensor is completely covered and 980 in bright sunlight. You would change your light conversion mapping as follows:

```
float lightLevel = map(analogRead(lightSensorPin),5,980,0,100);
```

This converts the values you are likely to get for the light level to a standard range between 0 and 100.

After you are satisfied that the code is working correctly, you can build your sensor probes and your sensor shield. Later, you create your Xively account and upload code for your three sensors. If your output doesn't seem right, first check your connections and then verify that your code is correct before going further. You need to make sure this circuit works before you make your sensors and shield.

Save this sketch; you need it when you write your code to post to Xively.

Building your sensor probes

You build three sensor probes for this project, so you can save time by making all of them at once. For each temperature sensor you build, you solder three wires in your multicore cable to the TMP36 sensor and then enclose it in a short piece of drinking straw for protection. The light sensor is almost the same, but uses only two wires.

Before you get started, measure out enough sensor cable to reach from where you want to place each of the sensors to where you want your Arduino situated. You need to get these lengths approximately correct before you start cutting the wire and soldering.

To fabricate your probes, do the following steps:

1. **Cut the cable for your temperature probes to length.**

2. **Strip about 2cm (1") of the outer insulation off the cable and then strip three of the internal wires.**

   You can cut off any additional wires because you need only three conductors for each temperature sensor: power, ground, and signal. If your cable has red, black, and yellow insulation, use those wires so that you don't get confused when you build your shield. The insulation color is arbitrary, really. Just keep track of which is which.

3. **Use your soldering iron to tin the wires with a little bit of solder so they adhere well to the sensors.**

   It can be tricky to solder wires directly to your sensor's legs, especially without four hands. One method is to melt a little extra blob of solder onto your sensor wire. When you solder it to the sensor, this blob will flow onto the sensor's legs so that you have a strong bond. You can always go back and add a little extra. When the joint is cold, inspect it to make sure it's good and then tug gently on the wire to test its strength.

4. **Splay the legs of your TMP36 and solder your three wires to its legs, as shown in Figure 12-5. With the flat face of the sensor toward you, the order to solder, from left to right, is: positive wire, signal wire, negative wire.**

5. **Solder the second temperature sensor the same way.**

6. **For the light sensor, solder only two wires to your LDR, one for power and one for signal, as shown in Figure 12-6.**

   I used red and yellow.

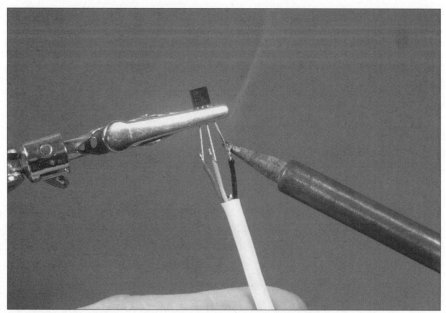

Figure 12-5:
Soldering
your tem-
perature
sensor.

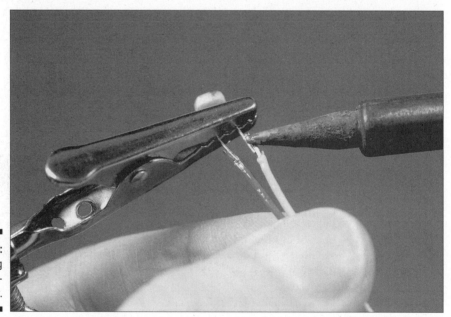

Figure 12-6:
Soldering
your light-
level sensor.

7. **For each of your three probes, cut a 5cm (2") piece from your drinking straw.**

   Each sensor straw should be long enough to cover your sensor and any exposed wires.

8. **For each sensor, use a dab of hot glue to keep the legs from touching, as shown in Figure 12-7.**

   Don't put too much glue on, or the sensors won't fit inside the straws. Wait for the glue to cool completely.

9. **After the glue cools, test that each sensor fits snugly into its straw, as shown in Figure 12-8. But make sure the leads don't touch each other or you'll have a short circuit.**

   The hot glue should prevent this from happening.

10. **Slip your sensors into the straws so that the sensor is near the end of the straw. Apply a bit of hot glue to the end of each sensor, as shown in Figure 12-9.**

    Make sure not to put too much glue on the light sensor.

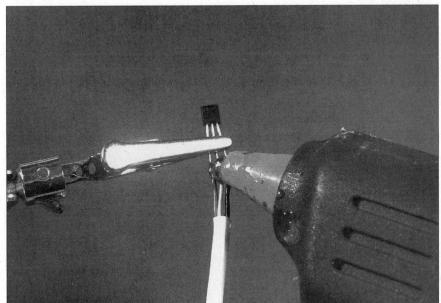

Figure 12-7:
Keeping the legs in position with hot glue.

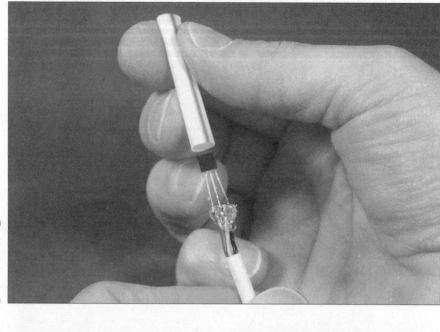

11. **Before the glue cools, draw each sensor back inside the straw just a little bit, creating a concave depression in the surface of the glue.**

    This reveals any air gaps. You want to make sure the seal is watertight. Add a little glue if necessary, and wait for it to cool.

12. **Turn the sensor over, and apply glue to the area where the cable enters the straw, again making sure you have a watertight seal, as shown in Figure 12-10.**

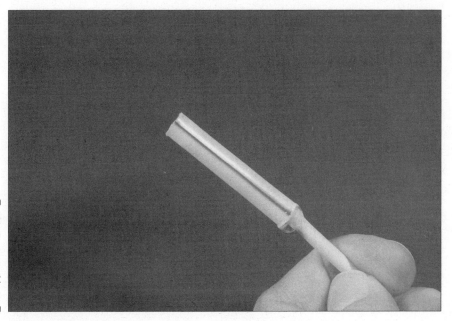

Figure 12-10:
Finishing up your sensors for a watertight seal.

Building your sensor shield

The sensor shield provides a tidy way to connect your probes to your Arduino and makes it easy to remove them should you need to. The shield performs a similar function to a breadboard, giving you multiple connections to power and ground, but it's a more permanent and reliable solution. You can expand it with up to two more sensors on an Arduino Uno.

After you've built this shield, you can adopt the same technique for other Arduino projects.

To create your sensor shield, do the following steps:

1. **Use your Arduino to hold your pin headers steady while you solder them your stripboard.**

   If your pin headers are attached to one another, split them into groups of two, two, and three.

2. **Insert the pins into the header sockets on your Arduino, as shown in Figure 12-11.**

Two pins go into digital Pins 6 and 7. Two pins go into headers for +5V and GND. Three pins go into the analog 2, 3, and 4 header sockets.

Digital Pins 7 and 6

Figure 12-11:
Using your
Arduino to
hold your
pin headers
securely for
soldering.

5V and GND Pins

Analog Pins 2, 3, 4

3. **Carefully place the stripboard onto your pin headers, with the copper strips facing upward.**

Make sure you don't get it crooked.

The pin headers on digital Pins 7 and 8 will not be connected to your sensor circuit. They are merely there to give your sensor shield physical stability.

4. **Carefully solder the pins to the copper strips, as shown in Figure 12-12, making sure that you don't create a solder bridge between any of the strips of copper.**

You don't want the strips to be electrically connected to each other.

5. **Remove the board from your Arduino and inspect the pins to make sure the connections are good.**

The leftmost two pins form your power and ground rails. The rightmost three pins are analog inputs. The other two are not connected to the circuit you're building.

Figure 12-12: Soldering your pins in place.

6. **Now add your 10kΩ resistor to the stripboard.**

   One edge of the board now has five pins soldered to it. With those pins at the top, insert the legs of your resistor through the non-copper side of the stripboard. The legs should be in the second and eighth copper strips, as shown in Figure 12-13. It doesn't really matter what row you place the resistor in. Any row will do, but you need to leave room for your sensor wires.

7. **Bend the resistor's legs slightly to hold it in place. Then, flip the board over and solder your resistor onto the copper strips, as shown in Figure 12-13.**

Figure 12-13: Adding the resistor to your sensor shield.

8. **Now connect your light sensor to the stripboard. Strip off about 5mm (¼") of insulation from your sensor cable and feed one of its two wires into the leftmost column of holes, which is your power rail. Feed the other wire into the same column as the right side of your resistor, which is connected to the pin that goes into the analog 2 input on your Arduino.**

   It should look like the top cable in Figure 12-14.

9. **Flip the board over and solder your cable onto the copper strips on the back.**

10. **Connect your temperature sensor cables below your light sensor cable, as shown in Figure 12-14.**

    Strip and feed the wires through the holes and solder the 5V power supply wires to your leftmost power rail.

11. **Solder your ground wires to the next column of holes, which is your ground rail.**

12. **Solder the signal wires to the columns for analog Pins 3 and 4, respectively. Check Figure 12-14 to make sure that you've soldered your connections correctly.**

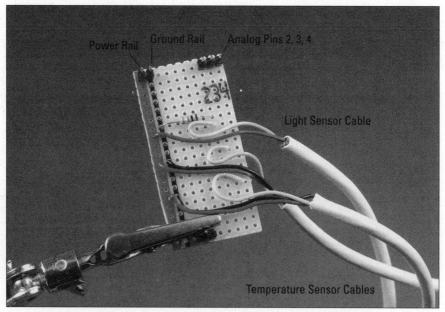

Figure 12-14: Soldering the sensor cables to your sensor shield.

13. **Insert your sensor shield back into the headers on your Arduino.**

Make sure that your analog pins align with the holes for your analog inputs 2, 3, and 4, as shown in Figure 12-15.

You don't want to get this wrong, so double-check that you are inserting your sensor shield correctly!

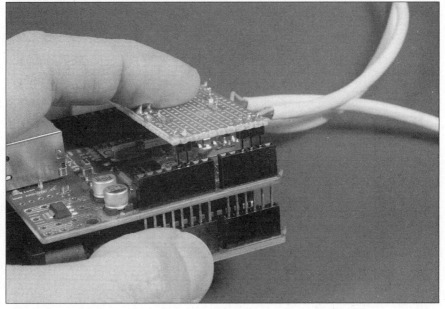

Figure 12-15:
Inserting your sensor shield onto your Arduino. Double-check your pins!

When you've finished building and installing your shield, you can put your sensor station into an enclosure. The specialty one shown in Figure 12-16 not only accommodates the cables, but it also has a special knockout plate for an Ethernet shield. This alone makes it worth the ten bucks or so it costs. Secure your sensor cables into the enclosure with cable ties or even hot glue. A bit of duct tape will do, if all else fails.

With the build complete, test your sensor shield by using the sensor code. When you are satisfied that it's working as well as it was on the breadboard, you can create an account on Xively to post your data to the Internet.

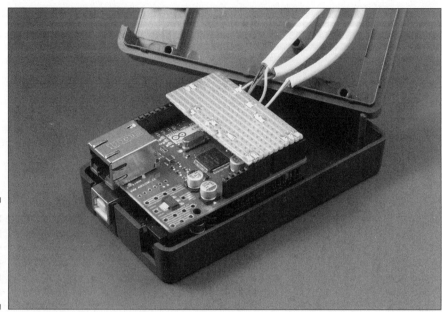

Figure 12-16:
Installing your sensing station into an enclosure.

Creating a Xively Account

It is certainly possible to set up your own website to receive data from your Arduino and display it in real time, but that takes a good deal of know-how, effort, and patience. So, why do all that work when someone else has done the tedious stuff for you? You can use a free service provided by Xively.com (an "Internet-of-Things" company) to do all the backend work of collecting data for you. You can even build charts and graphs of your data feeds that you can share with friends or embed into your own website. And the price couldn't be better!

On Xively, you set up *devices* and assign one or more *channels* to your device. You set up your Arduino as a device and assign each of your sensors a channel. That, in turn, displays them on your Xively device's webpage, or *feed*. You manage them using your Xively Workbench.

To set up your Arduino to post data to Xively, you need a Xively developer account. Xively then provides you with a Feed ID for your account and an Application Programming Interface (API) key for your device (your Arduino). Your API key allows you to post your home sensing data and provides a bit of security so only you have access to your data feed.

To set it all up, follow these steps:

1. **Open your web browser to Xively.com and click the Get Started button to create a Xively user account and activate it.**

   You will receive an account activation link by e-mail. When you activate, you'll see a Test Drive tutorial page; you can ignore it for now. You can go through the tutorial later to learn how Xively works in greater detail.

2. **To connect your Arduino, click the Develop button at the top of the page. On the Development Devices page, click the Add Device button, as shown in Figure 12-17.**

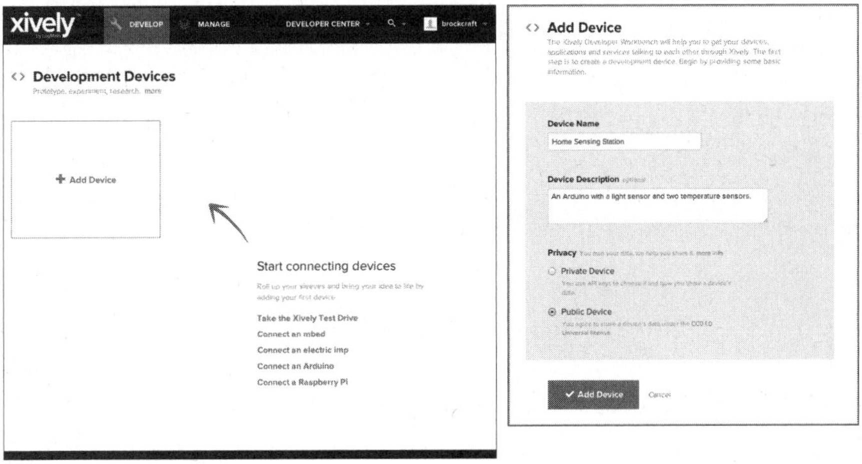

Figure 12-17:
Adding a device in your Xively Developer Workbench.

3. **Type a descriptive name for your home sensing station.**

4. **Select whether you want your data to be public or private.**

   When a device is private, the device and its data are accessible only to you (and those to whom you grant access); the information is not listed in Xively's online public directory. When a device is public, all data about and created by it can be copied, shared, and modified by anyone, including for commercial purposes.

5. **Click the Add Device button at the bottom of the page.**

   After you add your Arduino, you are taken to the Xively Workbench. This is where you manage your device and its channels. At the top of the page, you are provided with a Feed ID and API key, as shown in Figure 12-18.

Figure 12-18:
Setting up
your data
channels.
Take note
of your Feed
ID and API
key.

6. **Click the Add Channel button to create a light level channel for your device.**

7. **Configure the ID of your channel, as shown in Figure 12-19.**

    The first sensor is for light level, so type the word **light** into the ID field.

8. **Configure the characteristics of your channel.**

    You can add tags if you want, but they are optional. Leave the Units field blank. Because you are measuring light levels on an arbitrary scale from 0 to 100, type **of 100** into the Symbol field.

9. **Click the Save Channel button.**

10. **Repeat Steps 6 through 9 to add two more channels for temperature to your device, called temp1 and temp2.**

    In this project, I use the Celsius scale. But you can use Fahrenheit if you change the code, as I described earlier in this chapter. In the Units field type Celsius (or Fahrenheit). In the Symbol field, type C (or F).

    The channel names are used in your code. Make sure you use the *exact* channel names you use here. If you use different ones, you will have to modify your code to match them, or your sensor data won't be posted to Xively.

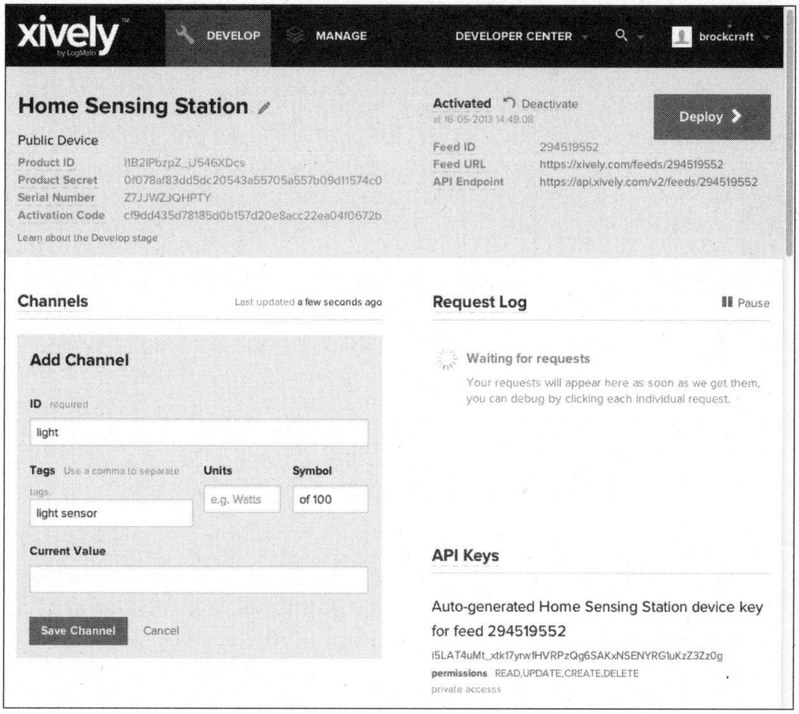

Figure 12-19:
Configuring
your device
on Xively.

11. **Note your Feed ID and API key.**

    Your Arduino's Feed ID and API key are shown in the lower-right corner of the page (refer to Figure 12-19). You need these for your code. The API is very long, so you should cut and paste it into a blank document or directly into your code. After you start posting data, you'll be able to access graphs at the Feed URL shown at the top-right of the page.

12. **To get ready for coding, open the example code for Chapter 12 from this book's companion website, copy the code, paste it into a new Arduino sketch, and save the sketch.**

    Get the example code from this book's companion website (www. dummies.com/go/arduinoprojectsfordummies). You modify it in the next section. You should now have a newly enabled Xively account with three channels but no data. These will be updated with data automatically when you send your data the first time.

Programming Your Sensing Station

When you set up your Arduino as a device on Xively, the Feed ID for your account and your device's API key are assigned automatically. You program your Arduino to use your unique feed's API key every time it updates your feed with new data. You modify the example code for this chapter to post data using the unique Feed ID and API key assigned by Xively.

To program your Arduino to post data to Xively, you need to obtain two code libraries: one for connecting to Xively and the other for using Hypertext Transport Protocol (called HttpClient), which allows your Arduino to send data via the web. The code libraries for Xively and HttpClient are included on the companion website with the code examples for all the projects at www. dummies.com/go/arduinoprojectsfordummies. Install the libraries into the Arduino Libraries folder for your operating system. If you are unsure about how to do this, it's explained in Chapter 3.

The Xively and HttpClient code libraries are updated regularly. You can also get them from their code repository on a service called github, where developers store the latest versions. The github URLs for the two libraries are also provided in the code comments.

Understanding the code

With the libraries installed, you tweak the example code to communicate with your feed and device. The listing that follows shows how you alter the example code:

```
#include <SPI.h>
#include <Ethernet.h>
#include <HttpClient.h>
#include <Xively.h>

#define API_KEY "***** YOUR API KEY GOES HERE *****"
#define FEED_ID ***** YOUR FEED ID GOES HERE *****

byte mac[] = { 0xDE, 0xAD, 0xBE, 0xEF, 0xFE, 0xED };

const int lightSensorPin=2;
const int tempPin1=3;
```

```
const int tempPin2=4;

unsigned long lastConnectionTime = 0
const unsigned long connectionInterval = 15000

char sensorId1[] = "light";
char sensorId2[] = "temp1";
char sensorId3[] = "temp2";

// Create three datastreams for the feed
XivelyDatastream datastreams[] = {
  XivelyDatastream(sensorId1, strlen(sensorId1), DATASTREAM_FLOAT),
  XivelyDatastream(sensorId2, strlen(sensorId2), DATASTREAM_FLOAT),
  XivelyDatastream(sensorId3, strlen(sensorId3), DATASTREAM_FLOAT),
};

// Wrap the 3 datastreams into one feed
XivelyFeed feed(FEED_ID, datastreams, 3);

// Create the ethernet client and Xively client
EthernetClient client;
XivelyClient xivelyclient(client);

void setup() {
  Serial.begin(9600);
  Serial.println("Initializing network");
  while (Ethernet.begin(mac) != 1) {
    Serial.println("Error getting IP address via DHCP, trying again...");
    delay(15000);
  }
  Serial.println("Network initialized");
  Serial.println("Ready.");
}
```

The important things to note in the preceding code are your FEED_ID and your API_KEY. You need to replace these with the ones assigned by Xively to your account and device, respectively. Cut and paste them into your code to make sure they are identical. Your Arduino uses them every time you upload data to your data feed to authenticate to the Xively servers.

Above those are the four libraries you include in the sketch. In addition to Xively and HttpClient, you also are using SPI and Ethernet, which provide communication to your Ethernet shield and specify how it operates.

Every device connected to an Ethernet network has what's called a Media Access Control (MAC) address. You've no doubt heard of IP addresses. MAC addresses sit "below" IP addresses, at the hardware level. Each piece of Ethernet hardware on a network has to have a unique address. Normally, these are burned onto the board at the manufacturer, but you can assign your own, as I show in this code. Newer Ethernet shields have a label on the bottom with a MAC address. You can put that number here, or simply ignore it.

As long as every MAC address is unique on your network, it won't pose a problem. But if you have two Ethernet shields running this code on your network, you will need to set different MAC addresses for them.

After the MAC address, the example sketch uses the three integers for the three analog pins from your test sketch:

```
const int lightSensorPin=2;
const int tempPin1=3;
const int tempPin2=4;
```

Next, the code declares two *long integers* to store the time in milliseconds, and the time you last posted data to Xively. You use these to set an update interval. The code specifies 15,000 milliseconds (15 seconds). If you want to update at a different interval, change it here.

Your sensors have their own IDs, which correspond to the channels you created on Xively:

```
char sensorId1[] = "light";
char sensorId2[] = "temp1";
char sensorId3[] = "temp2";
```

Make sure the names in the quotation marks are identical to the names you created for the three channels of your device.

The channels are updated by a Xively *data stream object* called datastreams, which is an array containing the three sensors. These three char variables uniquely identify each data stream used in your Xively account's feed, which correspond to the three channels you set up when you created your device:

```
XivelyDatastream datastreams[] = {
  XivelyDatastream(sensorId1, strlen(sensorId1), DATASTREAM_FLOAT),
  XivelyDatastream(sensorId2, strlen(sensorId2), DATASTREAM_FLOAT),
  XivelyDatastream(sensorId3, strlen(sensorId3), DATASTREAM_FLOAT),
};
```

Each data stream consists of its `sensorID`, which you created earlier, a variable to specify the length of the data being sent, and a `float` variable that contains the data itself (you can also use other kinds of variables). These values are added when your readings are posted to Xively. You could create many more streams here, limited only by your Arduino's memory.

Each data stream corresponds to the channels you set up for your Xively devices, so you need a data stream for each channel.

You *wrap* these three streams together to send them to your feed. The FEED_ID comes from the variable declaration at the top of the code that Xively created for you. The last value in the parentheses (3) specifies how many data streams you have:

```
XivelyFeed feed(FEED_ID, datastreams, 3);
```

The next lines create an Ethernet client and a Xively client for your Arduino to use to send data. The `setup()` section creates a serial port so that you can display what's going on for testing and debugging. It also establishes the Ethernet connection on your network, using an automatically assigned IP address. If you want to use a static IP address, you can do that, too. Chapter 11 describes how to use a static IP address with your Ethernet shield.

Understanding the main loop

In the main `loop()`, readings are posted to Xively with the `sendData()` function, which follows the main `loop()`. There's also a `getData()` function that verifies what was posted to Xively and prints it to the serial monitor. The `getData()` function is not essential, but it's good for debugging or live monitoring. Later, you use the `getVoltage()` function from your test sketch.

First, you use your three temperature sensors and the `sendData()` and `getData()` functions so that you can send three sensor readings. Remember to change the values in the `map()` function of your `lightLevel` reading (shown in bold) to correspond to the values you obtained from testing your sensors, as described in the previous section.

```
void loop() {
  if (millis() - lastConnectionTime > connectionInterval) {
    float lightLevel = map(analogRead(lightSensorPin),0,1023,0,100);
    sendData(0, lightLevel);
```

```
    getData(0);

    float temperature1 = ((getVoltage(tempPin1) -.5) * 100L);
    sendData(1, temperature1);
    getData(1);

    float temperature2 = ((getVoltage(tempPin2) -.5) * 100L);
    sendData(2, temperature2);
    getData(2);

    Serial.println("Waiting for next reading");
    Serial.println("========================");

    lastConnectionTime = millis();
    }
}
```

In this code, you use the same method to get the sensor readings you used in the test sketch and employ the sendData() and getData() *function calls* to send the values to Xively. The sendData() function sends the values to each channel and the getData() function allows you to read back the data from Xively, to make sure your code is working properly.

The sendData function takes a parameter for which sensor to send and also the value to send. Recall that your sensor values are stored in a data stream array called datastreams[]. Each sensor has a position in that array, starting with the light sensor, which is at position 0. This number is the first value you put into the sendData() function call, followed by the lightLevel reading just taken. The getData() function contains the same number, 0, which refers to the light sensor:

```
    sendData(0, lightLevel);
    getData(0);
```

You use the same code to take the temperature readings that you used in your test sketch. Because the positions for the temperature data streams in the datastreams[] array are 1 and 2, you use those numbers for the send-Data() and getData() function calls:

```
    sendData(1, temperature1);
    getData(1);
```

Take a moment to understand how the sendData() and getData() functions work. The sendData() function accepts two values, one for the position of the sensor in the datastreams[] array, and a second for the reading just taken. The *local integer variable* streamIndexNumber contains the number you used in the sendData() function call:

```
void sendData(int streamIndexNumber, float sensorValue) {
  datastreams[streamIndexNumber].setFloat(sensorValue);

  Serial.print("Sensor value is: ");
  Serial.println(datastreams[streamIndexNumber].getFloat());

  Serial.println("Uploading to Xively");
  int ret = xivelyclient.put(feed, API_KEY);
}
```

The next line actually stores the value of the reading just taken into the datastreams[] array at the position that was specified by your function call (0, 1, or 2, depending on which sensor was read), and sets the reading's value as a float:

```
datastreams[streamIndexNumber].setFloat(sensorValue);
```

The value is then printed to the serial monitor. The last line in the function finally sends the data to Xively, using a function from the Xively library, xivelyclient.put(). This is where your API key is needed. It's used to verify that you are allowed to post data to the feed. Don't share the key with others, or they'll be able to post to and read from your feed, too.

The getData() function allows you to read back what you've posted (or read data from other feeds, if you have the API key). It takes an integer as input, and that integer specifies the position of the data stream (that is, the channel) in the feed that contains your sensor data:

```
void getData(int stream) {
  Serial.println("Reading the data back from Xively");

  int request = xivelyclient.get(feed, API_KEY);

  if (request > 0) {
    Serial.print("Datastream: ");
    Serial.println(feed[stream]);

    Serial.print("Sensor value: ");
    Serial.println(feed[stream].getFloat());
    Serial.println("=========================");
  }
}
```

This function uses another built-in function from the Xively library, `xively client.get()`, which gets your Xively feed using your `FEED_ID` and your `API_KEY`. In the printed output, you specify exactly which stream from your feed you want to print:

```
Serial.println(feed[stream]);
```

The stream you are printing is one of the three you've been posting from your `datastreams[]` array.

Finally, you simply use the `getVoltage()` function from your test sketch and — voilà! — your code is complete.

Making sense of your sensor readings

Now take it for a test drive. Upload the code to your Arduino and turn on your serial monitor. You should see something similar to the output shown in Figure 12-20.

Figure 12-20: Monitoring your Xively feed posts in the serial monitor.

To see what it looks like on Xively, go to your feed's URL on Xively. You can find your feed's URL in the upper-right corner of your Xively Developer's Workbench. My feed is at: `https://xively.com/feeds/1424780519`. Simply replace the number at the end with your `FEED_ID`.

The reporting screen should look somewhat like mine, shown in Figure 12-21. You can use the gear widget to alter how your graphs look and to get custom embedded code that you can paste into your website, blog, or Twitter. If you are sharing tweets with your Facebook account, you can post them on Facebook, too.

You will likely agree that using an Arduino and Xively to post your sensor data to the Internet makes a lot of sense!

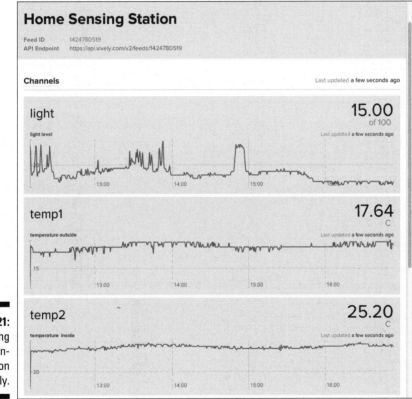

Figure 12-21:
Displaying
your sen-
sor data on
Xively.

Part IV
Advanced Arduino Projects

In this part . . .

✔ Learn about GPS and Arduino

✔ Build a GPS data logger

✔ Build a programmable LED cube

✔ Decode remote controls lying around your house

✔ Learn to program servo motors

Chapter 13

Building a GPS Data Logger

In This Chapter

▶ Understanding GPS

▶ Building a GPS data logger shield

▶ Collecting data with your data logger

▶ Plotting your course using online maps and Google Earth

*Y*ou've no doubt used the Global Positioning System (GPS) either in your car or on your phone. GPS is everywhere — literally over our heads, all the time. Designed for the United States military to aid with defense systems, GPS uses a constellation of satellites to provide precise location information to any receiver that can receive and decode the GPS signal. This task was challenging, as you can imagine. GPSs in the early days were as big as a small suitcase. But these days, you can get a GPS receiver on a wristwatch!

Only trouble is, many of the consumer products out there don't give you the flexibility to do whatever you want with the GPS data. That's where Arduino comes to the rescue! In this project, you can use an Arduino and a GPS shield kit to build a battery-powered GPS receiver that logs data to a mini SD card for several hours. You program your Arduino to collect the data, and you can then use it however you wish. Track your bicycle trips, hiking excursions, or walking tours. You could even stick the logger in a car to build up a log of driving habits and destinations. Ever have trouble remembering what parts of a city you explored while on vacation? Not anymore. Because you store the data in a standard format, you can make a plot of your trail, using tools online or applications, such as Google Earth.

Building the GPS data logger shield itself is easy and takes under an hour. If you haven't tried soldering before, this project is a good one to start with because it is pretty easy to do and you won't be at much risk of damaging things if you have trouble getting the hang of it. You then test your data logger to make sure it is working properly. It will take another hour or so to get everything into your enclosure. Finally, you go out and collect some GPS data. You can then plot the map online, get the data converted for use with software, such as Google Earth, and even download an image file if you need one.

Understanding GPS

The Global Positioning System is a constellation of 32 satellites that are whizzing around about 20,200km (12,600 miles) above your head. They orbit once every 12 hours and are arranged so that at least 6 satellites are always visible from anywhere on earth. Each satellite sends signals that include its exact position and the time when its message was sent. With this information from a minimum of 3 satellites, a GPS receiver can calculate your position based upon the transit time of the messages.

Because GPS relies on signals from several satellites, it can take time for your GPS receiver to "get a fix." GPS relies on line-of-sight, meaning signals from the satellites will be blocked by tall structures. If only two are visible from your location, it won't be possible to calculate your latitude, longitude, and altitude until at least one more satellite pops into view. When you first build and test your project, it can take a while to get a fix, so it's a good idea to place your receiver (or optional antenna) where it can get a good unobstructed view of the heavens above.

Selecting Your Parts

First, get together the parts and tools you need to build the data logger. You put everything into an enclosure, so you will need to do a little bit of light drilling for the power switch and the optional external antenna, if you choose to use one.

You need the following parts, shown in Figure 13-1:

- ✔ An Arduino Uno
- ✔ An Adafruit Industries Ultimate GPS logger shield
- ✔ A micro SD or micro SDHC card
- ✔ A 9V DC battery and snap connector
- ✔ A single-pole, single throw (SPST) rocker switch, such as Jameco #316451 or Maplin # N19CL
- ✔ An enclosure, such as Jameco #2134926 or Farnell #1848692, or a translucent one from Maplin, #N07GC
- ✔ A scrap of pine wood or wooden strips about 1cm (¼") thick and cut to the same width as your enclosure (optional)
- ✔ Three or four short pan head screws, about 1cm (¼") long. You can also use pan head wood screws (#6 screws should do).

✔ A 3-5V external magnetic mount GPS antenna, available from Adafruit or Jameco #2153297 (optional)

✔ An SMA to uFL/u.FL/IPX/IPEX RF "pigtail" adapter cable (optional) from Adafruit or other online sellers

✔ An adaptor to read the micro SD card, using your computer or laptop

You need to build this project with an Arduino Uno, Arduino Duemilanove, or Diecimila. You can also use an Arduino Leonardo or a Mega, but they need some modifications to the code to work correctly that I don't cover here. If you plan to use one of the latter, you should check out the Adafruit website that has detailed instructions for using other Arduinos.

The workhorse of this project is the Adafruit Ultimate GPS Logger Shield. It contains all the key components needed to get and record GPS data, including the GPS receiver, and an SD card slot. It also has a prototyping area in case you want to add additional features to your data logger. Getting a GPS module to work can be kind of tricky because you need some additional components to be able to connect it to an Arduino. The cool thing about this shield is that all these components are already connected, tested, and ready to go, so you can focus on building the project and not on troubleshooting why your GPS receiver isn't working.

You can download schematics and full-color parts placement diagrams from the companion website (www.dummies.com/go/arduinoprojectsfor dummies).

Figure 13-1: The parts you need for this project.

You can find a micro SD or SDHC card just about anywhere these days. I picked one up from the supermarket for about five bucks. You are only recording text data to it, so you don't need a big one. Go for cheap. Even with a 2GB card, at one reading per second, you'll be able to store millions of positions before you run out of room on it. And your battery will die long before that. You need to make sure you have a micro SD card reader so that you can copy the data from the card to your computer or laptop. You can get a micro SD to USB adaptor for about five bucks on Amazon or eBay.

To take your data logger into the wild, without your computer or laptop, you need to keep it powered up and you need a way to turn it on and off. This means a battery power supply and power switch. To get everything into a portable, small enclosure, use a standard 9V DC battery and 9V battery snap connector. You power the Arduino directly from the clip, which you solder onto the GPS shield. My tests conclude that a standard rectangular 9V battery lasted about five and a half hours. Because battery life is directly related to the chemical action of the battery materials, larger batteries will yield longer life. If you decide you want longer staying power, you can replace the 9V battery with a 9V battery pack that holds six AA cells, using the same style snap connector. These will substantially extend how much data you can collect.

To switch it on and off, I used a *slimline* rocker switch that gives the project a nice professional finish and is very inexpensive. The tricky part of using square-shaped rocker switches is that you need to bore a square hole in your enclosure. You can also use simple toggle switches that use a single, round bore hole, but these will stick out from the side of the box and could be easily switched off accidentally.

You need a small plastic enclosure to protect your project. An ABS plastic one is fine and is easy to cut into for the power switch and antenna. Jameco and Farnell offer a made-for-Arduino custom enclosure that works well, but you won't be able to see the status lights and you need an antenna. I found a translucent blue one from Maplin, which means I can also see the status lights on the shield. If you use a clear box, you might be able to get away without using an antenna at all, but you'll have to try it out to be sure. A metal box blocks the signal, so get the antenna if you are using one.

You need to hold your Arduino firmly in the box, but project enclosures rarely have the right internal supports (called "bosses") for your Arduino. Instead of screwing your Arduino into the plastic, you glue the short strips of wood into your project enclosure so that you can attach your Arduino to it with three or four pan head or #6 wood screws. The length of the screws should be about the same as the thickness of the wood strips, or slightly longer, as your Arduino will not sit completely flush against the wood.

If you are using an enclosure specially designed for Arduinos, you won't need the strips of wood or the screws.

GPS requires an unobstructed, line-of-sight view to the satellites that provide the tracking signal. Your GPS shield has an integrated antenna onboard. However, its sensitivity is limited. A plastic enclosure shouldn't interfere with the antenna, but using an external antenna provides greater sensitivity, although it will draw a little more power. Many GPS extension antennas are out there, and the magnetically mountable ones can be easily slapped onto the top of a car or a bicycle frame. If your antenna has an SMA connector and is made for GPS, it should work.

The antenna connector on the shield is a tiny little u.FL connector, which keeps the shield compact. However, most GPS antennas use a co-axial "subminiature version A" (SMA) connecter, which is threaded. So, to connect the GPS antenna to the shield, you also need a short "pigtail" SMA to u.FL adapter.

The u.FL connector is known by several industry names, including IPX, IPEX, and UMCC, but they are all the same design. You can easily find a pigtail adaptor for one of these connectors on eBay or Amazon and Adafruit also sells them.

If you are using a plastic enclosure like the one in the parts list, you need a couple of tools for cutting the holes in the enclosure for the power switch and the antenna. You need either a hand drill or a power drill and approximately 7mm (¼") drill bit for your switch. If you are using a square toggle switch, you'll need to square up the holes with a fine hand file.

Building Your Project

Building your project is done in three steps. First, you assemble the GPS shield and test to make sure it's working correctly. You then program and upload code to enable the data logger. Finally, you check to make sure you are logging data to your SD card. This project is really simple, so there's no wiring schematic, and you don't need to prototype it on breadboard.

Assembling and testing the GPS shield

Putting the shield together is really easy. All you have to do is attach the pin headers and insert a battery. What could be simpler? First, fire up your soldering iron and make sure that it's ready to go. Then do the following steps to put it together:

1. **Separate the strip of pin headers included with your shield into groups that match your Arduino's header sockets.**

   It's a good idea to use a pair of needle nose pliers to snap off the required number, as shown in Figure 13-2. That way, you can be sure that you've got the right number of pins in each segment and they break off cleanly. You also won't inadvertently snap the strip where you don't intend.

   Make sure that you count carefully. The Arduino header sockets do not all have the same number of holes!

2. **You use your Arduino as a support for your pin headers while you solder them onto the shield. Insert the pin headers into your Arduino's header sockets, as in Figure 13-3.**

3. **Seat your GPS shield onto the pin headers.**

   You may need to wiggle things around a bit in order to get the shield in place. Make sure all the pins extend through the top of your shield and that there are no missing pins, as shown in Figure 13-4.

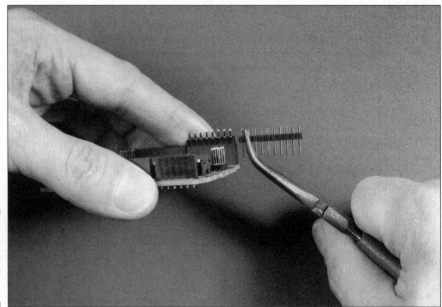

Figure 13-2:
Snapping off the right number of pin headers.

Figure 13-3:
Using your
Arduino as
a soldering
support.

Figure 13-4:
Placing your
shield into
position for
soldering.

4. Now use your soldering iron to solder each of the pins to your shield.

If you are right handed, start at the left side (and start at the right if you are left handed). That way you will be able to see your work as you go along. Refer to Figure 13-5.

After you've soldered the shield to your pins, you're almost ready to perform your maiden voyage — a test to make sure your GPS shield is working.

Your shield has two operating modes: *direct connection* and *software serial,* which are selected by a tiny switch on the shield, shown in Figure 13-6. In the direct connection mode, your Arduino doesn't run any code. Instead, it acts as an intermediary to your shield, so that you can communicate directly with the GPS module's *serial interface.* You use Arduino IDE serial monitor to send and receive commands directly to the GPS module on your shield. This is useful for testing the GPS unit, and for sending configuration commands if you want to change how it operates. When you are satisfied with the tests, you can put the GPS shield into software serial mode.

Your Arduino has one serial port, which it uses to communicate with your computer. It's physically connected both to your USB port and digital Pins 0 and 1. However, when you want your Arduino to control your GPS module, you also need a second serial port to connect to it and send commands. That's where the software serial port comes in. Software Serial is a library that allows your Arduino to use additional pins for serial communication. It's the only way you can send and receive serial data to other devices while you also monitor your Arduino with your computer. The soft serial switch lets you switch between the two.

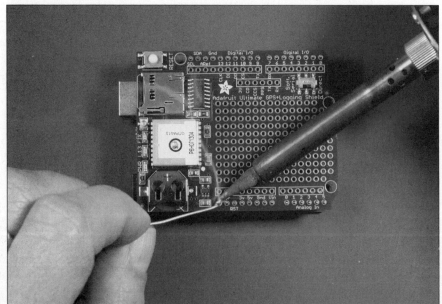

Figure 13-5:
Soldering
your shield
to your pin
headers.

Because of the digital pin layout, direct connection using this switch only
works on the Arduino Uno, Duemilanove, Diecimila, Arduino compatible, or
Arduino Mega.

To use direct connection mode for testing the GPS module, you first upload
a "blank" sketch onto your Arduino. Open your Arduino IDE and type the following into a new sketch:

```
void setup() {}
void loop() {}
```

Save this sketch with a name you'll remember, such as "blank." Switch your
shield to "Soft Serial" mode so that you can send this code to your Arduino.
Then, connect your USB cable and upload the blank sketch.

Now that the code is loaded, you can test your GPS module and monitor its
output directly from the GPS chip. Flip the switch on your shield to Direct,
as shown in Figure 13-7. This connects your USB serial connection directly
to the GPS module. Later, when you are ready to use your shield for data logging, you will switch it back to the "Soft Serial" setting.

If you have uploaded your blank sketch code, the red "FIX" LED should be
flashing once per second. If not, you may need to cycle the power. Unplug
your USB cable, make sure that you have set your switch to "Direct," and then
plug it back in. If the red LED still isn't flashing, you might have a problem with
your soldering or your board.

Figure 13-7:
Switching
to Direct
Connection
mode to test
the GPS
module.

Open your Arduino IDE and click on Serial Monitor, making sure it is set to 9600 baud in its drop-down menu. You should see output similar to that in Figure 13-8. If you do, your module is working correctly, though it hasn't picked up any satellites yet. Nonetheless, it still sends data so you know it's working.

```
●○○                    /dev/tty.usbmodem1421
[                                              ]  ( Send )
$GPGGA,235949.799,,,,,0,0,,,M,,M,,*4F
$GPGSA,A,1,,,,,,,,,,,,,,*1E
$GPGSV,1,1,00*79
$GPRMC,235949.799,V,,,,,0.00,0.00,050180,,,N*46
$GPVTG,0.00,T,,M,0.00,N,0.00,K,N*32
$GPGGA,235950.799,,,,,0,0,,,M,,M,,*47
$GPGSA,A,1,,,,,,,,,,,,,,*1E
$GPRMC,235950.799,V,,,,,0.00,0.00,050180,,,N*4E
$GPVTG,0.00,T,,M,0.00,N,0.00,K,N*32
$GPGGA,235951.799,,,,,0,0,,,M,,M,,*46
$GPGSA,A,1,,,,,,,,,,,,,,*1E
$GPRMC,235951.799,V,,,,,0.00,0.00,050180,,,N*4F
$GPVTG,0.00,T,,M,0.00,N,0.00,K,N*32
$GPGGA,235952.799,,,,,0,0,,,M,,M,,*45
$GPGSA,A,1,,,,,,,,,,,,,,*1E
$GPRMC,235952.799,V,,,,,0.00,0.00,050180,,,N*4C
$GPVTG,0.00,T,,M,0.00,N,0.00,K,N*32
[✓] Autoscroll          ( No line ending ◆ ) ( 9600 baud ◆ )
```

Figure 13-8:
Viewing out-
put directly
from your
GPS module.

This text is pretty hard to interpret unless you know what the GPS module is saying. It uses the National Marine Electronics Association (NMEA) format and outputs data for four different GPS data standards, each on a separate line and preceded by a "$" sign. The one you are interested in is the Global Positioning Recommended Minimum sentence ($GPRMC). This line gives you the following information, as shown in Figure 13-9:

- ✔ The NMEA sentence format used
- ✔ Time in Greenwich Mean Time (GMT)
- ✔ A satellite "fix" code: Active (A) or Invalid/Void (V)
- ✔ The longitude in decimal degrees
- ✔ The longitude hemisphere, north (N) or south (S)
- ✔ The latitude in decimal degrees
- ✔ The latitude hemisphere, east (E) or west (W)

The latitude, longitude, and hemispheres contain nothing if there is no fix — so you will just see commas with no data until you go outdoors to get a fix!

- ✔ The speed of travel over land (in knots).
- ✔ The "azimuth" or direction of travel. An azimuth is just a "compass" direction, which is a horizontal angle around the horizon, measured in degrees (0–360). 0 is north, 90 is east, 180 is south, and 270, west.
- ✔ The Coordinated Universal Time (UTC) date, starting from Week 1 in "GPS time" (which started in January 1980). This is updated when your GPS receives the correct current GMT from satellites — but it hasn't seen one yet.
- ✔ A checksum, preceded by an asterisk, which tests the raw data for transmission errors.

When you can see this information, you know the GPS unit is alive and well. You're now ready to hunt for satellites!

If you are using a laptop, you can go outside to check whether you can get a fix from the GPS satellites. If you are using a desktop and the optional extension cable and pigtail adaptor, you might be able to get a signal by sticking the antenna out of a nearby window. Attach the antenna as described at the end of this chapter to make sure your module is working before you build the enclosure.

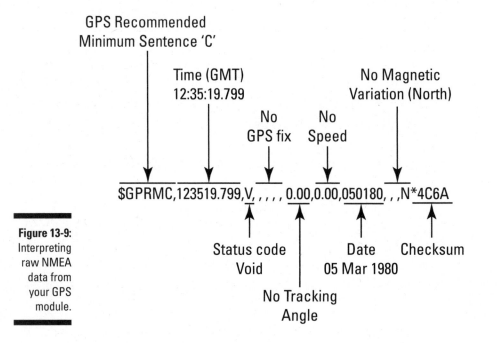

Figure 13-9:
Interpreting
raw NMEA
data from
your GPS
module.

Be patient! It can take a while to get a fix from the GPS satellites. In the best case, you'll get a fix in about a minute. However, you may have to wait 10 or 15 minutes or even longer, depending on the situation overhead. But after you do get a fix, you'll receive updated tracking data every second. Your GPS module will also start reporting the position data to your serial monitor.

The red LED labeled "FIX" on your shield will flash once every second until you get a fix. Afterward, it will flash once every 15 seconds as long as it has a fix. If it loses the fix, it will revert to flashing once per second.

If you are able to take your GPS module outside or if you have are using the optional long antenna, you may be able to get a fix while you are connected directly to the GPS module. Your status code will change to "A" and you will receive latitude and longitude information.

The GPS logger shield has an onboard Real Time Clock (RTC). The button battery is to keep this powered up when you aren't using it. However, your GPS module gets the time for the satellites. So you don't need this unless you write code to support it. If you do insert your button battery, your GPS module might stop operating after about 20 seconds unless you've set up the RTC. So keep it out during testing.

Programming your data logger

Now that you've communicated directly with your GPS module, you can upload code to log data to your SD module.

You need to switch the GPS module back to Soft Serial if you aren't communicating directly to the GPS module. All the code you'll upload to the board requires Soft Serial.

The code for this project is on the companion website for the book, www. dummies.com/go/arduinoprojectsfordummies, and is in a zipped file containing the files you need:

- ✔ The data logging sketch that runs on your Arduino, called shield_sdlog.
- ✔ A library that interfaces with the GPS module, called Adafruit_GPS.
- ✔ A library that writes data to the SD card, called SD.
- ✔ The library that allows you to create "virtual" serial ports, called Software Serial.

Software Serial is a "core library," so it is part of the Arduino IDE 1.0 installation. If you are using an older version of the IDE, you should update it.

You can hunt for these yourself online or on github, the code sharing website (see: https://github.com/adafruit/Adafruit-GPS-Library). But to make things easier, these are all in the Zip file for Chapter 13, on this book's website. You should download the Zip file now and extract the files to your system.

To make things easier, I've renamed the Adafruit library on the companion website to Adafruit_GPS. The Adafruit library on github extracts to Adafruit-GPS-Library-master and you'll need to rename it for the code to work properly. Refer to the instructions on installing libraries in Chapter 3.

After you've downloaded the files, fire up the Arduino IDE. If it's already running, you need to restart it so that the new libraries will appear in your Application menus. Now, navigate through the menus and select File⇨ Examples⇨Adafruit_GPS⇨shieldlog_sd. It's not necessary to go into the gory details of how each of the code lines work. But you should focus your attention on the following lines:

```
// see if the card is present and can be initialized:
  if (!SD.begin(chipSelect, 11, 12, 13)) {
  //if (!SD.begin(chipSelect)) {      // if you're using an UNO, you can use
              this line instead
    Serial.println("Card init. failed!");
    error(2);
  }
```

This project uses an Arduino Uno, so you need to add two forward slashes to comment out the first line and then remove the comment from the second line beginning `if (!SD.begin`. Otherwise you will get an error.

The rest of the code handles the following things:

- ✔ It creates the variable GPSECHO, which you should leave set to true while you are testing your module. It sends all that data to the serial port so you can see what's happening. Later, you can turn it off, if you wish.

- ✔ It creates the variable LOG_FIXONLY, which makes sure that entries are only recorded to your SD card if your GPS module has a fix. Leave this "false" until you are finished testing.

- ✔ It makes sure that you are able to write a fresh file to the SD card, and sequentially numbering new files.

- ✔ It establishes communication with the GPS module and kick-starts it.

- ✔ It writes the data received from your GPS module onto the SD card, inside the newly created file.

A new file with a two-digit sequence number is created whenever you power up your module. Take a moment to look through the code before uploading it to your Arduino.

If you plan to try out any of the other example sketches included in the Adafruit library (which I highly recommend), be sure to change the lines referring to Software Serial at the top of the sketch so that you are using Pins 7, 8 and not Pins 2, 3. Otherwise you won't see any output in the serial monitor.

Testing your data logger

After you've made the changes to your code, connect your USB cable to your USB port, select the correct serial port for your Arduino from the Arduino IDE, and upload your code. You don't need to remove the GPS shield before you upload your code. Make sure the switch is set to Soft Serial.

When uploading is finished, enable the serial monitor in your IDE. Make sure your baud rate is now set to 115200, or you will see gibberish on the serial monitor.

If you are indoors, you should see output very much like what you saw when you were directly connected to the GPS module during testing. If you happen to be outdoors, or you have used the GPS extension antenna and placed it outside a window, you may just start to see some GPS data after a while.

Figure 13-10 shows a diagram of the output from your GPS module when you are receiving data. You should see output similar to this in the serial monitor.

It's much the same as your earlier test, but now it has information in the previously blank fields.

Remember, it can take anywhere from a minute to 15 minutes before you see any GPS data.

Once you are happy that you've got it working properly, make two final changes to the code:

1. **Set the** GPSECHO **variable to false.**

   You don't need to echo data to the serial monitor when you are logging data and not connected to a computer.

2. **Set** LOG_FIXONLY **to true.**

   You are only logging data when you have a fix on GPS satellites.

When you've edited these values, you can disconnect your data logger from your computer.

Make sure that the switch on top of the GPS shield is set to Soft Serial. Now you are ready to build your enclosure and secure the module inside its new home!

Making the enclosure

Assembling and programming the shield was the easy part. Making the enclosure is just about as easy. All you need to do is provide holes for the switch and the antenna connector, solder the power switch, and solder the snap connector for your battery onto the shield.

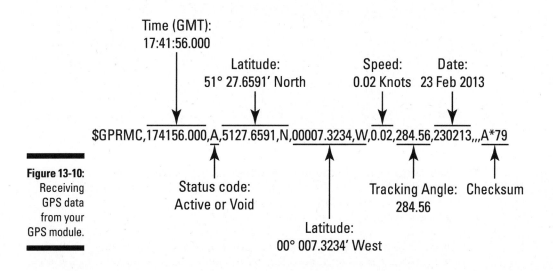

Figure 13-10:
Receiving
GPS data
from your
GPS module.

You need your hot glue gun for this part, so plug it in and allow it to warm up while you do the following steps, referring to Figures 13-11 through 13-14:

1. **Use your drill bit to bore out the hole for the rocker switch.**

   It may be easier to bore two adjacent holes and then remove the material between them.

2. **If you are using the optional antenna, bore a hole for it using the same bit.**

   I placed mine next to the hole for the rocker switch, as shown in Figure 13-11.

3. **Use a small file to make the hole for the power switch nice and square. See Figure 13-12.**

   I did not drill a hole for the USB connector because I wanted a tightly enclosed box. You might find it easier to bore a hole for your USB connector if you plan on frequently programming your GPS module. I've found it's more likely that I just "set it and forget it," so I didn't bother to create a hole in the enclosure for my USB connector.

4. **Insert your power switch into the enclosure.**

Figure 13-11:
Drilling holes for your power switch and antenna.

Figure 13-12:
Filing the hole for your rocker switch.

5. **If you are using an external antenna, insert your antenna pigtail adapter into the enclosure.**

   Be sure to use the washers provided, with the serrated washer on the inside of the enclosure and the lock washer and retaining nut on the outside of the enclosure, as shown in Figure 13-13.

6. **Now insert your scraps of pine into your enclosure to estimate where you want to place your Arduino.**

   You need to leave enough room for the 9V battery and to make sure your power switch won't touch your Arduino.

7. **Use your hot glue gun to apply glue to the wood and press it firmly into the bottom of the enclosure. See Figure 13-14.**

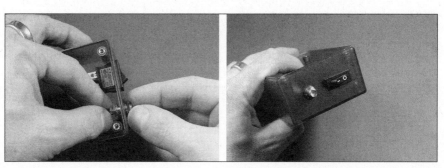

Figure 13-13:
Mounting your power switch and pigtail SMA antenna adapter.

Figure 13-14:
Positioning
your
Arduino and
gluing your
wood on the
enclosure.

8. **Test the position of your Arduino and GPS shield "sandwich" on the wood inside your enclosure, making sure that it doesn't touch the contacts of your power switch.**

Adding the power supply

The power supply is simply your 9V battery connected to the switch. The positive lead is connected to one side of the rocker switch. The other side is connected to the Vin pin on your GPS shield, which is connected to your Arduino's power input pin (through a pin header on the shield). The negative lead goes straight to your ground pin. Do the following steps, as shown in Figures 13-15 and 13-16:

1. **Solder the red, positive wire from your 9 volt battery clip to one side of the switch. It doesn't matter which side. (The battery clip should not be connected to any battery.)**

2. **Solder a jumper wire or other spare piece of wire to the other side of your switch. If you have a red one, that's even better.**

3. **Separate your GPS shield from your Arduino and use three or four of your wood screws to secure your Arduino to the wood, as shown in Figure 13-15.**

4. **Insert your mini SD card into the shield, as in Figure 13-16.**

   Be careful when you insert it. The spring inside has a tendency to make the card fly out of your hands if you don't hold it steady. Don't insert the small button battery until you are finished testing.

5. **Now insert your GPS shield back onto your Arduino, taking care to make sure you've slotted it into the right holes.**

Figure 13-15: Soldering the power switch connections and installing your Arduino.

Figure 13-16: Installing your mini SD card and battery (after testing).

6. **If you are using an external antenna, insert the u.FL connector into the socket on your GPS shield, as shown in Figure 13-17.**

   It's a tiny little socket located just below your mini SD card slot. The u.FL connector is not made for heavy use. Instead, it's optimized for size. After you've connected your pigtail adapter to it, you should leave it in place and try to avoid connecting and disconnecting it repeatedly. To keep the cable out of the way, I routed the cable underneath, between the shield and the Arduino.

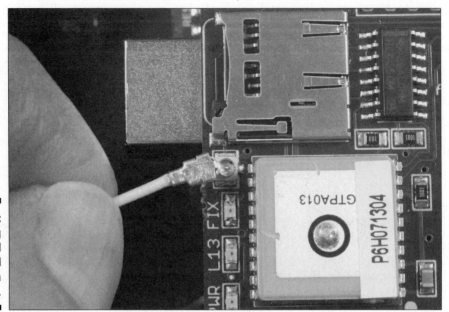

Figure 13-17:
Connecting
the optional
external
antenna
adapter.

7. Now, solder the red power wire from your power switch to the input power pin labeled Vin, as shown in Figure 13-18.

8. Carefully solder your black ground connection from your battery connector (still not connected to any battery) to the input labeled GND on your shield, which is connected directly to the GND input on your Arduino.

   Actually, there are two holes labeled GND. You can use either one of them, but I find the hole that is farther away from the Vin pin is easier to solder.

9. Make sure your power switch is turned off and attach your battery, as shown in Figure 13-19.

10. Screw the lid back onto your enclosure.

11. Attach the optional external GPS antenna.

12. Turn the power switch on.

Figure 13-18:
Soldering
your power
input wire.

Figure 13-19:
Connecting
your battery
and external
antenna.

Collecting and Plotting GPS Data

Now you are ready to go out into the wild and start collecting routing data. If you're using it, you can slap the external antenna onto your car or bicycle or any other ferrous metal surface. The steel panels of a car work great. I snaked my antenna through the sunroof and hit the road.

Tracking your path

Before you set off on your data logging adventure, make sure that the "FIX" LED is blinking once every 15 seconds. If it is blinking once per second it has not yet acquired the signal of at least three satellites and so won't write data to your SD card.

If you are using a single 9V battery, you can expect about three to five hours of tracking time. If you switch off the receiver during your journey, the code will automatically create a new log file. It automatically increments the numbers on the suffix of the filename. When you've got your data collected, you can switch off the unit and remove the SD card.

Plotting your data

Depending on how long you were tracking, your log file will contain a long list of GPRMC sentences, with each reading on a separate line. You should see text like that in Figure 13-10, but with geographic coordinates that match your own trek.

If your log file looks similar to this, you are ready to plot the data as a map. There are several ways to do this, but the raw GPRMC sentence is not in a format that can be easily read by most mapping websites and software. If you want to plot the coordinates using a tool like Google Earth, you will need to convert your raw data into the .kml format. You can do that and a whole lot more using Adam Schneider's excellent gpsvisualizer.com website.

To plot your map, do the following steps, as shown in Figure 13-20:

1. **Open your web browser and navigate to** gpsvisualizer.com.

2. **In the box labeled Get Started Now, click the Choose File button and locate your data file on your computer.**

3. **Choose an output format from the drop-down menu.**

   The default is Google Maps. If you want to get an image file you can download, you should select the image file output format that you want from the menu. Depending on the size of your file, it will take a few moments to process the data. You should soon see output like that in Figure 13-20.

4. **You can select the link at the top of the page to download an HTML file that contains a link to Google Maps, which will draw the map for you.**

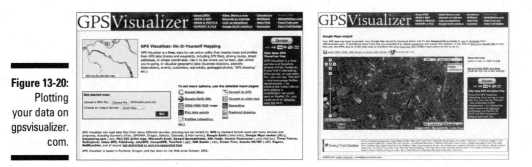

Figure 13-20:
Plotting
your data on
gpsvisualizer.
com.

If you would like to explore the map in Google Earth, which also allows you to save an image file, you can also select the output as a `.kml` file on the main landing page for `gpsvisualizer.com`.

The text files generated by your data logger are pretty small. The 5½-hour log file I generated in Figure 13-20 contains 24,380 lines of text, but only takes up 1.7MB of space on the card. So even with a small 2GB card, you can leave your data files on the SD card and keep on adding more for a long time. However, it is a good idea to occasionally copy them to your local system for safekeeping.

Now head out there and get tracking 'til you drop!

Chapter 14

Building a Remote-Controlled Car

*Y*ou can buy remote-controlled car kits in hobby shops, but building your own is much more fun — and it's easy to do with an Arduino and a little ingenuity. In this project, you create a fully drivable remote-controlled (RC) car by using an ordinary household remote control, an Arduino, and servo motors. You use your Arduino to decode the signals coming from any of your remotes and then use the decoded signal to tell your car to move forward, backward, and turn.

One cool thing about this project is that after you figure out how to use any old remote control with your Arduino, you can transfer this capability to just about any other project that you want to add a remote control to!

You can download schematics and full-color parts placement diagrams from the companion website (www.dummies.com/go/arduinoprojectsfor dummies).

Selecting and Preparing Your Parts

The parts you need are shown in Figure 14-1. You should get together the following components to build your car, which will take about five hours from starting gun to finish line:

- ✔ An Arduino

- ✔ A remote control

- ✔ TSOP2438 or TSOP4838 Infrared Receiver Module (Vishay Semiconductor) (Mouser Electronics 782-TSOP2438, and RS Components #708-5070). Alternatively, use a PNA4602 module.

✔ Two continuous-rotation servo motors (such as GoTeck GS-3360BB, Futaba 900-00008, Jameco #283039, or the Arduino Servo Module, Rapid #73-4464)

✔ A battery holder for six AA batteries and a 9V battery clip

✔ Six AA batteries

✔ Eight pin headers

✔ A breadboard

For the chassis:

✔ Two cylindrical cans of Pringles brand potato chips

✔ Two rubber bands about 8cm (3-4 inches)

✔ A piece of scrap plywood or balsa wood, at least 11 x 17cm (4 x 7 inches)

✔ A ball caster kit (Tamiya Brand — or Jameco #358336 or Cool Components #000984)

✔ Mounting hardware or hot glue

✔ Self-adhesive hook-and-loop fastener (optional)

Figure 14-1:
The parts you need for this project.

You can use any Arduino for this project. An Arduino Uno is shown in the figures.

The awesome thing about this project is that you can use pretty much any remote control you have in your house. You don't have to use the Toshiba remote shown in Figure 14-1. We have six of them, and we only use two, so I grabbed a spare one. You should select a remote that has arrows in the directions that you want to drive: left, right, forward, reverse, and — the all-important — stop! I got one of our old television remotes because it has a circular input pad, with a button in the center, which is a good place for the "brakes." It is possible that during testing, your remote will not be detectable. You might need to try a different one if you can't detect it during your testing.

The key component of this system is the Infrared (IR) Receiver module, a Vishay Electronics TSOP2438, which operates on the 38KHz carrier frequency. Other frequencies are used as well, but you need to detect 38KHz, one that is most common to household remote controls. The component works by sensing the infrared light patterns emitted by your remote and translating them into digital output signals your Arduino can read using a special IR library.

Only infrared light can be detected by the sensor — its epoxy case acts as a filter on other light frequencies. However, ambient light has infrared signatures, too. For example, a fireplace is a great source of heat and is also in the infrared spectrum. So this component is designed to ignore such stray noise.

Servo motors come in two flavors: 180 degree sweeping motion, or continuous rotation. Because you are using these motors for propulsion, you must get continuously rotating servos, such as the ones listed. The servos operate at 5V DC and can be somewhat power hungry. They also come with an accessory kit that contains mounting plates and armatures and an assortment of screws for mounting them. You need an additional angle bracket if you want to mount the servos using this hardware. You can also simply mount them to your car with hot glue.

You use a 9V battery pack for the project. You could use a single, rectangular 9V cell, but it won't last very long. The servo motors are pretty power hungry. You should get a 9V battery pack that holds six AA cells. They offer a nice balance between lifespan and weight. The heavier C or D cells last longer, but they may be too heavy for your car to move easily. Look for a battery holder that has a snap connector like those used for 9V batteries. This makes it easier to detach your battery pack from your car when it's time to reload. Figure 14-1 appears to show a pack containing two cells, but that's because the other four batteries are underneath the top two.

You need eight pin headers. The longer ones are easier to work with. You use two for your battery pack, and the other six to connect your servos to the breadboard. Pin headers usually come in long strips, so just break off a short section of two pins and two short sections of three pins each.

For the chassis, you can use any small piece of wood you might have lying around. The styling of the chassis is up to you, but the frame itself is carrying the weight of the components and the more weight you have, the more durable your design needs to be. A piece of scrap plywood should do nicely. You can also use plastic, balsa wood, or even cardboard, as long as it's large enough to support all your components and the material is not too heavy.

Probably the tastiest part of the project is the two cans of Pringles, which you use as the car's wheels — sadly, not the fuel. You can use almost any kind of rigid disc as a wheel, but Pringles (in addition to being edible) are easy to get, cheap, and the cans have a metal base. You need two wheels, so that's two cans. You can use small or large cans, since you are only using the metal base. I'd recommend large cans (more chips to eat!). You also need two rubber bands that can fit snugly around the cans without distorting them. Without them, your wheels won't get very good traction.

If you want to get fancy, you can buy a huge variety of remote-controlled car wheels at hobby shops or online. Just make sure that you can easily attach them to the shaft of your servo motors.

You also need a hammer and a small nail to attach the wheels to your servos, and a hot glue gun, if you wish to glue the servos to your chassis instead of mounting them with bolts. The benefit of hot gluing your servos to your chassis is that it's quick and easy. The drawback is that you will have to rip them off if you ever want to reuse them for another project. You can use a small section of self-adhesive hook-and-loop fastener (commonly called Velcro) to affix your battery pack.

Building Your Detector and Drive

The most important step comes at the beginning. Eat one of the cans of Pringles! You'll need to empty the cans before you build the car. After that's out of the way, you can proceed with getting your remote control to talk to your Arduino. After you decode your remote control, you can test your servo motors and program them to drive your car.

Building your circuit on the breadboard

The schematic in Figure 14-2 shows the circuit diagram of the car. The design is simple because both the IR sensor and the servos can be controlled without any additional components.

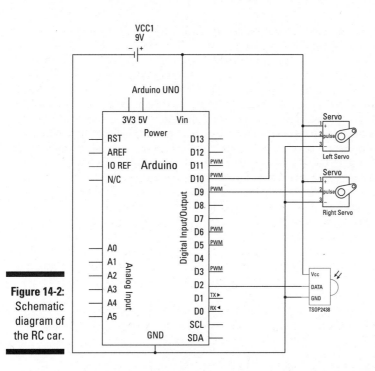

Figure 14-2:
Schematic
diagram of
the RC car.

Follow the parts placement diagram in Figure 14-3 to hook up the detector
and motors to your Arduino. The infrared receiver module is inserted into
the breadboard, facing upward so that it can see the signals emitted by your
remote control.

During final assembly, you attach the breadboard directly to your car's chassis, so if you want a clean look, keep the wiring tidy.

The IR receiver module only requires connections for power, ground, and
the signal output. It detects infrared signals that are sent from the front of
your remote control. There is an infrared LED on your remote control (it may
be behind a little plastic window) that sends out coded pulses of infrared
light that correspond to each button. Because the light pulses are infrared,
your eyes can't detect them. The infrared receiver module can though, and it
decodes these infrared pulses into digital high (+5V) and low (0V) voltages,
which are sent to the module's output pin.

To test whether your remote is working, you can point it to a digital camera or
some smartphone cameras, which can see the pulses. This is especially useful
if you are using a remote control that has been separated from the appliance
that it was originally paired with.

Connect the IR receiver module, as shown in Figure 14-3, with the output connection going to digital Pin 2. Make sure that the dome of the IR receiver is pointing upward or it may not be able to detect your remote when you send commands.

Using the pin headers makes it easy to attach and remove your servos. Use the pin header strips with three pins each to connect the servo motors to your breadboard. Connect the signal wires to digital Pins 9 and 10. In fact, as long as your code specifies the correct pins, you can use any pins labeled with a tilde "~" because those pins can output *pulse-width modulation (PWM)*. You use PWM to control the movement of the servo motors.

Your Arduino employs pulse-width modulation to generate smoothly changing output, which approximates an analog signal. I describe pulse-width modulation in more detail in Chapter 5.

You add the battery pack later. Right now, you need to connect your Arduino to your computer so that you can use the serial port to display the pulses that are decoded by the IR receiver.

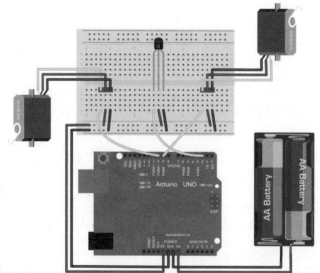

Figure 14-3:
Parts placement on the breadboard.

Coding the detector

After you've placed the components, you need to test your remote control so that you know the values that it spits out for different buttons. Take a look at the following code to make sure it makes sense to you, and then upload it so you can test your remote control.

```
#include <IRremote.h>

const int irReceivePin = 2;    // pin connected to IR detector output
IRrecv irrecv(irReceivePin);   // create the IR library
decode_results results;        // IR results are stored here

void setup()
{
  Serial.begin(9600);
  irrecv.enableIRIn();         // Start the IR receiver
}

void loop() {
  if(irrecv.decode(&results))
  {
    showReceivedData();
    irrecv.resume(); // Receive the next value
  }
  delay(250);
}

void showReceivedData()
{
  if (results.decode_type == UNKNOWN)
  {
    Serial.println("-Could not decode message");
  }
  else
  {
    if (results.decode_type == NEC) {
      Serial.print("- decoded NEC: ");
    }
    else if (results.decode_type == SONY) {
      Serial.print("- decoded SONY: ");
    }
    else if (results.decode_type == RC5) {
      Serial.print("- decoded RC5: ");
    }
    else if (results.decode_type == RC6) {
      Serial.print("- decoded RC6: ");
    }
    Serial.print("Value = ");
    Serial.println(results.value, DEC);  // Print the results as a decimal value
  }
}
```

The first line imports the Infrared Receiver library. This library is an excellent resource that was written by Ken Shirriff. The library decodes the raw data pulses that your IR receiver is sending to Pin 2. Download a Zip file of the library from this book's companion website, `www.dummies.com/go/arduinoprojectsfordummies`, or from `https://github.com/shirriff/Arduino-IRremote`, where the latest version of the libraries is hosted. To install, do the following:

1. **Extract the zipped archive.**

2. **Rename the directory, which will be named something similar to "shirriff-Arduino-IRremote-*xxx*" to IRremote.**

3. **Move the IRremote directory to your Arduino libraries folder.**

   On a Mac, this is typically just `Documents/Arduino/libraries/libraryname/libraryname.cpp`, and on Windows `My Documents/Arduino/libraries/ libraryname/libraryname.cpp`.

4. **Restart the Arduino IDE.**

   You should see some example sketches under the menu: File⇨ Examples⇨IRRemote.

If you aren't sure how to install libraries to the libraries folder on your system, refer to Chapter 3, which has general instructions on what you need to do.

This library handles four of the most common types of remote control signals: NEC, SONY, RC5, and RC6. Different manufacturers use different encoding *protocols,* but your remote is probably using one of these standards. There is also support for other kinds of remote control in the library, but you have to go digging around in the library code files to enable them.

The first variable, `irReceivePin`, stores the pin number your IR module is connected to. Then you create an IR receiver *object* called `irrecv`, which takes as a parameter the variable that specifies to which pin (Pin 2) the module is connected.

The data that is decoded by the library is presented within a special `decode_results` object called `results`.

After specifying these variables, you use `setup()` to open a serial communication channel, so you can report the decoded key codes. You then enable the input by using a function of the `irrecv` object called `irrecv.enableIRIn()`.

The `main loop()` decodes the results and displays them. The `irrecv` object you created has a `decode()` function, which knows whether there are decoded values. The `if` statement tests whether there are results to look at and if so, executes the showReceivedData() function. After that, the irrecv.resume() function prepares the module to get the next button pressed. The delay in the loop is to provide you time to read the results on the output window.

If there is no delay, the button presses will spew out of the Arduino very quickly. This would not normally pose a problem. However, when you hold down a button or press the same one many times, some remote controls send a "repeated key" result instead of simply repeating the last button you pressed.

The showReceivedData() function does the work of displaying the key code for the button you pressed. The value of the last key press is stored within a results *class* that knows about the different types of remote control protocols. The if statement tests whether the decoded results are of a known protocol type and if not, reports an error. Otherwise, the further series of if statements tests to determine which type of result was received and prints this to the serial monitor. The last statement prints the actual value that was decoded:

```
Serial.println(results.value, DEC);
```

You can output several different data formats, so DEC specifies that you want to get it as a regular old decimal number.

Reading your remote control codes

To check your remote, open the serial monitor in your Arduino IDE and press a few buttons on your remote control. You should see something similar to Figure 14-4. This is the result of pressing the numbers 0–9 on my Toshiba LCD TV remote control.

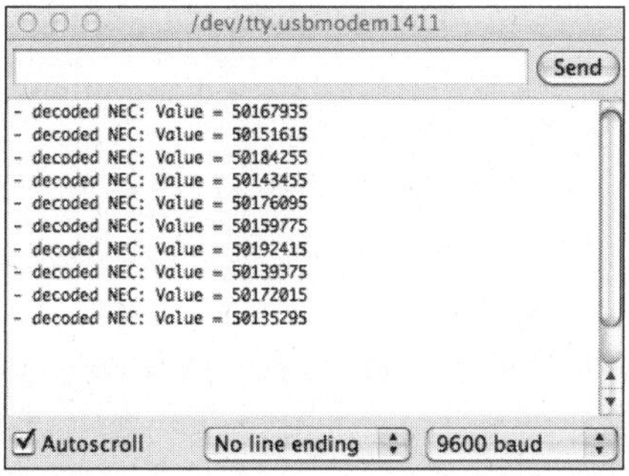

Figure 14-4: Example output of remote control codes.

After you've got some readings on your monitor, press the buttons you want to use to control your car. You need forward, reverse, left, right, and the all-important STOP, which is essential for avoiding collisions. I added one last button (a red one), for "Turbo!" mode, which really pours on a bunch of speed. Choose a good button for Turbo mode. Make a note of the codes that your remote generated, because you need these for the next part of the sketch.

Coding the drive motors

When you've got the six codes, you just need to associate them with actions to drive your motors. Add the next part of the Arduino sketch so that you can test your motors.

Before `setup()`, add the following code (new code in bold):

```
#include <Servo.h>

#include <IRremote.h>
IRrecv irrecv(irReceivePin);
decode_results results;

const int rightMotorPin = 9;
const int leftMotorPin = 10;

Servo rightServo;
Servo leftServo;

int rightSpeed=90;
int leftSpeed=90;

long keyCode=0;
```

The first instruction adds a Servo control library, one of the standard ones that's included with your Arduino IDE. The Servo library contains all the instructions needed to send pulses to your servo motors by using PWM. You don't want to have to write these yourself (which truly would be akin to reinventing the wheel!). It's customary to put all the libraries at the top of your code. That way, you can refer to them later when you create objects that use their capabilities.

You next create two *integer constant* variables to keep track of the pins you've got your servos attached to and assign these the values of the digital pins you used, 9 and 10. Two slightly cryptic lines each create a Servo *object,* one called `rightServo` and one called `leftServo`. You can now send instructions to the servo objects, and they'll respond to them.

The main instruction you're sending is the direction the objects should turn. Continuous rotation servo motors take values from 0–180 degrees, and the center point, 90, means stationary. Sending a value below 90 rotates the shaft left, and above 90 rotates right. The farther from 90 you go, the faster the rotation speed, up to the limits of the servos' capabilities.

You need to store the value that you are sending to your servos, so the variables leftSpeed and rightSpeed take care of this. You increment and decrement these values to turn your servos. Setting them to start at 90 means your car will remain stationary when you start it up.

The last *long integer* variable, keyCode, stores the decoded value that you will obtain from the IR library. You use this value to determine which rotation rules to apply to your servos.

If you find that one of your servo motors is turning consistently too slowly, you can increase the value by which its speed is incremented. Just make sure that you use whole numbers only. You use PWM for the motors and PWM values can only be whole numbers from 0 to 255.

Now add the following code to your setup() (new code in bold):

```
void setup()
{
  Serial.begin(9600);
  irrecv.enableIRIn();            // Start the IR receiver

  leftServo.attach(9);
  rightServo.attach(10);

  pinMode(rightMotorPin, OUTPUT);
  pinMode(leftMotorPin, OUTPUT);

}
```

As you might deduce, you have to "attach" your servos so that you can address them from your Arduino. You then specify that the rightMotorPin and left-MotorPin will be used for OUTPUT because those are the pins you are using to send PWM control signals to your servos.

Now, you can assign your button codes to the movement of your motors. Add the following to the main loop:

```
void loop() {
  if(irrecv.decode(&results))
  {
  showReceivedData();

  keyCode=results.value;
    if(keyCode != -1)
    {
      switch (keyCode){
        case 50174055:  // Replace this code with the one from your remote!
        Serial.println("Forward");
        leftSpeed-=1;  // Opposite values propel the wheels forward
        rightSpeed+=1;
        break;

        case 50182215:  // Replace this code with the one from your remote!
        Serial.println("Backward");
        leftSpeed-=1;  // Opposite values propel the wheels backward
        rightSpeed+=1;
        break;

        case 50168955:  // Replace this code with the one from your remote!
        Serial.println("Stop");
        leftSpeed=90;  // A value of 90 stops the servos from turning
        rightSpeed=90;
        break;

        case 50152125:  // Replace this code with the one from your remote!
        Serial.println("Turn Left"); // Wheels move in opposite directions
        leftSpeed-=1;
        rightSpeed-=1;
        break;

        case 50135805:  // Replace this code with the one from your remote!
        Serial.println("Turn Right");  // Wheels move in opposite directions
        leftSpeed+=1;
        rightSpeed+=1;
        break;

        case 50139885:  // Replace this code with the one from your remote!
        Serial.println("TURBO!!");  // need to move left servo to go right
        leftSpeed=leftSpeed-50;
        rightSpeed=rightSpeed+50;
        break;

      }
    }
  }
  delay(250);
}
```

In this code, the first thing that happens is the decoded `results.value` is assigned to the integer `keyCode`. If the value is not -1, that means there is something to act on — a button has been pressed. This is tested by the next `if` statement. If a button has been pressed, you check to see whether it is one of the buttons you chose to control movement, using a `switch...case` statement.

The `switch...case` conditional structure is used to test a variable among a number of possible situations. The variable `keyCode` is the test variable and its value is passed to the switch function, which determines which case is applicable. These cases are defined within the curly brackets. You can have as many cases as you want (limited by memory). Only the one that matches your criterion will be performed.

The first case is moving the car forward:

```
switch (keyCode){
    case 50174055:  // Replace this code with the one from your remote!
    Serial.println("Forward");
    leftSpeed-=1;
    rightSpeed+=1;
    break;
```

My Toshiba remote control sends an infrared signal for the value "50174055" whenever the up arrow is pressed. That's the case I want to test against. The switch statement looks at the value of `keyCode`, and in the case that it matches the number 50174055, executes everything after the colon until the statement break. At this point, no more test cases are evaluated, and the Arduino skips to the last curly bracket that ends the `switch()` statement. Anything else within the statement will be ignored.

If the forward button is pressed, you need to turn the servos in the appropriate direction for the way they are mounted on the chassis. However, when you mount the servos to the chassis, they will be facing away from each other, and thus, pointed in *opposite* directions. So, the left servo has to turn counterclockwise to propel the car forward and the right servo has to turn clockwise to propel the car forward. That is, the speed for both servos has to change at the same rate, but in *opposite* directions. To go forward, `leftSpeed` is decreased by 1 and `rightSpeed` is increased by 1, and to go backward, just the opposite. You do this in the `case` statement:

```
    case 50182215:  // Replace this code with the one from your remote!
    Serial.println("Backward");
    leftSpeed+=1;  //  Opposite values propel the wheels backward
    rightSpeed-=1;
    break;
```

The third case in the *switch...case* structure is when the car stops. Both the speed values are set to 90, which the servo interprets as stationary.

The next two statements handle turning — this baby *can* turn on a dime! That's because the wheels move in opposite directions. To go left, the left servo speed is decreased, turning it counterclockwise. The right servo has to turn clockwise. If both servos were facing the same way, this would mean that its `rightSpeed` variable has to be increased. However, because the right servo is mounted in the opposite orientation to the left servo, its speed variable *also* has to be decreased. It's a bit counterintuitive, but it works. And when you want to turn right, you just do the opposite, increasing the speed variable for both wheels.

The last case statement is for Turbo! mode. It adds forward (or negative) speed in an increment of 50, rather than 1.

Make sure to change the key codes to match the ones you decoded for your remote.

Now that you have the speed variables under control, you need to send the values to the servos. You do this with a function that updates the motors. Add an instruction to *call* this function at the end of your main program loop:

```
Void loop(){

    ...

    updateMotors();
    delay(10);
}
```

You also can change the delay timer to 10 milliseconds. You don't need the longer 250ms delay any more. You can also delete the `showReceivedData` function if you want, because you won't be needing it any more.

Now define the `updateMotors()` function at the very bottom of your code:

```
void updateMotors(){
    leftServo.write(leftSpeed);
    rightServo.write(rightSpeed);
}
```

Testing the drive motors

After you've checked your code, upload it to the breadboard test bed and check out the action. You should be able to point your remote in the general direction of your breadboard and get the motors turning. You may even be able to detect infrared light bounced off of the ceiling or adjacent walls. Try it.

When your code is running, you may notice that your motors are turning slightly, even when they are supposed to be stationary. This is probably due to a slight calibration problem. There is a tiny hole on the top of your servo motor, underneath which is a tiny potentiometer you use to fine-tune the servo. To calibrate your motors, insert a small screwdriver into this hole until you feel it click into the potentiometer's head. Adjust left and right and the motor will turn. Do this until you get a feel for the range of movement. Then, center the potentiometer so that the servo shaft does not move. You may hear a slight clicking sound, after you've got it centered, but this is normal. I think of it as the sound of the engines idling!

Test that all your remote control commands are accurately detected and that your servos are turning correctly. Servos are power hungry. If you test the motors in "Turbo!" mode, there's a chance you might draw too much current from your USB port all at once, in which case your Arduino will be disconnected from your USB port. You'll have to reboot it to start the sketch running again. If this happens, you won't be able to test drive in Turbo mode until you connect your battery pack.

The final test is solo operation. You need to connect your AA battery pack — the power plant — to your system. Fire up your soldering iron and grab the remaining two pin headers. Clamp these into your helping hands and *tin* the pins by applying a bit of solder to them. Then tin the leads of your battery connector and solder them to the pin headers, as shown in Figure 14-5.

You should do this quickly and precisely. If you heat the pins too long, the plastic that holds them will melt and you'll need to start all over.

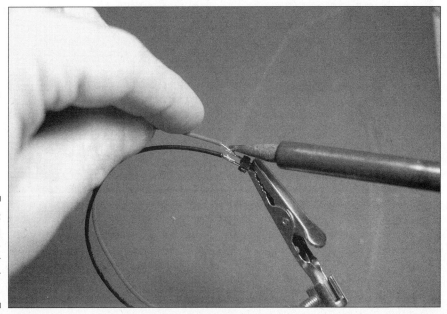

Figure 14-5:
Soldering pin headers to your power leads.

Take time to let the pins cool down between tinning them and attaching the power leads.

After you've soldered them together you are ready to test. Disconnect your Arduino from your computer. Next, plug in your battery pack to the Vin and GND connections on your Arduino's power headers.

It's very important to make sure you get the polarity right! Do not insert the power leads into the wrong headers and do not insert them backward. If you do, you could damage your Arduino permanently.

When the power is connected, you should be able to do the computer-free operational test, as shown in Figure 14-6. After you've finished building the brains and the power plant, you can move on to assembling the car's frame, or *chassis*.

Figure 14-6:
Testing your system before assembly.

Building Your Chassis

Now lay your Arduino, breadboard, and battery pack on the scrap wood to judge their size. Then mark the outside dimensions and cut the wood to size.

Because your car is using three-point suspension, with a ball caster serving as the front wheel, you want to make sure you have balanced all your components and the weight is distributed evenly. So, mark the centerline of the wooden platform, as shown in Figure 14-7. Next, close to the one end, mark the centerline for the servo motor axles. There should be enough room to mount the servos to your chassis. If you are using screws or bolts, make sure that they are positioned on the platform so that the axles of the servos will be on the same axis. You also need to be sure that they are parallel to one another. If your wheels are not parallel, your motors will be working against one another and your car will be hard to control.

If you want to bolt your Arduino to the chassis (instead of using tape or hot glue), take a moment to mark bore holes on the top end of your chassis, at the back. Use your Arduino as a template and use the holes in the corners of your Arduino's PCB.

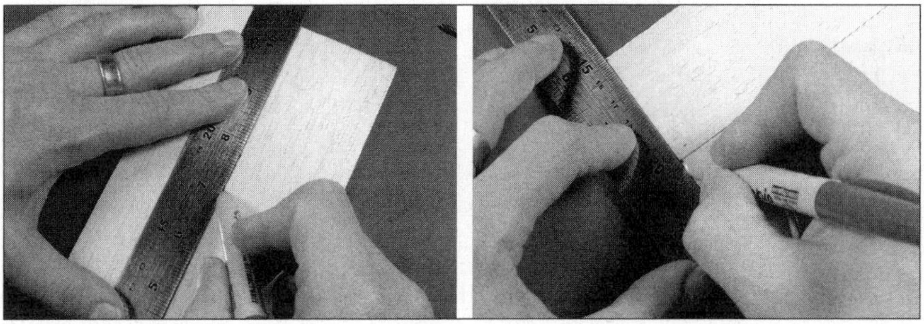

Figure 14-7:
Marking
your
centerline.

Now assemble and mount the ball caster kit, as shown in Figure 14-8. Use the enclosed instructions as a guide and brush up on your Japanese! The ball caster has a clever way of setting the height. There are several shafts sticking out of the plastic base. Depending on which way you orient the plate that holds the ball bearing in place, you can get a final height of either 25mm or 35mm. Because the Pringles can wheels are pretty high, use the 35mm setting. The kit comes with a bunch of extra mounting screws. You can either use these to mount the bearing to your chassis, or you can use hot glue, which is not as reliable, but is easier. Mount your ball caster on the centerline, as shown in Figure 14-9.

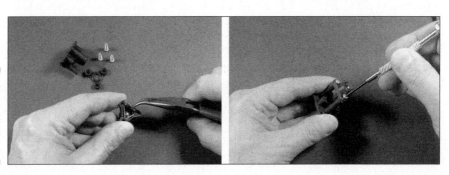

Figure 14-8:
Assembling
and setting
the ball
caster.

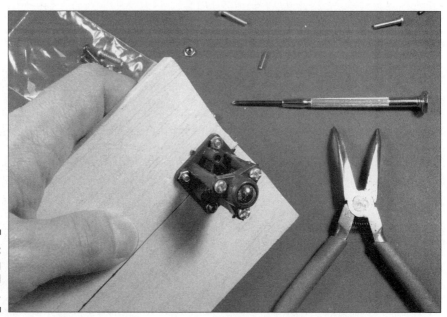

Figure 14-9:
Mounting
the ball
caster.

Next, prepare the wheels. If you haven't already done so, eat the second can of Pringles. Save the plastic lid!

Then mark a line about 1cm (½ inch) up from the bottom of the can. This is easy to do if you set your Sharpie on a book about that thickness and hold it so that it is touching the side of the can. Then simply rotate the can to make a consistent mark around its circumference. Using this line as a guide, carefully cut off the bottom of both cans using a sharp hobby knife, as shown in Figure 14-10.

With the wheels removed, use a hobby knife to bore a small hole in the plastic lid at the tiny dimple in the exact center. It should be big enough to fit your pen through. Then, use the lid as a template to mark a guide mark on the metal discs from the bottom of the can, as shown in Figure 14-11.

Now grab your hammer and nail. Also, locate the mounting screw that secures the header plates onto your servo. This should be in the accessory pack that came with your servos. The shaft plate mounting screw is usually the single black one and not the shiny silver ones that are used for mounting your servo motor.

The nail should be the same thickness as the plate mounting screw but no thicker than its head. Otherwise the wheel won't stay on!

Figure 14-10:
Slicing
off your
wheels.

Use your hammer and the nail to punch a hole in the center of the metal disc, as shown in Figure 14-11. Do this on a surface that you don't mind nailing into a bit. When you've punched a hole, carefully fold the metal burrs outward a bit. Then use your hammer to tap them so that they are flush with the metal surface.

Watch out for those burrs — they are sharp. This thing has drawn blood — I can tell you!

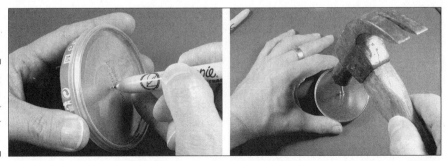

Figure 14-11:
Marking
the center
of your
wheels.

Now that you have a hole for the axle shaft, fit the rubber bands around the circumference of your wheels and attach one of the servo header plates in your accessory kit to each of the shafts of your servos. They should fit snugly but are removable if you ever need to do any tire service.

Thread the shaft mounting screw through your wheel and screw it securely onto the drive shaft of the servo, as shown in Figure 14-12.

Figure 14-12: Mounting your wheels to the servo motors.

Next you attach the servo motors to your chassis. (First, unplug the power from your Arduino.) Use the axle center line you made earlier as a guide for the placement of your motors, as shown in Figure 14-13.

Remember, the motors are mounted in opposite orientations! The left motor is mounted on the right side of the undercarriage and the right motor is on the opposite side. You can use hot glue to affix them, or use mounting hardware, as shown in Figure 14-13. If you use the mounting hardware, you'll need to bore additional holes into your chassis to attach the motors.

When you've finished, your car should look more or less like the one in Figure 14-14. There is a slight downward incline toward the front. This is to improve aerodynamic stability, of course! Note the carefully placed "DIY" sticker from my Arduino kit, which is subtly masking a hole in the chassis —

and improving the coolness factor at the same time. You can mount some spoilers later (should you choose to make any), but for now, it's time to add the rest of your parts and get motoring.

Figure 14-13:
Attaching
your servo
motors to
the chassis.

Figure 14-14:
Checking
your
chassis.

The final step before road testing is assembling everything. Your breadboard probably has a patch of adhesive foam tape on the bottom. Peel off the protective film and affix it to the center of your car's chassis. Mount the Arduino over the wheels, as shown in Figure 14-15. It's also okay to use tape or even a couple of dabs of hot glue.

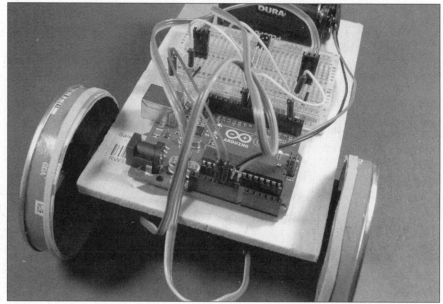

Figure 14-15:
Attaching
your control
and power
plant.

Next, run the servo control wires around the back end of the vehicle. It's a good idea to tie them down with some extra wire ties so that they don't get entangled in the wheels. You can mount the battery pack on the front of the vehicle with a bit of self adhesive hook-and-loop fastener (or even a bit of duct tape, for a truly homebrew approach).

Congratulations, your masterpiece is ready for road testing! I prefer a stripped down design, as shown in Figure 14-16. Just the basics and nothing fancy. But you can add just about anything to spruce up the frame as long as it's not too heavy or out of balance.

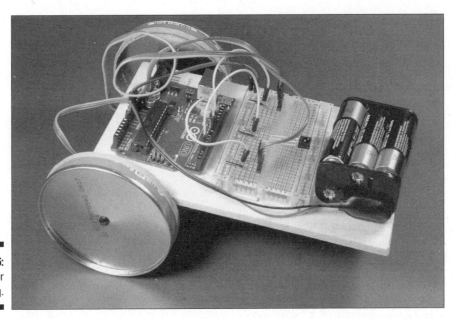

Figure 14-16:
Ready for
road testing.

Put on your driving gloves and goggles. Grab your remote control and plug the power connection from your battery pack into the Arduino power headers, making sure to get the polarity right. Set your car on a suitable, smooth surface and put the pedal to the metal. Stamp on the "Turbo!" button to release your inner Formula 1 champion.

If you're lucky, you can get an action shot that's suitable for the automobile hall of fame!

Chapter 15

Building an LED Cube

*I*f you haven't seen one already, you will soon! LED cubes are getting really popular, and it's easy to build a simple one with an Arduino Uno. This project shows you how to create a 3 x 3 x 3 LED cube with just a few inexpensive parts. It's easy and fun to build and you can get really creative with the patterns it displays. In the process, you get to brush up on your soldering skills. After you understand how it works, you can expand to 4 x 4 x 4 or larger cubes with an Arduino Mega.

Building it is only half the fun. If you're like me, you'll get really absorbed in designing animated patterns for your cube. The companion website for the book, www.dummies.com/go/arduinoprojectsfordummies, has an LED cube pattern generator, which will help you to try out different animation sequences and will also generate the code you need *automagically*.

You can expect to spend about five hours building your first cube project. Getting your soldering technique down is pretty easy, once you get going, and there are other ways to speed up your assembly process. After you get it built and tested, you'll definitely want to spend some time playing around with programming the patterns, which can be a lot of fun, and even compulsive!

The LED cube is made of three layers of nine LEDs. But, like the scrolling sign in Chapter 6, only one of the LEDs is ever lit at a time. You just switch the LEDs on and off so quickly that the persistence of vision (POV) effect means that you perceive many LEDs to be lit up at once.

You can download schematics and full-color parts placement diagrams from the companion website (www.dummies.com/go/arduinoprojectsfor dummies).

Selecting Your Parts

To get the ball rolling, pull together your parts and get your tools ready, as shown in Figure 15-1. The parts you need are

- An Arduino
- Twenty-seven 5mm LEDs of the same color and specification
- Three resistors (not shown) with a value between 220 ohms – 270 ohms
- A 9V DC battery and battery clip
- A single-pole, single-throw (SPST) rocker switch, such as Jameco #316451 or Maplin # N19CL
- A small piece of stripboard or perfboard
- Thirteen jumper wires
- A small scrap of foam core board or corrugated cardboard
- An enclosure sized about 80 x 12 x 40 mm (3" x 4.5" x 1.5"), such as Jameco #675489 or Maplin# LH14

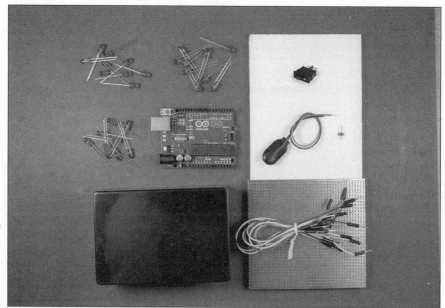

Figure 15-1:
The parts you need for this project.

This project can be easily built by using any Arduino, but I used an Uno. If you want to expand the project to make a bigger cube, or to make the LEDs to fade in and out using pulse-width modulation (PWM), you need to use a board that accommodates more PWM outputs, such as an Arduino Mega.

Your LEDs should all be of the same size, color, and specification. Or perhaps you want to get creative and use different colors. Of course, you can use whatever you like, but you should at least make sure that the power requirements are the same so that your cube operates correctly, and the LEDs light up consistently. If you use LEDs with different specifications, individual LEDs will stand out from their neighbors, which is visually distracting, especially during animations. You use three resistors to control current flow to the LEDs. 250 to 270 ohm resistors are fine. You can use higher values but your LEDs will be dimmer.

Because your cube doesn't need to be connected to a computer to work, you need a battery power supply and way to turn it on and off. Because you're powering both the Arduino and the Cube matrix and you need to fit it into a small enclosure, get a standard 9V DC battery and 9V battery clip. You power the Arduino directly from the clip, so get two pin headers. That way, you can plug the clip directly into your power headers.

To switch it on and off, I found a very nice looking slimline rocker switch that gives the project a nice professional finish and is very inexpensive. The main challenge to using rocker switches is that you need to bore a square hole in your enclosure. You can also use simple toggle switches that use a single, round bore hole.

You need a small piece of stripboard or perfboard, to which you mount the LED cube assembly for stability. If you use stripboard, you'll have to sever the copper traces so that the LED columns aren't shorted together. Perfboard only has metal plating around each individual hole, which eliminates this problem. Both will work fine, but I tend to have lots of stripboard lying around, so that's what's shown in the figures.

Unlike most of the projects in the book, this one doesn't use a breadboard. The project requires 13 jumper wires. Twelve of these connect to your Arduino's output pins. One wire connects the power switch to the Vin pin on your Arduino.

To lay out your LEDs into a cube, you need a jig that can hold them securely while you solder the LEDs together. You can bore holes in wood, but I've found it's just as easy to use a piece of foam core (also called "foam board") or a piece of heavy corrugated cardboard. This will be sufficient, unless you plan to make a lot of cubes, in which case it's worth it to make a more durable jig from a piece of wood.

If you are using an ABS plastic enclosure like the one in the parts list, you will need a few tools for cutting the holes in the enclosure that accommodate the LED leads and the power switch. You need either a hand drill or a power drill. You need two bits: a small 1mm (⅟₁₆") bit for the LED leads and a large bit about 7mm (¼") for your switch. If you are using a square toggle switch, you'll need to square up the holes with a fine hand file.

After you get your parts together, you can get right down to building the project and then upload code to start the light show.

Building Your Cube

Building your cube is done in three steps. First you prepare each layer of the cube. Then, you modify your enclosure to accommodate the cube and Arduino. Finally you add your power supply to the project so the LED cube can go roaming around without a computer.

Assembling the LED matrix

The cube matrix is built out of three layers of 9 LEDs, for a total of 27 LEDs. The layers are identical, which makes it easy to build them. You solder together each of the layers separately and then you assemble the layers like a little LED cube layer cake. After your cube is assembled, you solder it to your stripboard.

The positive "+" leg (or *anode*) of each LED on a given layer has a connection to one of the digital outputs of your Arduino, which provides power. On each layer, all the negative "–" (or *cathode*) legs are connected together and only one ground pin is used for the whole layer. A total of three ground wires, one for each layer, are connected to the digital pins of your Arduino.

Only a single LED lights up at a time. You just cycle through them so quickly it looks like lots of them are on simultaneously.

You control which LED is lit by turning on one of the nine pins on a layer — the "active" layer — and then connecting that layer to ground. Meanwhile, the other inactive layers are not connected to ground, so the corresponding LEDs in those columns remain unlit.

Prepare your soldering jig

To get started with the first layer, you need to prepare your soldering jig, which is made from your foam core, cardboard, or wood. You need to bore a grid of nine holes into this material. Mark off a 3-x-3 grid of dots on your material with a ruler and pen. The dots should be spaced 25mm (1") apart.

It's important to measure carefully to make sure they are very precise and squared with each other. Otherwise, the layers won't match up when you stack the layers together.

If you are using foam core, cut X-shaped crosses that are centered on the marking dots. Then at the center of the X-cuts carefully press the lens of an LED into the foam to make holes, as shown in Figure 15-2. If you are using a harder material, you'll need to drill them out. Your LED should stay vertical, snugly in the hole, and shouldn't fall to the side. If the LED is loose, it will be difficult to solder, so start over if the holes don't provide a good fit.

You need to test each of your layers as you build them. Arduino to the rescue! Open up the Arduino IDE and load up the "Blink" sketch on your Uno. Pin 13 should be blinking once per second. Get long jumper wires to use as test leads. Insert one into the Pin 13 and the other into GND. You'll use these probes to make sure that all your LEDs are working as you build.

Figure 15-2:
Making your soldering jig.

Lay out and solder your layer

The cathode "–" leg of each LED is connected to its neighbor so that an entire layer of cathodes forms an "S" shape. Fire up your soldering iron so that you can join the cathodes. To build your layers, perform the following steps, as shown in Figures 15-3 and 15-4:

1. **Bend the shorter, cathode (–) leg of eight of the nine LEDs so that each is flat against the bottom of its exterior resin base, perpendicular to the longer anode (+) leg. Make the "V" for victory sign with your index and middle finger, line up your middle finger with the longer anode (+) leg and your index finger with the shorter cathode (–) leg, and then fold your index finger forward.**

   That's the way to bend your LEDs' legs (see Figure 15-3). It doesn't matter whether you use your right or left hand, as long as you use the same hand for the entire project.

2. **Place the LEDs into the jig to form an "S" shape out of the bent cathode legs, with the anode leg just touching the anode of its neighbor.**

3. **Use a small bead of solder to make a firm connection between the tip of one cathode leg and the folded cathode leg of the next LED in the series.**

4. **Keep going until you get to the end of the S shape.**

   Don't bend the two legs of the last LED. You'll deal with those when you stack the layers.

5. **While the layer is still in the jig, connect the ground jumper of your test probes to one of the horizontal cathode legs. Use an alligator clip from your "helping hands" to hold it in place.**

6. **Now touch the other probe that's connected to Pin 13 to each of the LED anode legs that is sticking up, as shown in Figure 15-4.**

   It should blink once per second. If it doesn't, check that all your solder joints are good and try again.

7. **After testing, set aside the layer and do the next one until you have three layers. Leave the last layer in the jig so you can start building the cube.**

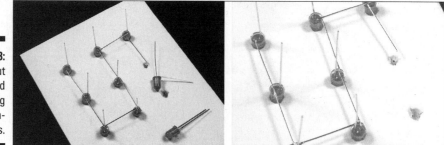

Figure 15-3:
Laying out
LEDs and
bending
your cath-
ode legs.

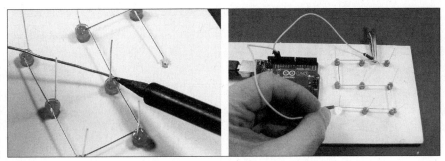

Figure 15-4:
Soldering
your cube
layers.

Assembling your cube

When you've completed three layers, you're ready to assemble the cube!
Hold one of the completed layers close to the one in the jig, matching up the
corners. But don't align the "S" shapes. Instead, rotate the layer in your hand
by 90 degrees so that the two layers are not matched up. Doing this provides more structural stability to your cube when all its layers are soldered
together. Also, you need to make sure that the two LEDs that have both
anode and cathode legs pointing up are not aligned on top of one another.
Refer to the connection diagrams in Figure 15-5. Do the following steps:

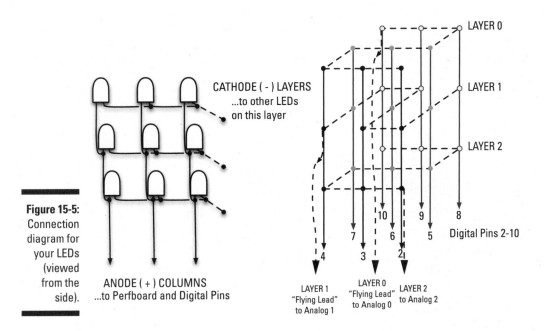

Figure 15-5:
Connection
diagram for
your LEDs
(viewed
from the
side).

CATHODE (-) LAYERS
...to other LEDs
on this layer

ANODE (+) COLUMNS
...to Perfboard and Digital Pins

LAYER 0
LAYER 1
LAYER 2

Digital Pins 2-10

LAYER 1
"Flying Lead"
to Analog 1

LAYER 0
"Flying Lead"
to Analog 0

LAYER 2
to Analog 2

1. **Align the corner LEDs of the two layers.**

2. **Using your needle nose pliers, make a small bend at the very tip of the anode (+) leg of the LED in the corner of the jig so that it can touch the anode leg of the corner LED in the layer in your hand.**

3. **Now, carefully solder the two anodes together.**

   This is the point when it's good to have about five limbs! Use your "helping hands" or an alligator clip to hold things together while you make the solder joint, as shown in Figure 15-6. Try to work quickly so that you don't overheat the LEDs.

4. **Now, move to the next LED in the series and repeat this operation.**

5. **Continue until you've soldered together all the anodes of the LEDs in the two layers.**

Make sure that you don't solder the cathode leg of the last LED in your cathode layer to an anode on the adjacent layer!

When you've connected the two layers, each LED on the top layer should have its anode leg soldered to the anode leg of the LED on the layer underneath it. The last LED in the series of each layer should have both its legs pointing down, and nothing connected to the cathode leg (and they are in different corners).

Figure 15-6:
Soldering
your anode
columns
together.

Now repeat the operation above to add your third layer. Make sure to rotate the layer again by 90 degrees so that the adjacent "S" shapes of the two layers are not aligned and the terminating LEDs with both legs sticking up are not on top of each other. The top and the bottom "S" shapes will be in the same orientation (refer to Figure 15-5).

After you've soldered all three layers of your LED layer cake together, you should have nine vertical columns of three connected anodes. You will also have a single LED at the corner of each layer with an unconnected cathode. You will solder a "flying lead" to this cathode so that you can connect each of the three layers to the Analog pins of your Arduino. You'll connect them to ground in your code.

Now test your LED cube to make sure that everything is working. Repeat the test procedure you did for the individual layers. This time, you should be able to light an LED by connecting its layer to ground and touching your positive probe to any anode in its column. For example, in Figure 15-7, the ground lead is connected to the topmost plane. You can light any LED in that plane by touching the connected anode wires of any column of LEDs. Because only the topmost plane is connected to ground, only a single LED lights up.

Figure 15-7:
Testing
your cube
assembly.

You use the same principle to create the animations on your LED cube but instead of manually connecting the power, your Arduino does it programmatically — and very fast!

After you test your cube and make sure every LED is working, take a moment to gently align all the LEDs and straighten up your cube. LEDs always get slightly bent out of shape during soldering.

Fabricating the enclosure

With you cube complete, you can fabricate the enclosure. The enclosure provides stability for your LEDs and hides the inner workings so you can bask in undistracted glowing glory. You need to drill holes in the right place for your cathodes and anodes and a separate hole for your power switch. You then connect your LEDs to your stripboard (or perfboard if you are using that instead) inside the enclosure, which provides stability and makes soldering your jumper wires easier. Do the following steps, referring to Figures 15-8 through 15-13:

1. **Set your LED cube on your stripboard and mark it so that there is a bit of extra room all the way around the LED grid but not so big that it won't fit into your enclosure.**

2. **Cut your stripboard to size.**

   You can use a hobby knife to do this. Score several times along the holes in the stripboard and you'll be able to cleanly snap it in two.

3. **Carefully slip the leads of your LEDs through the copper side of the board so that you can mark the top side of your stripboard.**

   On three corners of your stripboard, you mark two adjacent holes, as shown in Figure 15-8. One hole accommodates the anode and the other hole is for a connection to each cathode layer.

4. **Now use the stripboard as a drill hole marking template. Tape it onto the outside of your enclosure and use a hobby knife to lightly score guide marks into the surface of the plastic box, one for each anode and three for the cathodes.**

5. **Check that you have marked 12 bore holes — 9 anodes and 3 cathodes.**

Figure 15-8:
Marking
your drill
holes on the
stripboard.

6. **Measure and mark the position for your power switch.**

   I put it on what's usually considered the top half of the enclosure because it's a bit easier to do, and mounted the LED cube on the bottom cover. Mounting the cube on the bottom of the box is a little easier to do, but you might not like the look of the screws — it's up to you.

7. **Now use your small drill bit to bore out the grid of holes you marked.**

   You can do this on a desktop if you use an old catalog to protect its surface, as shown in Figure 15-9.

Figure 15-9:
Using your
stripboard
as a
template.

8. **Use your large drill bit to bore out the hole for the rocker switch, as shown in Figure 15-10.**

   You might find it is easier to bore two adjacent holes and then remove the material between them. Use a small file to make the hole nice and square. After you've finished, you should have an excellent looking power switch for your cube. Test the fit, as shown in Figure 15-11.

Figure 15-10: Drilling the hole for your power switch.

Figure 15-11: Testing the fit of the power switch.

9. **Now carefully feed the LED anodes and cathodes through the surface of your enclosure and through the stripboard.**

   This part is a little fiddly and you might find it easier to start at one corner of your cube, feeding in a single row and then working your way across the leads. Persevere! It can be done!

10. **Finally, flip over the assembly and tape the stripboard in place. Gently slide the cube so that the LED legs are square with reference to the enclosure's surface.**

11. **Use your soldering iron to solder the 12 anode leads onto the stripboard.**

12. **Sever the copper strips that are connecting the rows of LEDs. You can use a hobby knife to do this, or a small drill bit that is just wider than the copper strips. Bore six shallow holes to break the copper traces — but not all the way through the board.**

    You can see these in Figure 15-12.

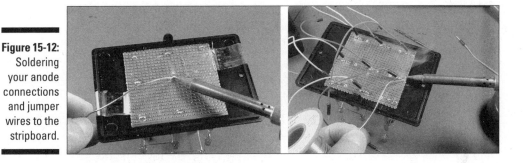

Figure 15-12: Soldering your anode connections and jumper wires to the stripboard.

Making the final connections

Each of your LED layers is connected through a resistor to an analog pin. Rather than being used for input, as is usually the case, the three analog pins provide a pathway to ground. Each of your LED layers is connected to one analog pin. But the cathodes for each layer are on the last LED for that layer.

To make the connection, you feed a "flying lead" up through the cathode hole you bored in your enclosure and solder it to the cathode leg of the LED in each of the three corners of your cube (refer to Figure 15-5).

1. **Create a "flying lead" for each LED layer. Feed a small length of wire through each of the cathode holes and solder the end to the free cathode of each LED layer. Wire with black insulation is best because it won't distract from the LEDs.**

You may have to ream this hole to be slightly larger so that it accommodates the insulation.

2. **Solder the other end of each flying lead to your perfboard, on a row that is not connected to any of the other anode leads.**

3. **For each flying lead, solder one leg of a 220 ohm resistor to the hole next to the flying lead and on the same strip of copper.**

4. **Solder the other leg or the resistor to an adjacent, unused row.**

   You use a jumper wire to connect the second leg of the resistor to the analog pins of your Arduino, providing a pathway to ground.

5. **To create the three connections to the analog pins, solder a jumper wire to your perfboard strip in a hole adjacent to each resistor.**

   This is a bit of an unusual way to solder wires to a stripboard. Usually you feed wires through the stripboard hole on the opposite side. Soldering the connections this way means that the stripboard remains flush against the enclosure. Figure 15-12 shows how this looks for Steps 5 and 6.

6. **Now grab nine of your jumper wires and solder them onto the sections of strip connected to each of the anode legs in the stripboard.**

7. **The final step is to warm up your hot glue gun and place a couple dollops of hot glue onto the sides of your board to keep it securely connected to the enclosure.**

   Set it aside to cool while you work on the power switch.

Testing your connections

After you have soldered all the jumper wires, you should test your cube to make sure there are no bad connections. Connect your ground wire probe from your Arduino to one of the three cathode leads. Figure 15-13 shows the wire ground connected to the middle layer and the positive wire connected to one of the anode jumper wires. Now, systematically go through each of the anode wires and make sure that they are working and make a note of which jumper wire goes to each of the nine columns.

If an LED fails to light up, you've got a broken connection in either its anode or its cathode. If the other LEDs in the same column fail to light up as well, the problem is with the anode connection for that column. If the other LEDs in the layer won't light up, your problem is with the cathode connection. The schematic diagram for the cube is shown in Figure 15-14.

Figure 15-13:
Testing
the entire
cube circuit
assembly.

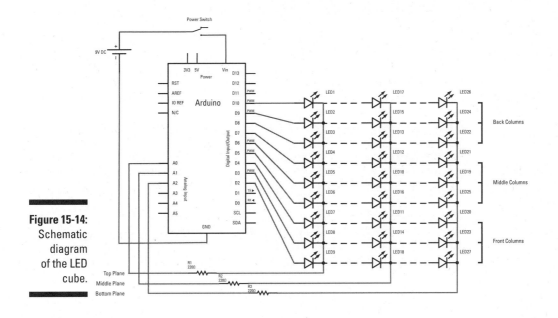

Figure 15-14:
Schematic
diagram
of the LED
cube.

If two or more LEDs light up when you make a connection, you have a solder "bridge" connecting them. Check all your joints going to that column and layer to make sure there aren't any fat blobs of solder making unwanted connections. After you've tested everything, move on to the power supply and switch.

Adding the power supply

The power supply is simply your 9V battery connected to the switch. The positive lead is connected to one side of the rocker switch. The other side is connected to the Vin pin on your Arduino. The negative lead goes straight to your ground pin. Do the following steps, as shown in Figure 15-15:

1. **Solder the red, positive wire from your 9 volt battery clip to one side of the switch.**

   It doesn't matter which side.

2. **Solder one of your jumper wires to the other side of your switch.**

   If you have a red one, that's even better.

3. **Get your pin headers and solder the black negative lead to one (or both) of them.**

   You use two pin headers because there are two adjacent GND connections on your Arduino and using two pins gives a more secure physical connection.

Set the battery aside until later so you can program your animation patterns. Figure 15-16 shows what your project will look like after you've installed everything into the enclosure.

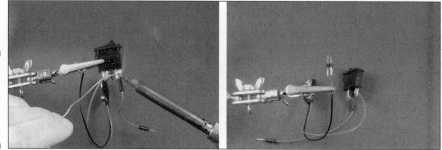

Figure 15-15: Soldering the power switch connections.

Figure 15-16:
Putting
everything
into your
enclosure.

Connecting your Arduino

Now connect your Arduino to the cube. Plug in the nine anode jumper wire connections to your digital pins, as shown in Figure 15-5. Connect the three cathode connections to analog Pins 0, 1, and 2.

In your program, you use the analog input pins as connections to ground, rather than as analog inputs.

Now plug in your Arduino to the USB connection and get down to tweaking the code.

Programming Your Cube

The code for this project is on the companion website for the book, www. dummies.com/go/arduinoprojectsfordummies. You should download it now so that you can send it to your Arduino after you understand how the code works. This program is long because it contains several example animations to get you started.

It's easy to make an error manually typing in the patterns, so the companion website also has a pattern generation tool, described in the next section.

Just as with movie animations, the dancing patterns on your LED cube are created as sequences of frames and displayed rapidly in sequence to give the illusion of movement. That means you have to define whether an LED is on or off for each frame of the animation, represented by a 1 or a 0. Your code then reads these sequences of bits and "paints" the pattern for each frame onto the entire cube. Unlike movie animations, however, you can set the display duration for each frame independently, in increments of 100 milliseconds.

It's actually slightly more complicated than that, because for each frame, only one LED is lit at any given moment. Imagine you have the top nine LEDs lit up in a single animation frame. Your code determines that the top nine LEDs should be lit up for that frame and then lights each one in order, one at a time. Because this is done in microseconds, it appears that the entire top plane is illuminated simultaneously.

You only have 2,048 *bytes* of working memory, called *static random access memory* (SRAM), which is used for storing and manipulating variables when your program is running. To save on this running memory space, the pattern is defined by a table of individual *bits* ("on" or "off") you store in a single large array in an extra room on your Arduino that is normally used to store the program itself, the *flash memory.* This array is read from there when the program is running, instead of from SRAM.

Take a moment to understand how the code works before you hook up your Arduino.

Variable declarations

Here's the first part of the code your Arduino will run, which contains all the program variables and defines the animation sequence(s). The code listing for the pattern data is truncated, because it is too long to put in this book, but you can refer to it in your IDE.

Understanding the pattern structure

```
#include <avr/pgmspace.h>

prog_uchar PROGMEM patternData[] = {
  // Blink all LEDs on and off
  B111, B111, B111, B111, B111, B111, B111, B111, B111, 10,
  B000, B000, B000, B000, B000, B000, B000, B000, B000, 10,

  . . .
};
```

The first part of the code contains includes a library called `avr/pgmspace.h` that allows you to get the animation pattern from program memory space. This comes with the standard Arduino software distribution.

After this, the `patternData[]` array is the next huge chunk of code (only part of which is shown above), and it defines each frame of your animation sequence. It is an array of *unsigned char* values (unsigned means they are not negative) stored in program memory, as indicated by the `prog_uchar PROGMEM` prefix. Each grouping of bytes contains the values for your LEDs. The first 9 bytes are the on or off states of your 27 LEDs for a frame. The lines of data are laid out in rows of frames, consisting of 10 values. This is easier to read, but you'll notice there's a comma after every line, because this data table is really just one long list of numbers.

The tenth byte stores the duration that you want to display this frame, in increments of 100ms. So a value of 10 displays the frame for 1 second. The first frame sequence turns on all the LEDs for one second:

```
B111, B111, B111, B111, B111, B111, B111, B111, B111, 10,
```

Here's how the sequence of bits relates to the LEDs on your cube (the "mapping"). The binary values are preceded by the letter *B*. Take a look at this hypothetical line:

```
      Top Plane, |   Middle Plane, |    Bottom Plane, ms
Front, Mid, Back, | Front, Mid, Back, | Front, Mid, Back,
 B111, B000, B000, | B010, B010, B010, | B111, B111, B111, 10,
```

The first value, B111, lights up the top three LEDs on the front row of your cube. The top three LEDs in the middle and back rows are off, as indicated by the three zeros, one for each LED in the row. From this pattern, you can see the middle plane values would illuminate a line of LEDs in the middle of each row, extending from the front of the cube to the rear of the cube. The Bottom Plane is entirely lit up — all the LEDs are on. The final value is the duration: 10 times 100ms, or 1 second.

Defining your variables

Now take a look at the rest of the variables:

```
const int cubeSize=3;    // the dimensions of the cube, in LEDs
const int planeSize=9;   // the number of LEDs on each plane of the cube
const int planeDisplayTime=1000; // time each plane is displayed in microseconds
const int updateSpeed=100; // multiplies displayTime to get milliseconds

byte patternBuffer[planeSize]; // Stores the current pattern from patternData
int patternIndex; // Keeps track of the data value containing the duration
```

```
int patternBufferIndex; // Counts where we are while painting the display
byte displayTime; // Multiplied by 100ms to set the frame duration
unsigned long endTime; // Tracks when we are finished with the frame

int plane; // Loop counter for painting the cube
int ledrow; // Counts LED rows in the refresh loop
int ledcol; // Counts LEDs columns in the refresh loop
int ledpin; // Counts LEDs in the refresh loop

int LEDPin[] = {2,3,4,5,6,7,8,9,10};
int PlanePin[] = {14,15,16};
```

The first four *const inst* variables define the size of the cube in LEDs (3^3, which is 3 cubed, or 27), and the size of each plane. You could increase this to four or more if you were to build a larger cube — but then you'd need a larger Arduino! The planeDisplayTime controls the refresh rate that each frame is painted at in millionths of a second. The updateSpeed variable controls how long each frame is displayed. You multiply this by the last value on each line of your data table to determine how long each frame is displayed. If you change the value for update speed, it will affect all the frames of your whole animation sequence.

The *byte* variable called patternBuffer[] is a temporary array that holds the data values of the frames that you read from program memory when the program is running. The patternIndex integer is used to keep track of the elements of the array when loading from program memory so that you know which one contains the duration in milliseconds. The patternBuffer Index is merely a counter used when you are painting the display. The byte displayTime is a temporary variable that stores the time each frame is displayed when you read it from program memory. The endTime value is a counter used to determine if you are finished painting the frame.

The next four integers are used as utility counters while the display is being painted.

The last two arrays store the pins you are using for the cube. The LEDPin[] array stores the anode connections and the PlanePin[] array stores the cathode connections. You turn these pins on and off when you are refreshing the display. Pins 14, 15, and 16 are merely the Arduino's analog input pins labeled A0, A1, and A2.

Setup

Setup is very simple. It consists of two *for* loops to initialize the pins using the pinMode command. The pins are all set for OUTPUT. Because you are storing the pin numbers in two arrays, you need two *for* loops to iterate through them, setting each pin's mode, in turn.

The main loop

The main loop is where the action happens. You are only getting the data you need to work with for each frame, one frame at a time. But the program memory space contains all the frames. You use the patternIndex to keep track of where you are, and to start, you set the patternIndex to 0. You then load up the temporary buffer with the data for a single frame from program memory (nine values plus the duration). Then you execute a *do...while* loop to paint this frame for the entire main loop of the program. You continue in this loop for as long as there is data in displayTime — the last value of each frame. When you reach the end of the pattern, there won't be any more frames, so the displayTime will be *null*. Then the loop quits and the main loop starts it up all over again.

Here's how it works:

```
patternIndex = 0;
do {
 memcpy_P( patternBuffer, patternData+patternIndex, planeSize );
 patternIndex += planeSize;
 displayTime = pgm_read_byte_near( patternData + patternIndex++ );
 endTime = millis() + displayTime * updateSpeed;

 while ( millis() < endTime ) {
     patternBufferIndex = 0;

     // Loop over the planes of the cube
     for (int plane=0; plane<cubeSize; plane++) {
       // Turn the previous plane off
       if (plane==0) {
         digitalWrite(PlanePin[cubeSize-1], HIGH);
       }
       else {
         digitalWrite(PlanePin[plane-1], HIGH);
       }

       // Prepare the digital pins to light up LEDs
       ledpin = 0;
       for (ledrow=0; ledrow<cubeSize; ledrow++) {
         for (ledcol=0; ledcol<cubeSize; ledcol++) {
             digitalWrite( LEDPin[ledpin++], patternBuffer[patternBufferIndex] &
               (1 << ledcol) );
         }
         patternBufferIndex++;
```

```
            }

            // Turn on the current plane
            digitalWrite(PlanePin[plane], LOW);
            // delay planeDisplayTime us
            delayMicroseconds(planeDisplayTime);
         }
      } // End of the while loop
   }
   while (displayTime > 0
}
```

Loading the frame

First, you start at the `patternIndex` of 0 and load the first nine values of the pattern from program memory space into the temporary buffer so you can work with it. You get the first nine values because `planeSize` is 9. This is the data for your first animation frame.

Array indexing starts from zero, so you will get the values of array elements 0 to 8.

You use a special C programming language instruction `memcp_P` to copy the data from program memory into the variable `patternBuffer[]`. The data is coming from the `patternData` that you just copied from program memory and you are getting nine values, because `planeSize` is 9.

Next, you increment the `patternIndex` by the `planeSize` (9), so that you will be able to load the next frame of data after you paint this one.

You use another C command, `pgm_read_byte_near()`, to read the value just after the values for the LEDs, which contains the duration you want to display this frame.

The last step before painting the display is to set the `endTime` for this frame. This is the current number of milliseconds on the Arduino's internal timer, which you get using the `millis()` function, plus the `displayTime` in milliseconds, multiplied by the update speed.

Painting the frame

Now you use the `patternBuffer` to update your LEDs. As long as the clock has not run out on the `endTime`, you display the frame. You use two nested *for* loops to iterate over the three planes of the cube, setting all the pins to HIGH, which prevents electricity from flowing through the planes, turning off all the LEDs on the whole cube.

Then, you iterate over the LEDs for the data you loaded into the pattern buffer. You use `ledpin` as an *array index counter* to get the values from the arrays that contain the locations of the connections to your digital pins. That way you can specify whether or not to light up an LED.

Two nested *for* loops turn your `LEDPin` on or off. The first loop keeps track of which row you are on and the inner loop keeps track of which column you are in in that row. Then, you turn the LED on or off in a clever way:

```
digitalWrite(LEDPin[ledpin++], patternBuffer[patternBufferIndex] & (1<<ledcol)
          );
```

Recall that the `digitalWrite(pin, value)` function takes two parameters, the pin and whether to write it HIGH (1) or LOW (0). The pin to turn on is specified as the one from the `LEDPin` array you are currently working on. The `LEDPin` specifies which of the three LEDs you are working on. The "++" increments this index variable so that you grab the next element of the `LEDPin` array in the next iteration of the *for* loop so you can do the next LED.

The value to write is taken from the `patternBuffer` array, using *bit shifting*. The binary values in the `ledcol` variable are shifted left by the value of `ledcol`, indicated by `1 << ledcol`, which has the effect of skipping through the batches of columns to find the value for the next LED column. The "&" is a bitwise AND. If both `patternBuffer` and the new value coming in from `ledcol` are 1, the resulting output is HIGH and the LED is turned on; otherwise the output is LOW.

Even though you might have written an LED pin HIGH, it won't light up yet. There's no pathway to ground, because the analog pins are all still HIGH.

The next time you render a frame, you need to jump ahead to get the next 27 binary values for your LEDs from the `patternBuffer`. You increment `patternBufferIndex` to do this.

Now you activate the current plane by setting its cathode pin to LOW, allowing electricity to pass from the activated anode pin through the cathode pin to ground. The LED lights up and you can move to the next one. The `delay Microseconds()` function provides a very slight delay. If you don't have this instruction, the code will execute so quickly that the LEDs will all appear to be on and the animation effect won't work.

The very last line of code keeps advancing this process until the `patternData` is consumed. After this, the *do...while* loop ends and the main `loop()` just starts the whole animation sequence all over again.

Figure 15-17 shows what your LED cube will look like when you've finished building it and have uploaded code to animate the LEDs.

Editing your patterns

You can edit any of the animation sequences by changing the values in pat-ternData[]. There are several sample animations to get you started. You change the patterns and then upload the code to your Arduino to see the effect of the animation. Of course, you need to have the Arduino connected to your USB port to make changes, so you need to test out all your ideas before you detach the umbilical and go to battery power.

Figure 15-17:
What your LED cube will look like when it's built.

Using the LED Cube Pattern Designer

Obviously, tweaking each of the individual bits of data is pretty tedious, especially when you want to test out your creative animation ideas. It's very hard to imagine what an animation will look like unless you "took the red pill" and your brain is able to see the raw code of the matrix! Having a visual interface makes things a little easier.

The companion website for this book has a browser-based LED cube pattern designer to help you out with making your own designs. Go to www.dummies.com/go.arduinoprojectsfordummies and look for the pattern designer in Chapter 15, as shown in Figure 15-18.

You can use the website to create sequences of animation frames and play them back. You click on the grey boxes to turn them orange, which means the corresponding LED will be illuminated in that frame. You can preview the results in an isometric preview window on the right.

When you are happy with your frame, set its duration and click the Apply button. Click on the Insert button to the lower right to create a new frame and determine which of its LEDs are turned on. Keep going until you've created your animation sequence. When you're ready to preview the animation, click the Play button. The animation will be played at approximately the same speed as you'll see it when it's uploaded to your cube.

When you are satisfied with the animation, click on the Get Code button. You can cut and paste the results in the textbox directly into your Arduino sketch! What could be easier? Then upload your code and enjoy the three-dimensional show!

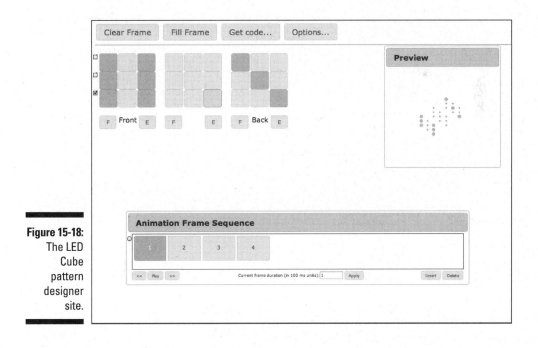

Figure 15-18:
The LED Cube pattern designer site.

Part V
The Part of Tens

Enjoy an additional *Arduino Projects For Dummies* Part of Tens chapter about online learning resources for Arduino and electronics in general at www.dummies.com/extras/arduinoprojects.

In this part . . .

✔ Find out about the best forums, tutorials, and other resources for Arduino

✔ Discover the top 10 troubleshooting techniques

Chapter 16

Ten Great Arduino Resources

In This Chapter

▶ Finding the learning resources you need online

▶ Discovering the best Arduino communities

▶ Supplying the key books in your Arduino library

*I*f you've made it this far, you are undoubtedly an Arduino aficionado. That's why this chapter describes some great resources for learning about the Arduino platform.

The Arduino world has come a long way in less than a decade. There are dozens of online learning resources and many suppliers of all things Arduino, shields, and related products. Most of them have tutorials, datasheets, or video demos that you can learn from, which may inspire your own projects. There are several online forums where you can chat with others who are creating Arduino projects and even the technical gurus who create code libraries, such as the ones used in this book.

There are a lot of great Arduino resources out there and it was pretty hard to narrow them down to just the best ten. Actually, I couldn't quite do it. So there are ten plus one. It never hurts to get a little bit of extra help.

You can download schematics and full-color parts placement diagrams from the companion website (www.dummies.com/go/arduinoprojectsfor dummies).

Websites

The Internet is obviously the best source of current information, and a great place to find ideas and troubleshoot problems. I've pulled together a list of my favorites sites here.

Arduino.cc and related forums

www.arduino.cc

The first stopping point for all things Arduino is undoubtedly, the official website, which is the home of the Arduino project and has the key resources you need to support your projects and further explorations. The latest news and developments are featured on the main page, which is a handy at-a-glance news ticker for what's going on lately. For a more personal take, and some behind-the-scenes opinions and interviews, check out the blog of the Arduino team.

Probably the handiest resource on an everyday basis is the Reference page, which contains a comprehensive list of all the Arduino commands, their syntax, and examples of use. The Learning area features major topics and concepts with numerous practical examples, and lists details about the many Arduino libraries for things like Communication, Motor Control, and Ethernet.

But just as handy is the online community, the Arduino Playground. If you ever are stumped by a particularly intransigent problem, or haven't been able to find any help, the community in the forums is always willing to lend a hand, especially for newbies and people who are not especially technical. It's okay to learn here! Best of all, there's often no waiting for a solution — you'll probably find that your question has already been asked — and answered.

Fritzing

www.fritzing.org

Fritzing is a free, open-source, and easy-to-use electronics design automation (EDA) software package created at the University of Applied Sciences, Potsdam. You can use Fritzing to lay out your project designs and it will automatically generate the schematics. You can also place virtual parts into a breadboard, generate resulting circuit diagrams, and even create the necessary files to order custom-made printed circuit boards. Another nice feature is its capability to export .jpg and .png files of your projects. All the parts layouts in this book were created with Fritzing.

Fritzing has been closely linked to the Arduino project from the beginning, so it's got lots of support for Arduino projects. There is a "parts bin" containing all the types of Arduino boards from the Mini, to the Uno, to the Mega, and beyond. Also, many of the products from companies like Adafruit and Parallax are in the parts library, so you can easily create your own projects using parts and kits such as 16x2 LCD displays and the Real Time Clock breakout board.

Download the software for Mac, Windows, or Linux on the Fritzing website.

Hack-a-day

www.hackaday.com

On the Internet, it's hard to suggest that anything is the "grand-daddy" of anything, but I think Hack-a-day is a strong contender in terms of hacking projects. They've been making daily posts for years now, with literally hundreds of amazing and clever hacks, which usually have links to pictures, videos, and the source code. There's a whole section called Arduino Hacks that showcases a huge variety of cool Arduino projects. This is a real source of inspiration and if you're looking for something to do over a long weekend, this is a great place to go for inspiration.

Also, a large proportion of the posts on Hack-a-day showcase the projects of some serious experts in the subject area. These often link Arduino to broader hacking topics such as mobile platforms like iOS and Android, physical prototyping/3D printing, or electronics in general, to name a few. You'd be hard-pressed not to learn some new techniques from simply browsing through the posts. It's a great resource for connecting with people with very advanced skills in a wide range of hacking interests and abilities.

Instructables

www.Instructables.com

Instructables is sort of the Wikipedia of tutorials. It has a large library of user-contributed step-by-step projects and how-to guides. This means that the variety is huge — as diverse as the interests of its contributors. There's a large trove of Arduino projects on the site and most of them are well documented and explained. You can browse through them step-by-step online, or for a small premium membership fee, you can download .pdf files of the projects.

On the downside, because it errs on the side of inclusiveness and a light editorial touch, you'll not infrequently come across projects that are thin on explanation. Also, because the photographs are all home-brewed, it's not uncommon to find shots that are blurry, poorly lit, or otherwise difficult to make out. Even with these minor complaints, the site is a pretty useful resource, and I often find myself trawling through it for ideas or solutions to problems.

Learn.adafruit.com

www.learn.adafruit.com

This is the home of Adafruit Industries' huge collection of how-tos and instructions about its products and projects, most of which are Arduino related. Adafruit has the homey mom-and-pop, you-can-do-it attitude that makes you feel warm and snuggly about prototyping with Arduino and electronics. Yes, warm and snuggly about electronics!

The best thing about Adafruit is the careful explanation and clear guidance provided. The photography is exceptionally good and the descriptions are clear, easy to understand, and focused on getting you up to speed very quickly. After reading a few of the tutorials, you'll be inspired to try some new projects yourself and push your boundaries. You'll be pretty convinced there's not a topic or concept you can't quickly get up to speed with.

On top of that, many of the tutorials are about Adafruit Industries' exceptional products, several of which I use in this book. Honestly, sometimes you just want to crow about something because it's great. Adafruit's stuff is consistently excellent, and comes with probably the best product guides out there in the Arduino supplier community.

Make:

www.makezine.com

Make: magazine and its companion websites have been at the forefront of the making/hacking "movement" (if you can call it that) and they have always been strong supporters of the Arduino initiative. There's a special Arduino section on the Make: website, which has plenty of project examples, in case you are hungry for more. Other topics, such as 3D printing, robots, and Raspberry Pi, have their own specialty areas, too, which makes sense, because some of the best projects are those that arise from cross-pollinating diverse subjects.

Make: also hosts regular MakerFaire events, which are hugely popular and a great place to meet fellow enthusiasts and witness exotic, robotic, and neurotic concoctions that exhibitors and speakers have been working on. If you have a chance to attend a MakerFaire near you, don't miss out!

element14

www.element14.com

element14 is an online resource and community for engineers that focuses on electronics geared toward professionals and electronics hobbyists alike. It's an initiative of the electronics equipment supplier Farnell (which also owns Newark). Because microcontrollers are based on silicon, the 14th element in the periodic table, it's an appropriate name! In addition to a number of subject interest communities, there's a special subgroup called the Arduino group that has hundreds of members and an active discussion area.

Perhaps the best offering from element14 for Arduino enthusiasts is a series of detailed video tutorials on useful topics. There are several Arduino project videos on topics such as Arduino-based robots and remote controls. Aside from the Arduino-specific videos, there are also a number of more general-interest tutorials related to electronics and prototyping, as well as a video area called element14 TV.

YouTube

www.youtube.com

Sounds unlikely maybe, but YouTube is a great resource for building Arduino projects. There are more than 100,000 videos listed and the number is growing all the time. I often browse the videos when I'm looking for inspiration or trying to figure out how to solve a particularly tricky problem.

Don't miss out on the Arduino tutorials from element14, which are all here on YouTube and cover topics like wireless communication, electrical engineering, motors and transducers, and serial communication, to name a few.

You can also get familiar with some of the Arduino team members, including Massimo Banzi and Tom Igoe, by watching their presentations and TED Talks. There's even a documentary of the Arduino project.

Books and eBooks

Books are another great resource, and are often better than the Internet, because they've been carefully composed and edited to provide the information and help you need — like this one! I have stocked my lab with a few key texts that are dog-eared from constant use.

Arduino For Dummies

If you haven't already cracked it open, it's worth getting a copy of the companion book to this one, *Arduino For Dummies* by John Nussey (John Wiley & Sons, Inc.). It's a very straightforward, but in-depth guide to the Arduino platform and goes into much more detail about the Arduino itself than I had space for in this book. If you want to get to grips with the basics a bit more thoroughly, it's a great place to start.

There are several useful and fun projects to help you get familiar with key topic areas, such as installing your Arduino, the basics of electronics, soldering, using sensors, and also connecting your Arduino to other programs like Processing, and for music, MAX/MSP.

Of course, the best plan would be to have both books in your arsenal!

The Arduino Cookbook

This book by Michael Margolis is exactly what its title suggests. It's especially useful because it gives short, simple examples to specific problems. Want to connect to a servo motor? There's a recipe for that. Want to drive shift registers? There's one for that, too. There are even clear examples of how to use Arduino's built-in EEPROM or build your own custom Arduino libraries.

Unlike in this book, all the recipes contain just the basics that you need to enhance your own Arduino projects. There are no pictures, but plenty of diagrams, and the explanations are simple and easy to understand. It's one of the most used books in my collection. I can't recommend this book enough!

Making Things Talk

This book, now in its second edition, is by Tom Igoe, one of the founding members of the Arduino project, and a teacher at NYU's acclaimed Interactive Telecommunications Program. It gives clear explanations of interactive projects in Tom's accessible and amusing style, and has tons of color photos and illustrations.

Because it was written early in the development of Arduino, the first edition describes interactive projects as they might be built using a number of different microprocessor platforms — not just Arduino. This is very useful for getting an idea of the broader spectrum of microcontrollers. However, the second edition takes a more focused approach and all its projects use Arduino. If you are focused on Arduino, you should hunt for the second edition.

The great thing about *Making Things Talk* is that it is both project based and theory grounded. After trying out a few of the projects in it, you won't be able to get away with *not* learning something about the underlying theories on which the projects are based. The topics are wide ranging and very practical, including electronics, networking and communication protocols, sensing and detection, and wireless communications. It's essential reading for anyone who wants to know both *how* to build a project, and *why* it works the way it does.

Chapter 17

Ten Troubleshooting Tips

Sometimes things just don't go according to plan. It happens. And even if you've followed the instructions in this book pretty carefully, your project may not be working quite right.

Figuring out what's wrong with an Arduino project is a bit different. With electronics-only projects, you just have to focus on the hardware. With software-only projects, you just need to go over your code. But with Arduino projects, you could have a problem either in the hardware *or* the software. Therefore, you may have to check both, to see what's going wrong.

Fortunately, there are a few simple things to try out when your project is just not working, is broken, or is working, but not quite according to plan. I almost always start out with my hardware and if that doesn't sort it out, take a look at the code to see if there's some kind of problem with it. Sometimes you can tell whether to look at the software or hardware first because of the kind of behavior you're seeing (or not seeing) in your project.

Here's what to do when you are having trouble.

Troubleshooting Your Hardware

There are at least five things (and probably more) that you should do to make sure your hardware is working properly. I've listed these in the order of importance — the order I try to do them, anyway. The first order of business though, is to *disconnect the power* if your circuit is still running. You don't want stray currents flowing around your project while you are testing for bad connections. Always troubleshoot the hardware with your circuit powered down. Then, check the following five things.

Checking Your Connections

I was a network administrator for a long time, which means I connected a lot of computers to a lot of other computers. The most frequent cause of problems in my work was things simply being disconnected. So my first rule of thumb was to check my connections — and the same goes for Arduino projects. Look for wires that have come loose, pin headers that aren't pushed in, and things that have come detached from where they should be. If things have come out from where they should be, double-check that you are reconnecting them properly. More than one time, I've reinserted a connection into the wrong hole on my breadboard, which just means more troubleshooting when it fails to work again! If you have any soldered joints, test those, too. You might have had a "cold" joint, which means the junction is brittle and conducts poorly. Gently wiggle or tug on the connections to make sure that they are solidly joined. Hunt for cloudy-looking solder connections or dirty or oily joints. You may need to resolder them. Finally, use a multimeter to test the continuity of suspected problem wires. It could be that a connection you've assumed is good is actually not connected at all.

You've checked for disconnected wires (or "opens"), now check for short-circuits. This is anywhere wires are touching or connected that they shouldn't be. They are called short circuits because the unintended connection provides a pathway for electricity to flow where you don't want it to, usually to ground. Electricity, like water, follows the path of least resistance, and a shorter circuit often offers just that. Look for wires with missing insulation that might be touching. Double-check your breadboard to ensure that your wires are not placed in the wrong column or row, providing a short circuit to ground. Also, make sure that the legs of your components aren't touching each other.

 If you power up your Arduino (either from your USB connection or a battery) and the power LED doesn't light up, disconnect it immediately. You should definitely look for short circuits, in which the power rail is connected directly to ground. Your board has a protective polyfuse, a solid-state fuse that automatically resets itself to prevent short circuits from blowing your microcontroller, but it won't protect you against all such "ground fault" errors.

If you have soldered connections, make sure that there aren't any blobs of solder and that adjacent connections aren't, in fact, soldered together. This is known as a *solder bridge.* If you have one, use a desoldering wick or a desoldering tool to remove the excess solder. Then try again and solder a better connection. This is particularly difficult to do if you've got a problem with an integrated circuit (IC), because you don't want to overheat it. When desoldering ICs, transistors, or other sensitive parts, make sure that you don't apply the heat too long, or you could burn up a component simply by overheating it. Most components can handle a couple hundred degrees for 3 to 5 seconds or so, but not more than that. My rule of thumb is that if it's too hot to touch, it's getting too hot!

Confirming Your Power Is Correct

First, make sure that you have enough power and then make sure it's getting to the right place. Double-check your resistor values and ensure that you didn't substitute any values that are dramatically different from the one specified. For example, if you use a 100KΩ resistor to reduce the current flowing to an LED instead of a 1KΩ resistor, your LED probably won't light up at all. Similarly, if you are expecting a part to be working and it isn't, you may be supplying either too little or too much power to it.

If you are powering external components from your Arduino but they don't seem to be working, try powering them completely independently from your Arduino by using a battery or external power supply. If the component is still not working, it may be broken. Also, if you are supplying power from the 5V power supply pin on the bottom of your Arduino, make sure that you haven't mistakenly inserted your wire into the adjacent 3.3V power supply (see Figure 17-1). If you do, the device won't be getting enough power to operate. Conversely, if you've powered a 3.3V device from the 5V rail, you've over-driven it, and it might already be too late for that part. Remember that 3.3V devices can be very sensitive to being overdriven.

Figure 17-1:
Avoid making an incorrect connection in the power area.

Another problem in the same area could be that you have connected one of your ground wires to the Vin pin. The Vin pin is connected to the center post of the power input "barrel" connector on the lower left of your Arduino. The opposite case is that you connected a wire that was supposed to supply power to the Vin into one of the two GND pins. The polyfuse should protect you against problems, but you want to avoid this.

Make sure that you are using a common ground. Especially when you are controlling devices by switching power to a transistor, it is often the case that your transistor's ground rail needs to be shared with the ground rail of the device you are controlling. Double-check your schematic to determine if this is the case and confirm you've built the circuit correctly.

We all make mistakes, even on a good day. I have fried more than my fair share of components. I started to feel kind of bad when I went through a handful of infrared LEDs on one project, so I started a little LED graveyard (see Figure 17-2). I keep it on my workbench as a reminder to always check my connections before applying power!

Figure 17-2:
My LED
graveyard.
RIP, LED.

Hunting for Odors and Hot Components

It sounds funny, but if you are having trouble with your components, you might have overdriven them without knowing it. You should especially suspect this if your components are getting too hot to touch and if you start to notice any unusual odors. If something is burning, there is a big problem. Disconnect the power and start from the top to try to diagnose your connections. Sniff your circuits closely, and you might detect a melted plastic smell. That's usually a pretty bad sign, and the component is probably fried. Unfortunately, if you are getting to this stage, it's probably already too late and the damage is done. If you see smoke . . . there was probably fire. You should check your connections and replace that component for sure.

You might have already fried either the component in question or your Arduino, but you can at least replace the croaked component and try again. Even the ATmega328 microprocessor can be popped out and replaced. Just make sure that you figure out *why* something got fried before you replace it and fire up the power again!

Test Your Outputs on External Devices

Are you seeing what you'd expect to see? If not, you should check your digital outputs, both on your Arduino and external devices. If you are expecting +5V coming from an external device such as a sensor that you are using for digital input, use your multimeter to check that you are actually getting that voltage from your sensor. If not, your Arduino won't necessarily be able to read this signal as a digital HIGH input. If you are expecting to read an analog value as input and there is no voltage coming from the device, your Arduino won't give expected readings from the analog inputs. Again, use a multimeter to see exactly what values you are getting from the input device.

Also, make sure that if you are using a device that is supplying a digital output that it is going to a digital pin. If your sensor is supplying an analog output, make sure it's going to an analog input pin.

Testing Your Digital Pins

Check your pin(s) on your Arduino, too. If you have run too much current over it, you've *overdriven* the pin, and then it may have stopped operating. The maximum current is 40mA. It will withstand more than that for a short amount of time, but exceeding the maximum rating is never a good idea. If you suspect a pin is dead, you can check it to be sure. Connect a 220Ω resistor to an LED. Connect the short pin of the LED to ground and put the long pin into the suspected digital pin. Run the Blink sketch on your Arduino, substituting the pin in question for Pin 13. For example, if you think Pin 7 is dead, change the code so that `ledPin = 7` and send this to your Arduino. If it doesn't blink, then you know that pin has gone to the great big bucket in the sky.

Troubleshooting Your Software

After making sure that your hardware is not the source of the problem, it's time to check your software. Sometimes what might have seemed like a hardware problem is actually due to an error in your code. I've listed the things you should check, with the important ones up front.

Checking Your Syntax

Back in the dinosaur times when I was learning to program, the message I saw on my green computer screen most often was ?_SYNTAX ERROR. This slightly cryptic message usually meant there was a character out of place in my code, a missing space, or some other kind of typo. Your Arduino IDE has the equivalent in the console at the bottom of the window. When there's a problem, the window border changes to orange and the error message is displayed in white. Sometimes the error message can be a bit hard to interpret. But take the time to actually read the error and really try to understand what it's saying.

The compiler's trying to point you in the right direction! If there's an error in your code, it will usually highlight the line where the error occurred. The most common problem is a missing semicolon at the end of a line. Probably the second most common problem is a missing curly bracket, which yields the message `expected declaration before '}' token` or something similar. Don't worry about what a token is; just hunt for the missing bracket. The little number on the lower left of your IDE window will say what line the problem is on.

Your compiler is not a perfect debugger, though, so it sometimes may direct you to a problem in one area that is arising due to a typo or error in another section. Follow the trail from where the problem is identified and trace it back to the part of the program that may have led you to this point. You'll probably be able to fix the trouble there.

Using the Serial Monitor

Because your Arduino doesn't have its own screen, you can't really inspect what's happening with your hardware. Therefore, you just need to use your computer as your Arduino's screen and output anything you want to inspect to the serial monitor on your computer. Use `Serial.println()` statements at key points in your code to output the contents of variables to the serial monitor. You may need to also add a delay() statement to provide a moment, so you can read the value(s). Otherwise the numbers may fly right by on the monitor.

Your serial port is the only channel of communication between your computer and your Arduino. Your serial port runs on your USB cable, but it is also accessible on digital Pins 0 and 1. For this reason, you can't use the serial monitor to send and receive data from your computer at the same time as you are using digital Pins 0 or 1 for data interchange with a shield or other device.

Only one project in this book does that — the RFID card reader uses your Arduino's serial input pin (Pin 0, labeled 'RX') to get data from the RFID card reader. Therefore, you have to disconnect it from your serial port when you are sending software to your Arduino.

Checking Your Inputs and Outputs

Make sure that in your code, you have specified the input mode of your digital pins in the setup() section. They should be either set to pinMode(pin, INPUT) or pinMode(pin, OUTPUT). (Analog pins do not have to be declared if you are using them as analog inputs.) Also, if you are reading data from an external sensor, make sure it's one that provides the kind of signal you are expecting. For example, some Hall-effect sensors provide either a +5V or 0V digital output. If you are reading from the analog pins, this won't work as expected. Similarly, if you are trying to read a device that has a variable voltage output and it's connected to a digital pin, you may not get the expected behavior from the device. Connect it to an analog input pin instead.

Using a Simulator or an Emulator

If you are using Windows or Linux, you can use a "simulator" to operate a virtual Arduino on your computer. Sadly, I don't know of any Mac Arduino emulators . . . yet! Simulators are software applications that essentially pretend to be an Arduino, behaving exactly the way your hardware ATmega328 chip does, but running as a software program on your computer. You simply run the emulator and program it with the code that you would normally send to your Arduino.

The cool part is that you can see all the inputs and outputs, and can control the signal going to any of the analog or digital pins with virtual sliders and switches. The virtual Arduino shows exactly what a real Arduino would do, if you change the inputs and outputs. You can also inspect the contents of memory and trace what values variables have at any given time. Diagnosing memory problems can be especially difficult on microcontrollers unless you can inspect them in real time or use an emulator. Your chip is a sort of "black box" really, and emulators are a good way of opening it up to reveal its contents.

There are both Arduino *simulators* that mimic the behavior of the Arduino and *emulators* for the AVR chip family, which are technical tools aimed at engineers. The terms are often used interchangeably. Here are a few sources for both:

Arduino simulators

Try the following simulators:

✔ Simulator for Arduino in free and Pro versions (`virtronics.com.au` or `www.arduino.com.au/`)

✔ Arduino Simulator iPhone App ($8.49)

✔ Emulino (free) (`https://github.com/ghewgill/emulino`)

✔ Simuino (free) (`http://code.google.com/p/simuino/`)

AVR emulators

Here are some emulators you can use:

✔ AVR Studio 4, 5, or 6 (`www.atmel.com/microsite/atmel_studio6/`)

✔ Virtual Breadboard ($29.00) (`www.virtualbreadboard.com/`)

✔ Emulare (`http://emulare.sourceforge.net/`)

✔ SimAVR (`http://gitorious.org/simavr`)

When All Else Fails . . .

Read the manual! Actually, you can't really do that, because there is no manual for your Arduino. About the closest thing is the Arduino website (`http://arduino.cc`). The best thing about the site is the huge collection of discussion forums there. The forums are searchable using the search box in the upper-right corner. Believe me, if you are encountering a problem, someone has probably already been there! Choose your search terms carefully and you'll undoubtedly turn up your problem exactly or something very similar to it.

Adafruit, Sparkfun, and element14 also have Arduino forums where people post discussions. Those communities are filled with people like you and me who just want to get their Arduinos to do cool stuff. They are almost always helpful and supportive. Don't be afraid to out yourself as a newbie. You might actually get a faster answer.

Use your favorite search engine to hunt for other people who might have had the same trouble and above all, be persistent. Just when you think it's getting really tough to figure out your problem, you might just have that breakthrough you've been waiting for.

Hang in there, and keep on hacking!

Index

• M •

Apple & Mac

iPad For Dummies,
5th Edition
978-1-118-49823-1

iPhone 5 For Dummies,
6th Edition
978-1-118-35201-4

MacBook For Dummies,
4th Edition
978-1-118-20920-2

OS X Mountain Lion
For Dummies
978-1-118-39418-2

Blogging & Social Media

Facebook For Dummies,
4th Edition
978-1-118-09562-1

Mom Blogging
For Dummies
978-1-118-03843-7

Pinterest For Dummies
978-1-118-32800-2

WordPress For Dummies,
5th Edition
978-1-118-38318-6

Business

Commodities For Dummies,
2nd Edition
978-1-118-01687-9

Investing For Dummies,
6th Edition
978-0-470-90545-6

Personal Finance
For Dummies,
7th Edition
978-1-118-11785-9

QuickBooks 2013
For Dummies
978-1-118-35641-8

Small Business Marketing Kit
For Dummies,
3rd Edition
978-1-118-31183-7

Careers

Job Interviews
For Dummies,
4th Edition
978-1-118-11290-8

Job Searching with
Social Media
For Dummies
978-0-470-93072-4

Personal Branding
For Dummies
978-1-118-11792-7

Resumes For Dummies,
6th Edition
978-0-470-87361-8

Success as a Mediator
For Dummies
978-1-118-07862-4

Diet & Nutrition

Belly Fat Diet For Dummies
978-1-118-34585-6

Eating Clean For Dummies
978-1-118-00013-7

Nutrition For Dummies,
5th Edition
978-0-470-93231-5

Digital Photography

Digital Photography
For Dummies,
7th Edition
978-1-118-09203-3

Digital SLR Cameras &
Photography For Dummies,
4th Edition
978-1-118-14489-3

Photoshop Elements 11
For Dummies
978-1-118-40821-6

Gardening

Herb Gardening
For Dummies,
2nd Edition
978-0-470-61778-6

Vegetable Gardening
For Dummies,
2nd Edition
978-0-470-49870-5

Health

Anti-Inflammation Diet
For Dummies
978-1-118-02381-5

Diabetes For Dummies,
3rd Edition
978-0-470-27086-8

Living Paleo For Dummies
978-1-118-29405-5

Hobbies

Beekeeping
For Dummies
978-0-470-43065-1

eBay For Dummies,
7th Edition
978-1-118-09806-6

Raising Chickens
For Dummies
978-0-470-46544-8

Wine For Dummies,
5th Edition
978-1-118-28872-6

Writing Young Adult Fiction
For Dummies
978-0-470-94954-2

Language &
Foreign Language

500 Spanish Verbs
For Dummies
978-1-118-02382-2

English Grammar
For Dummies,
2nd Edition
978-0-470-54664-2

French All-in-One
For Dummies
978-1-118-22815-9

German Essentials
For Dummies
978-1-118-18422-6

Italian For Dummies
2nd Edition
978-1-118-00465-4

Available in print and e-book formats.

Math & Science

Algebra I For Dummies,
2nd Edition
978-0-470-55964-2

Anatomy and Physiology
For Dummies,
2nd Edition
978-0-470-92326-9

Astronomy For Dummies,
3rd Edition
978-1-118-37697-3

Biology For Dummies,
2nd Edition
978-0-470-59875-7

Chemistry For Dummies,
2nd Edition
978-1-1180-0730-3

Pre-Algebra Essentials
For Dummies
978-0-470-61838-7

Microsoft Office

Excel 2013 For Dummies
978-1-118-51012-4

Office 2013 All-in-One
For Dummies
978-1-118-51636-2

PowerPoint 2013
For Dummies
978-1-118-50253-2

Word 2013 For Dummies
978-1-118-49123-2

Music

Blues Harmonica
For Dummies
978-1-118-25269-7

Guitar For Dummies,
3rd Edition
978-1-118-11554-1

iPod & iTunes
For Dummies,
10th Edition
978-1-118-50864-0

Programming

Android Application
Development For
Dummies, 2nd Edition
978-1-118-38710-8

iOS 6 Application
Development For Dummies
978-1-118-50880-0

Java For Dummies,
5th Edition
978-0-470-37173-2

Religion & Inspiration

The Bible For Dummies
978-0-7645-5296-0

Buddhism For Dummies,
2nd Edition
978-1-118-02379-2

Catholicism For Dummies,
2nd Edition
978-1-118-07778-8

Self-Help & Relationships

Bipolar Disorder
For Dummies,
2nd Edition
978-1-118-33882-7

Meditation For Dummies,
3rd Edition
978-1-118-29144-3

Seniors

Computers For Seniors
For Dummies,
3rd Edition
978-1-118-11553-4

iPad For Seniors
For Dummies,
5th Edition
978-1-118-49708-1

Social Security
For Dummies
978-1-118-20573-0

Smartphones & Tablets

Android Phones
For Dummies
978-1-118-16952-0

Kindle Fire HD
For Dummies
978-1-118-42223-6

NOOK HD For Dummies,
Portable Edition
978-1-118-39498-4

Surface For Dummies
978-1-118-49634-3

Test Prep

ACT For Dummies,
5th Edition
978-1-118-01259-8

ASVAB For Dummies,
3rd Edition
978-0-470-63760-9

GRE For Dummies,
7th Edition
978-0-470-88921-3

Officer Candidate Tests
For Dummies
978-0-470-59876-4

Physician's Assistant Exam
For Dummies
978-1-118-11556-5

Series 7 Exam
For Dummies
978-0-470-09932-2

Windows 8

Windows 8 For Dummies
978-1-118-13461-0

Windows 8 For Dummies,
Book + DVD Bundle
978-1-118-27167-4

Windows 8 All-in-One
For Dummies
978-1-118-11920-4

Available in print and e-book formats.

Take Dummies with you everywhere you go!

Whether you're excited about e-books, want more from the web, must have your mobile apps, or have been swept up in social media, Dummies makes everything easier.

Dummies products make life easier!

- DIY
- Consumer Electronics
- Crafts
- Software
- Cookware
- Hobbies
- Videos
- Music
- Games
- and More!

For more information, go to **Dummies.com®** and search the store by category.

For Dummies is a registered trademark of John Wiley & Sons, Inc.

A Wiley Brand